You can return this item to any library but please
note that not all libraries are open every day.
Items must be returned on or before the due date.
Failure to do so will result in overdue charges.
Items may be renewed unless requested by
another customer, in person or by telephone, on
two occasions only. Your membership card
number will be required.
Please look after this item – you may be charged
for any damage.

BOURNEMOUTH LIBRARIES
Headquarters: Leisure & Tourism Directorate
Town Hall, Bournemouth, BH2 6DY

LONG WALK TO FREEDOM: VOLUME 2
1962–1994

From his imprisonment in Pretoria in 1962 to the long years on Robben Island and his eventual release, this second and final volume of Nelson Mandela's memoirs tells the extraordinary story of the quest for freedom and justice that saw him inaugurated as South African President. *Long Walk to Freedom: Volume 2* brilliantly recreates the drama of the experiences that helped shape Mandela's destiny and conveys the blossoming of a life that changed the face of South African politics for ever. This volume concludes an awe-inspiring story that makes for compulsive—and essential—reading.

LONG WALK TO FREEDOM

The Autobiography of
Nelson Mandela

Volume Two

1962–1994

WINDSOR

First published 1994
by
Little Brown and Company
This Large Print edition published 2004
by
BBC Audiobooks Ltd
by arrangement with
Time Warner Books Limited

ISBN 0 7540 8724 7

Reader's note: for editorial reasons, Part Seven: Rivonia commences at section 52, when in the original 1994 edition it began at section 49. No text, however, has been omitted in this two-volume edition.

British Library Cataloguing in Publication Data available

Printed and bound in Great Britain by
Antony Rowe Ltd., Chippenham, Wiltshire

I dedicate this book to my six children, Madiba and Makaziwe (my first daughter), who are now deceased, and to Makgatho, Makaziwe, Zenani and Zindzi, whose support and love I treasure; to my twenty-nine grandchildren and six great-grandchildren, who give me great pleasure; and to all my comrades, friends and fellow South Africans whom I serve and whose courage, determination and patriotism remain my source of inspiration.

CONTENTS

ACKNOWLEDGEMENTS

As readers will discover, this book has a long history. I began writing it clandestinely in 1974 during my imprisonment on Robben Island. Without the tireless labour of my old comrades Walter Sisulu and Ahmed Kathrada for reviving my memories, it is doubtful the manuscript would have been completed. The copy of the manuscript which I kept with me was discovered by the authorities and confiscated. However, in addition to their unique calligraphic skills, my co-prisoners Mac Maharaj and Isu Chiba had ensured that the original manuscript safely reached its destination. I resumed work on it after my release from prison in 1990.

Since my release, my schedule has been crowded with numerous duties and responsibilities, which have left me little free time for writing. Fortunately, I have had the assistance of dedicated colleagues, friends and professionals who have helped me complete my work at last, and to whom I would like to express my appreciation. Thanks again to my comrade Ahmed Kathrada for the long hours spent revising, correcting and giving accuracy to the story.

I am deeply grateful to Richard Stengel who collaborated with me in the creation of this book, providing invaluable assistance in editing and revising the first parts and in the writing of the latter parts. I recall with fondness our early morning walks in the Transkei and the many hours of interviews at Shell House in Johannesburg and my home in Houghton. A special tribute is owed to Mary Pfaff who assisted Richard in his work. I have also benefited from the advice and support of Fatima Meer, Peter Magubane, Nadine Gordimer and Ezekiel Mphahlele.

Many thanks to my ANC office staff who patiently dealt with the logistics of the making of this book, but in particular to Barbara Masekela for her efficient co-ordination. Likewise, Iqbal Meer has devoted many hours to watching over the business aspects of the book. I am grateful to my editor, William Phillips of Little, Brown, who has guided this project from early 1990 on, and edited the text. He was ably assisted by Jordan Pavlin and Steve Schneider. I would also like to thank Professor Gail Gerhart for her factual review of the manuscript.

LONG WALK
TO FREEDOM:

VOLUME 2
1962–1994

PART SEVEN

Rivonia

Prison not only robs you of your freedom, it attempts to take away your identity. Everyone wears a uniform, eats the same food, follows the same schedule. It is by definition a purely authoritarian state that tolerates no independence or individuality. As a freedom fighter and as a man, one must fight against the prison's attempt to rob one of these qualities.

From the courthouse, I was taken directly to Pretoria Local, the gloomy red-brick monstrosity that I knew so well. But I was now a convicted prisoner, not an awaiting-trial prisoner, and was treated without even the little deference that is afforded to the latter. I was stripped of my clothes and Colonel Jacobs was finally able to confiscate my *kaross*. I was issued the standard prison uniform for Africans: a pair of short trousers, a rough khaki shirt, a canvas jacket, socks, sandals and a cloth cap. Only Africans are given short trousers, for only African men are deemed 'boys' by the authorities.

I informed the authorities that I would under no circumstances wear shorts and told them I was prepared to go to court to protest. Later, when I was brought dinner, stiff cold porridge with half a teaspoonful of sugar, I refused to eat it. Colonel Jacobs pondered this and came up with a solution: I could wear long trousers and have my own food, if I agreed to be put in isolation. 'We were going to put you with the other politicals,' he said, 'but now you will be alone, man. I hope you enjoy it.' I assured him that solitary confinement would be fine as long as I could wear and eat what I chose.

*   *   *

For the next few weeks, I was completely and utterly isolated. I did not see the face or hear the voice of another prisoner. I was locked up for twenty-three hours a day, with thirty minutes of exercise in the morning and again in the afternoon. I had never been in isolation before, and every hour seemed like a year. There was no natural light in my cell; a single bulb burned overhead twenty-four hours a day. I did not have a wristwatch and I often thought it was the middle of the night when it was only late afternoon. I had nothing to read, nothing to write on or with, no one to talk to. The mind begins to turn in on itself, and one desperately wants something outside oneself on which to fix one's attention. I have known men who took half-a-dozen lashes in preference to being locked up alone. After a time in solitary, I relished the company even of the insects in my cell, and found myself on the verge of initiating conversations with a cockroach.

I had one middle-aged African warder whom I occasionally was able to see, and one day I tried to bribe him with an apple to get him to talk to me. '*Baba*,' I said, which means Father, and is a term of respect, 'can I give you an apple?' He turned away, and met all my subsequent overtures with silence. Finally he said, 'Man, you wanted long trousers and better food, and now you have them and you are still not happy.' He was right. Nothing is more dehumanizing than the absence of human

4

companionship. After a few weeks I was ready to swallow my pride and tell Colonel Jacobs that I would trade my long trousers for some company.

During those weeks I had plenty of time to ponder my fate. The place of a freedom fighter is beside his people, not behind bars. The knowledge and contacts I had recently made in Africa were going to be locked away rather than used in the struggle. I cursed the fact that my expertise would not be put to use in creating a freedom army.

I soon began to protest vigorously against my circumstances and demanded to be put with the other political prisoners at Pretoria Local. Among them was Robert Sobukwe. My request was ultimately granted, accompanied by a stern warning from Colonel Jacobs that serious consequences would result if I returned to my impudent ways. I don't think I ever looked forward to eating cold mealie pap so much in my life.

*　　　*　　　*

Apart from my desire for company, I was keen to talk with Sobukwe and the others, most of whom were PAC, because I thought that in prison we might forge a unity that we could not on the outside. Prison conditions have a way of tempering polemics, and making individuals see more what unites them than what divides them.

When I was taken to the courtyard with the others, we greeted each other warmly. Besides Sobukwe, there was also John Gaetsewe, a leading member of the South African Congress of Trade Unions; Aaron Molete, an ANC member who worked for *New Age*; and Stephen Tefu, a

5

prominent communist trade unionist, and PAC member. Robert asked me to give them an account of my African tour, which I did gladly. I was candid about how both the PAC and the ANC were perceived in the rest of Africa. At the end of my narrative I said there were issues that I wanted us to examine. But after initially allowing Sobukwe and me a certain proximity, the authorities took pains to keep us apart. We lived in single cells along a corridor and he and I were put at opposite ends.

Occasionally we did have a chance to talk as we sat next to each other on the ground of the prison courtyard sewing and patching up shabby old mailbags. I have always respected Sobukwe, and found him a balanced and reasonable man. But we differed markedly about the principal subject at hand: prison conditions. Sobukwe believed that to fight poor conditions would be to acknowledge the state's right to have him in prison in the first place. I responded that it was always unacceptable to live in degrading conditions and that political prisoners throughout history had considered it part of their duty to fight to improve them. Sobukwe responded that prison conditions would not change until the country changed. I completely agreed with this, but I did not see why that ought to prevent us from fighting in the only realm in which we now could fight. We never resolved this issue, but we did make some progress when we submitted a joint letter to the commanding officer setting out our complaints about prison conditions.

Sobukwe never broke in prison. But in Pretoria he was a bit sensitive and testy, and I attribute this to Stephen Tefu. Tefu had become a kind of goad to Sobukwe, teasing, taunting and challenging him. Even at the best of times, Tefu was a difficult fellow: dyspeptic, argumentative, overbearing. He was also articulate, knowledgeable, and an expert in Russian history. Above all, he was a fighter, but he would fight everyone, even his friends. Tefu and Sobukwe quarrelled every day.

I was keen to discuss policy issues with Sobukwe, and one of the matters I took up with him was the PAC slogan 'Freedom in 1963'. It was already 1963 and freedom was nowhere to be seen. 'My brother,' I said to Sobukwe, 'there is nothing so dangerous as a leader making a demand that he knows cannot be achieved. It creates false hopes among the people.'

I said this in a most respectful manner, but Tefu jumped in and started to berate Sobukwe. 'Bob,' he said, 'you have met your match with Mandela. You know he is right.' Tefu continued in this vein, annoying Sobukwe to the point where he would tell Tefu, 'Leave me alone.' But Tefu would not stop. 'Bob, the people are waiting for you. They are going to kill you because you have deceived them. You are just an amateur, Bob. You are not a real politician.'

Tefu did his best to alienate me as well. Every morning, when we were visited by the warders, he would complain to them about something—the food, the conditions, the heat or the cold. One day an officer said to Tefu: 'Look, man, why do you complain every morning?'

'I complain because it is my duty to complain,' Steve said.

'But, look at Mandela,' the officer said, 'he does not complain every day.'

7

'Ah,' said Tefu with disgust, 'Mandela is a little boy who is afraid of the white man. I don't even know who he is. One morning, I woke up and found every newspaper saying, "Mandela, Mandela, Mandela", and I said to myself, "Who is this Mandela?" I will tell you who Mandela is. He is a chap built up by you people for some reason that I don't understand. That is who Mandela is!'

*   *   *

We were joined for two weeks by Walter Sisulu, who had been on trial in Johannesburg for incitement to strike while I had been in Pretoria. He was sentenced to six years. We had a number of opportunities to talk in jail and we discussed Walter's application for bail while his appeal was pending, a move I wholeheartedly supported. After two weeks he was released on bail, and he was instructed by the movement to go underground, from where he was to continue to lead the struggle, which he ably did.

Not long after Walter left, I was walking to the prison hospital with Sobukwe when I spotted Nana Sita in the courtyard about twenty-five yards away. Sita, the distinguished Indian campaigner who had led our defiance at Boksburg in 1952, had just been convicted by a Pretoria magistrate for refusing to vacate his house—the house he had lived in for more than forty years—which was in a neighbourhood that had been proclaimed 'white' in terms of the Group Areas Act. He was hunched over, and the fact that he was barefoot despite an acute arthritic condition made me uncomfortable in my own sandals. I wanted to go over to greet

8

him, but we were marching under the eyes of half a dozen warders.

Suddenly and without warning, I suffered a blackout. I crumpled to the concrete and sustained a deep gash above my left eye, which required three stitches. I had been diagnosed back in the Fort with high blood pressure and had been given certain pills. The cause of the blackout was evidently an overdose of these pills; I was taken off them and put on a low-salt diet; this solved the problem.

That afternoon was my first scheduled visit from Winnie since I had been sentenced. Stitches or no stitches, I was not going to miss it. She was extremely concerned when she saw me but I assured her I was fine and explained what happened. Even so, rumours circulated that my health had broken down.

53

In October 1962, during my trial, the ANC held its first annual conference since 1959. Because the organization was illegal, the conference took place in Lobatse, just over the border in Bechuanaland. The conference was a milestone, for it explicitly linked the ANC and MK. Although the National Executive stated, 'Our emphasis still remains mass political action,' Umkhonto was referred to as the 'military wing of our struggle'. This was done in part to try to quell the more irresponsible acts of terrorism then being committed by Poqo. Poqo, Xhosa for 'independent' or 'standing alone', was loosely linked to the PAC, and their acts of terrorism targeted both African collaborators and whites. The ANC wanted the people to see its new militancy, but also to see that it was controlled and responsible.

The government had decided to accelerate the programme of 'separate development' to show the world that apartheid allowed races their individual 'freedom'. The prototype would be the Transkei. In January 1962, Verwoerd had announced that South Africa intended to grant the Transkei 'self-government'. In 1963 the Transkei became a 'self-governing' homeland. In November 1963, an election was held for the Transkei legislative assembly. But by a margin of more than three to one, Transkei voters elected members opposed to the homeland policy.

The Bantustan system was nevertheless instituted; the voters had opposed it, but participated in it simply by voting. Though I abhorred the Bantustan system, I felt the ANC should use both the system and those within it as a platform for our policies, particularly as so many of our leaders were now voiceless through imprisonment, banning or exile.

Terrorism against the Bantu Authorities increased. As acts of sabotage mounted, so did the government's vigilance. John Vorster, the new minister of justice, who had himself been detained during the Second World War for opposing the government's support of the Allies, was a man unsentimental in the extreme. For him, the iron fist was the best and only answer to subversion.

On 1 May 1963, the government enacted legislation designed 'to break the back' of

Umkhonto, as Vorster put it. The General Law Amendment Act, better known as the Ninety-Day Detention Law, waived the right of habeas corpus and empowered any police officer to detain any person without a warrant on grounds of suspicion of a political crime. Those arrested could be detained without trial, charge, access to a lawyer, or protection against self-incrimination for up to ninety days. The ninety-day detention could be extended, as Vorster ominously explained, until 'this side of eternity'. The law helped to transform the country into a police state; no dictator could covet more power than the Ninety-Day Detention Law gave to the authorities. As a result, the police became more savage: prisoners were routinely beaten and we soon heard reports of electric shock, suffocation and other forms of torture. In Parliament, Helen Suzman, the representative of the liberal Progressive Party, cast the lone vote against the act.

Increased penalties were ordered for membership of illegal organizations; sentences from five years to the death penalty were instituted for 'furthering the aims' of communism or of other banned organizations. Political prisoners were redetained, as I found out in May 1963 when Sobukwe's three-year sentence was up; instead of releasing him, the government simply redetained him without charging him, and then sent him to Robben Island.

Vorster also championed the Sabotage Act of June 1962, which allowed for house arrests and more stringent bannings not subject to challenge in the court, restricting the liberties of citizens to those in the most extreme fascist dictatorships.

Sabotage itself now carried a minimum penalty of five years without parole and a maximum of death. Because the wording of the act was so broad, even activities such as trespassing or illegal possession of weapons could constitute sabotage. Another act of Parliament prohibited the reproduction of any statement made by a banned person. Nothing I said or had ever said could be reported in the newspapers. *New Age* was banned at the end of 1962, and possession of a banned publication became a criminal offence, punishable by up to two years in prison. Provision was also made for house arrest, the best-known use of which was imposed on the white political activist Helen Joseph.

54

One night towards the end of May, a warder came to my cell and ordered me to pack my things. I asked him why, but he did not answer. In less than ten minutes, I was escorted down to the reception office where I found three other political prisoners: Tefu, John Gaetsewe and Aaron Molete. Colonel Aucamp curtly informed us that we were being transferred. Where? Tefu asked. Someplace very beautiful, Aucamp said. Where? said Tefu. '*Die Eiland,*' said Aucamp. The island. There was only one. Robben Island.

The four of us were shackled together and put in a windowless van that contained only a sanitary bucket. We drove all night to Cape Town, and arrived at the city's docks in the late afternoon. It is not an easy or pleasant task for men shackled together to use a sanitary bucket in a moving van.

The docks at Cape Town were swarming with armed police and nervous plain-clothed officials. We had to stand, still chained, in the hold of the old wooden ferry, which was difficult as the ship rocked in the swells off the coast. A small porthole above was the only source of light and air. The porthole served another purpose as well: the warders enjoyed urinating on us from above. It was still light when we were led on deck and we saw the island for the first time. Green and beautiful, it looked at first more like a resort than a prison.

'*Esiquithini.*' 'At the island.' That is how the Xhosa people describe the narrow, windswept outcrop of rock that lies eighteen miles off the coast of Cape Town. Everyone knows which island you are referring to. I first heard about the island as a child. Robben Island was well known among the Xhosas after Makanna (also known as Nxele), the six-foot six-inch commander of the Xhosa army in the Fourth Xhosa War, was banished there by the British after leading ten thousand warriors against Grahamstown in 1819. He tried to escape from Robben Island by boat, but drowned before reaching shore. The memory of that loss is woven into the language of my people who speak of a 'forlorn hope' by the phrase '*Ukuza kuka Nxele*'.

Makanna was not the first African hero confined on the island. In 1658, Autshumao, known to European historians as Harry the Strandloper, was banished by Jan van Riebeeck during a war between the Khoi Khoi and the Dutch. I took solace in the memory of Autshumao, for he is reputed to be the first and only man ever to escape from Robben Island, and he did so by rowing to the

13

mainland in a small boat.

The island takes its name from the Dutch word for seal, hundreds of which once cavorted in the icy Benguela currents that wash the shores. Later the island was turned into a leper colony, a lunatic asylum and a naval base. The government had only recently turned the island back into a prison.

*   *   *

We were met by a group of burly white warders shouting: *'Dis die Eiland! Hier gaan julle vrek!'* ('This is the island. Here you will die!') Ahead of us was a compound flanked by a number of guardhouses. Armed guards lined the path to the compound. It was extremely tense. A tall, red-faced warder yelled at us: *'Hier is ek you baas!'* 'Here I am your boss!' He was one of the notorious Kleynhans brothers, known for their brutality to prisoners. The warders always spoke in Afrikaans. If you replied in English they would say, *'Ek verstaan nie daardie kaffirboetie se taal nie.'* ('I don't understand that kaffir-lover's language.')

As we walked towards the prison, the guards shouted 'Two-two! Two-two!'—meaning we should walk in pairs, two in front, two behind. I linked up with Tefu. The guards started screaming, *'Haas! Haas!'* The word *haas* means 'move' in Afrikaans, but it is customarily reserved for cattle.

The warders were demanding that we jog, and I turned to Tefu and under my breath said that we must set an example; if we gave in now we would be at their mercy. Tefu nodded his head in agreement. We had to show them that we were not everyday criminals but political prisoners being

14

punished for our beliefs.

I motioned to Tefu that we two should walk in front, and we took the lead. Once in front, we actually decreased the pace, walking slowly and deliberately. The guards were incredulous. 'Listen,' Kleynhans said, 'this is not Johannesburg, this is not Pretoria, this is Robben Island, and we will tolerate no insubordination here. *Haas! Haas!*' But we continued at our stately pace. Kleynhans ordered us to halt, and stood in front of us: 'Look, man, we will kill you, we are not fooling around, your wives and children and mothers and fathers will never know what happened to you. This is the last warning. *Haas! Haas!*'

To this I said: 'You have your duty and we have ours.' I was determined that we would not give in, and we did not, for we were already at the cells. We were ushered into a rectangular stone building and taken to a large open room. The floor was covered with water a few inches deep. The guards yelled: '*Trek uit! Trek uit!*' ('Undress! Undress!') As we removed each item of clothing, the guards would grab it, search it quickly and then throw it in the water. Jacket off, searched, thrown in the water. Then the guards commanded us to get dressed, by which they meant for us to put on our soaking clothes.

Two officers entered the room. The less senior of the two was a captain whose name was Gericke. From the start, we could see that he was intent on manhandling us. The captain pointed to Aaron Molete, the youngest of the four of us and a very mild and gentle person, and said, 'Why is your hair so long?' Aaron said nothing. The captain shouted, 'I'm talking to you! Why is your hair so long? It is against regulations. Your hair should have been cut. Why is it long . . .' and then he paused and turned to look at me, and said, '. . . like this boy's?' pointing at me. I began to speak: 'Now, look here, the length of our hair is determined by the regulations . . .'

Before I could finish, he shouted in disbelief: 'Never talk to me that way, boy!' and began to advance. I was frightened; it is not a pleasant sensation to know that someone is about to hit you and you are unable to defend yourself.

When he was just a few feet from me, I said, as firmly as I could, 'If you so much as lay a hand on me, I will take you to the highest court in the land and when I finish with you, you will be as poor as a church mouse.' The moment I began speaking, he paused, and by the end of my speech he was staring at me with astonishment. I was a bit surprised myself. I had been afraid, and spoke not from courage but out of a kind of bravado. At such times, one must put up a bold front despite what one feels inside.

'Where's your ticket?' he asked, and I handed it to him. I could see he was nervous. 'What's your name?' he said. I nodded my head towards the ticket, and said, 'It is written there.' He said, 'How long are you in for?' I said again, gesturing towards the ticket, 'It is written there.' He looked down and said, 'Five years! You are in for five years and you are so arrogant! Do you know what it means to serve five years?' I said, 'That is my business. I am ready to serve five years but I am not prepared to be bullied. You must act within the law.'

No one had informed him who we were, or that we were political prisoners, or that I was a lawyer. I had not noticed it myself, but the other officer, a tall, quiet man, had vanished during our confrontation; I later discovered that he was Colonel Steyn, the commanding officer of Robben Island. The captain then left, much quieter than he had entered.

*   *   *

We were then by ourselves, and Steve, his nerves jangling, could not stop speaking. 'We have provoked the Boer,' he said. 'Now we are in for a rough time.' He was in the midst of speaking when a stocky fellow named Lieutenant Pretorius walked in. To our surprise, Pretorius spoke to us in Xhosa, which he seemed to know quite well. 'We have looked at your records and they are not so bad. All except this one,' he said, nodding towards Steve. 'Your record is filthy.'

Steve exploded. 'Who are you to talk to me like that? You say I have a filthy record. You have read my files, eh? Well, you will find that all those convictions were for cases I was fighting for the rights of my people. I am not a criminal; you are the criminal.' The lieutenant then warned Steve that he would charge him if he ever addressed him in that way again. Before leaving, Pretorius said he was placing us in a single large cell with windows that faced outside and then added, rather ominously, 'But I don't want you to talk to anyone through those windows, especially you, Mandela.'

We were then taken to our cell, one of the best I had ever seen. The windows were large and within easy reach. Through those in one wall we could see other prisoners and warders as they walked past. It was spacious, certainly large enough for the four of us, and had its own toilets and showers.

It had been an exhausting day and a short while later, after a supper of cold porridge, the others went to sleep. I was lying on my blanket on the floor, when I heard a tapping at the window. I looked up and saw a white man beckoning me to come to the glass. I remembered the lieutenant's admonition and stayed put.

Then I heard the fellow whisper: 'Nelson, come here.' The fact that he knew my name intrigued me and I decided to take a chance. I went over to the window and looked at him. He must have realized that I thought he was white, because the first thing he whispered was, 'I'm a Coloured warder from Bloemfontein.' He then gave me news of my wife. There had been a report in the Johannesburg newspapers that my wife had come to see me at Pretoria Local, but that they had not informed her that I had been taken to Robben Island. I thanked him for the information.

'Do you smoke?' he said. I told him that I did not and he seemed disappointed. I then got the idea: 'Yes, but my comrades do.' He brightened at this and said he would return in a few minutes with tobacco and sandwiches. Everyone was now awake. Tefu and John Gaetsewe smoked, and I split the pouch of tobacco between them, and we all divided the sandwiches.

For the next few weeks the Coloured warder came almost every night with tobacco and sandwiches. And each night I would divide up the tobacco evenly between Tefu and Gaetsewe. The warder was taking great risks, and he warned me that he was prepared to deal directly only with me, or the arrangement was off.

*   *   *

When we arrived on the island we had no idea how
many other prisoners were there. Within a few days
we learned there were about a thousand men, all
Africans, all recent arrivals. Most of these men
were common-law prisoners, but I knew there
would be some political prisoners among them. I
wanted to contact them, but we were completely
isolated. For the first few days we were kept locked
in our cell and not even permitted outside. We
demanded to be taken to work like the other
prisoners, and this was soon granted, but we were
taken out alone, supervised by Kleynhans. Our first
job was covering up some newly laid pipe, and we
were on a small hill and could see some of the
island, which was wild and lovely.

We worked hard that first day, but on each
succeeding day Kleynhans pushed us harder. He
did this crudely, as one would urge on a horse or
cow. *'Nee, man. Kom aan! Gaan aan!'* ('No, man.
Come on. Go on.') At one point, Steve, who was
older than the rest of us, put down his shovel and
was immediately threatened by Kleynhans. But
Steve, in Afrikaans, responded: 'You ignoramus
who cannot even speak your own language
properly—you cannot tell me what to do. I will
work at my own rate, that is what I am prepared to
do, and that is all I can do.' Then, with great
dignity, he picked up his shovel and resumed work.
Steve had been a teacher of Afrikaans, and he not
only spoke perfect Afrikaans but its antecedent,
High Dutch. Steve would speak to the warders in a

19

condescending and grandiloquent style that they probably did not understand. But they knew better than to engage him in a verbal battle.

There were two Kleynhans brothers on the island, both reputed to have viciously assaulted prisoners. We were looked after by the older brother, who must have been warned to restrain himself, for he never touched us. The younger one was under no such constraints. One day, we were walking back from work along a road and passed a workspan of several hundred prisoners carting sand in wheelbarrows. They were non-political prisoners and both of our groups were ordered to halt while the two brothers had a chat; the younger brother ordered one of his men to polish his boots while he talked. I recognized some of the men in the other workspan as those who had been sentenced to death in the Sekhukhuneland peasant revolt of 1958, and I turned round to get a better look at them. The younger brother rudely ordered me to look the other way. I do not know how I would have reacted had I not been standing in full view of the other prisoners, but my pride was now at stake. I refused to turn round. The younger Kleynhans advanced with the obvious intent of assaulting me, but when he was a few steps away, his brother ran over, grabbed him, whispered a few words, and the incident passed.

One day we were visited by the head of prison, who was responsible for running all of Robben Island and had come to hear our complaints. Theron was a sour fellow who did not like to deal with prisoners face to face. I did not want to alienate him but I was not going to cringe. 'We are grateful that you have come to see us,' I said,

20

speaking for the group, 'because we have a number of problems which I am certain you will be able to sort out.' I enumerated the problems, and when I finished, he said, 'I will see what I can do.'

Perhaps he thought he had given in too easily because as he was walking out he turned to Tefu, who had a large belly, and said, *'Jou groot pens sal in die plek verdwyn'*, Afrikaans for 'That great stomach of yours is going to disappear here in prison.' *Pens* means stomach, but is used to refer to the stomach of animals like sheep or cattle. The word for the stomach of a human being is *maag*.

Steve did not take kindly to the prison head's jibe, and he was incapable of letting an insult go unanswered. 'You know, Captain,' he said, 'there is nothing you can do to me that can truly affect me for I am a member of the most revolutionary political organization in the world, the Communist Party, which has a distinguished record of service to oppressed people around the globe. You and your poor National Party will be in the ash-heap of history while we are ruling the world. I am better known internationally than your witless state president. Who are you? A small functionary not even worth paying attention to. By the time I leave prison I won't even know your name.' Theron turned on his heel and left.

*   *   *

The nightly visits of our Coloured warder went a long way to mitigate the harshness of the island. But even with this luxury, Steve was still dissatisfied. Tefu was a heavy smoker; he would sometimes puff away the entire night leaving

21

himself no tobacco for the next day. Gaetsewe, however, conserved his tobacco, and never ran out. One evening, in a particularly irritable mood, Tefu confronted me. 'Nelson,' he said, 'you are short-changing me. You are giving Gaetsewe more tobacco than me.'

This was not true, but I thought I would play a game with him. 'Very well then,' I said. 'Every night when I get the tobacco I will first divide it into two portions and then I will let you choose which one you want.' That night, and each night afterwards, I separated the tobacco into equal piles and said to Steve, 'Choose.'

Tefu would be in an agony of indecision. He would look at both piles, his head swinging back and forth between the two. Finally, in frustration, he would grab one of the piles and go off and begin to smoke. Though this process seemed to me eminently fair—and also humorous—Tefu was still unhappy. He began to hover about when the warder came to the window in order to make sure that I was not hoarding the tobacco. This made the warder uncomfortable. 'Look,' he said to me, 'I deal only with you. It is a question of security.' I said I understood, and told Tefu that he could not be around when I was dealing with the warder.

The next night, however, when the warder came to the window, Tefu strode up to the bars and said to him, 'From now on I want my own tobacco. Just give it to me directly.' The warder panicked. 'Mandela,' he said, 'you have broken our agreement. No more. I won't be bringing you these things.' I shooed Tefu away and remonstrated with the warder. I said, 'Look, man, this is an old chap,' meaning Tefu. 'And he's not very normal,' I said, pointing to my head. 'Make an exception.' So he softened and gave me the supplies, but warned if it happened again, that would be the end.

That night, I thought it necessary to punish Tefu. I said, 'Now, look, you have jeopardized our supplies. You are not going to have any tobacco or sandwiches tonight. You have almost lost us these privileges. So we're cutting you off until you improve.' Tefu was silent.

We stayed in one corner of the cell that night, eating our sandwiches and reading the paper the warder also brought for us. Tefu sat by himself in the opposite corner. Eventually we drifted off to sleep. At about midnight, I felt an arm on my shoulder, jostling me awake.

'Nelson . . . Nelson.' It was Tefu. 'Nelson,' he said, speaking softly, 'you have hit me in a weak spot. You have deprived me of my tobacco. I am an old man. I have suffered for my commitment to my people. You are the leader here in jail, and you are punishing me like this. It is not fair, Nelson.'

He had hit *me* in a weak spot. I felt as though I had abused my power. He had indeed suffered, far more than I had. I had not eaten half my sandwich, and I immediately gave it to him. I roused Gaetsewe—I had given him all the tobacco—and asked him if he would share it with Tefu. Tefu was always difficult, but from that point on he behaved much better.

*   *   *

Once we started working, I got some sense of what life was like for other prisoners on the island. The authorities also moved some young political

23

prisoners from the PAC into the cells opposite ours. At night, we were able to talk with them through the barred door. Among these young men, I discovered, was Nqabeni Menye, a nephew of mine from Mqhekezweni whom I had last seen when he was a baby in 1941.

We conversed about the Transkei and caught up on family history. One night, while his friends were gathered around him, he said, 'Uncle, what organization do you belong to?' The ANC, I said, of course. My response caused consternation among those young men and suddenly their faces disappeared from the window. After some time, my nephew reappeared and asked me whether or not I had ever been a member of the PAC. I replied that I had not. He then said he had understood that I joined the PAC during my Africa tour. I told him that I had not, that I had always been a member of the ANC, and that I always would be. This again caused dismay among them and they vanished.

I later learned that PAC propaganda claimed that I had joined that organization when I was travelling elsewhere on the continent. Although I was not pleased to hear this, it did not surprise me. In politics, one can never underestimate how little people know about a situation. A short while later my nephew was back and asked me if I had met and talked with Sobukwe at Pretoria Local. I said that I had and that we had very good discussions. This pleased them, and they said good night and that was the last I saw of them.

*   *   *

A few hours later that same evening a captain came

24

to our cell and commanded the four of us to pack our belongings. Within minutes my comrades were taken away, leaving me in the cell by myself. In prison, one counts oneself lucky to be able to wave good-bye to one's comrades. One can be in extraordinarily intimate circumstances with someone for months, and then never see the person again. It is dehumanizing, for it forces one to adapt by becoming more self-contained and insulated.

Now that I was alone, I was also somewhat anxious. There is sometimes safety in numbers; when you are alone, there are no witnesses. I realized I had not been served any food, and banged on the door: 'Warder, I have not received my supper.'

'You must call me *baas*,' he yelled. I went hungry that night.

Very early the next morning I was taken back to Pretoria. The Department of Prisons released a statement to the press that I had been removed from the island for my own safety because PAC prisoners were planning to assault me. This was patently false; they had brought me back to Pretoria for their own motives, which soon became clear.

I was kept in solitary confinement at Pretoria Local. But prisoners are resourceful and I was soon receiving secret notes and other communications from some of the ANC people there. I had a communication from Henry Fazzie, one of the MK cadres who had undergone military training in Ethiopia and been arrested while attempting to return to South Africa. They were among the first ANC members to be tried under the Sabotage Act.

25

Through the prison grapevine, I attempted to help them with their defence and suggested they contact Harold Wolpe. I later heard that Wolpe was in police detention. This was my first intimation that something had gone seriously wrong. One day, as I was being led away from the courtyard after exercise, I saw Andrew Mlangeni. I had last seen him in September 1961 when he was leaving the country for military training. Wolpe, Mlangeni—who else was under arrest?

Early in 1961, Winnie had been banned for two years. I heard from another prisoner that Winnie had recently been charged with violating her bans, which could lead to imprisonment or house arrest. Winnie was headstrong; a banning order was just the type of thing that would make her angry. I had no doubt that she violated her orders, and I would never counsel her not to do so, but it concerned me greatly that she might spend time in prison.

One morning in July 1963, as I was walking along the corridor to my cell, I saw Thomas Mashifane, who had been the foreman at Liliesleaf Farm. I greeted him warmly, though I realized that the authorities had undoubtedly led him to my corridor to see if I recognized or acknowledged him. I could not but do otherwise. His presence there could mean only one thing: the authorities had discovered Rivonia.

A day or two later I was summoned to the prison office where I found Walter; Govan Mbeki; Ahmed Kathrada; Andrew Mlangeni; Bob Hepple; Raymond Mhlaba, a member of the MK High Command who had recently returned from training in China; Elias Motsoaledi, also a member of MK; Dennis Goldberg, an engineer and a member of

26

the Congress of Democrats; Rusty Bernstein, an architect and also a member of the COD; and Jimmy Kantor, an attorney who was Harold Wolpe's brother-in-law. We were all charged with sabotage, and scheduled to appear in court the next day. I had served just nine months of my five-year sentence.

*   *   *

In bits and pieces, I learned what had happened. On the afternoon of 11 July, a dry cleaner's van entered the long driveway of the farm. No one at Liliesleaf had ordered a delivery. The vehicle was stopped by a young African guard, but he was overwhelmed when dozens of armed policemen and several police dogs sprang from the vehicle. They surrounded the property and a handful of officers entered the main building and the principal outbuilding. In the latter they found a dozen men around a table discussing a document. Walter jumped out of a window but was cut off by a snarling police dog. The arrests also included Arthur Goldreich, who had driven into the farm as the police raid was in progress.

The police searched the entire farm and confiscated hundreds of documents and papers, though they found no weapons. One of the most important documents remained right on the table: Operation Mayibuye, a plan for guerrilla warfare in South Africa. In one fell swoop, the police had captured the entire High Command of Umkhonto we Sizwe. Everyone was detained under the new Ninety-Day Detention Law.

Joe Slovo and Bram Fischer were fortunately

27

not there at the time of the raid, but they often went to the farm two or three times a day. In hindsight, it is extraordinary that Liliesleaf was not discovered sooner. The regime had become stricter and more sophisticated. Wiretaps had become common as was twenty-four-hour surveillance. The raid was a coup for the state.

*   *   *

On our first day in court we were not given the opportunity to instruct counsel. We were brought before a magistrate and charged with sabotage. A few days later we were allowed to meet Bram, Vernon Berrangé, Joel Joffe, George Bizos and Arthur Chaskalson, all of whom were acting for us. I was still being kept separately as I was a convicted prisoner, and these sessions were my first opportunity to talk with my colleagues.

Bram was very sombre. In his quiet voice, he told us that we were facing an extremely serious trial and that the state had formally advised him they would ask for the supreme penalty permitted by law, the death sentence. Given the climate of the times, Bram said, this result was a very real possibility. From that moment on we lived in the shadow of the gallows. The mere possibility of a death sentence changes everything. From the start, we considered it the most likely outcome of the trial. Far lesser crimes than ours had recently been punished by life sentences.

Prison officials never let you forget that you might hang. That night, a warder rapped on my cell door at bedtime. 'Mandela, you don't have to worry about sleep,' he said. 'You are going to sleep for a

28

long, long time.' I waited a moment and said, 'All of us, you included, are going to sleep for a long, long time.' It was small consolation.

55

On 9 October 1963, we were picked up in a heavily fortified police van. It had a steel divider running along the centre, segregating the white prisoners from the Africans. We were driven to the Palace of Justice in Pretoria, where the Supreme Court sits, for the opening of 'The State versus the National High Command and others', that later become known as 'The State versus Nelson Mandela and others', and is still better known as the Rivonia Trial. Near the court stands a statue of Paul Kruger, the president of the Republic of the Transvaal who fought against British imperialism in the nineteenth century. Underneath this Afrikaner hero is a quotation from one of his speeches. The inscription reads: 'In confidence we lay our cause before the whole world. Whether we win or whether we die, freedom will rise in Africa like the sun from the morning clouds.'

Our van was in the centre of a convoy of police trucks. At the front of this motorcade were limousines carrying high police officials. The Palace of Justice was teeming with armed policemen. To avoid the enormous crowd of our supporters who had grouped in front of the building, we were driven to the rear of the building and taken in through great iron gates. All around the building police officers with machine guns stood at attention. As we descended from the van, we could hear the great crowd singing and chanting. Once inside, we were held in cells below the courtroom before the opening of what was depicted in the newspapers at home and around the world as the most significant political trial in the history of South Africa.

*　　　*　　　*

As we emerged from the cells, each of the accused was accompanied by two armed warders. When we entered the ornate, high-ceilinged courtroom, we each turned to the crowd and made a clenched-fist ANC salute. In the visitors' gallery our supporters shouted *'Amandla! Ngawethu!'* and *'Mayibuye Afrika!'* This was inspiring, but dangerous: the police took the names and addresses of all the spectators in the galleries, and photographed them as they left the court. The courtroom was filled with domestic and international journalists, and dozens of representatives of foreign governments.

After we filed in, a group of police officers formed a tight cordon between us and the spectators. I was disgusted to have to appear in court wearing my prison clothes of khaki shorts and flimsy sandals. As a convicted prisoner, I did not have the choice of wearing proper clothes. Many people later commented on how poorly I looked, and not just because of my wardrobe. I had been in and out of solitary confinement for months and I had lost more than twenty-five pounds. I took pains to smile at the gallery when I walked into the courtroom, and seeing our supporters was the best medicine I could have had.

Security was particularly tight as only a few weeks earlier Arthur Goldreich, Harold Wolpe, Mosie Moola and Abdulhay Jassat had bribed a young guard and escaped from jail. Arthur and Harold made their way to Swaziland disguised as priests, then flew to Tanganyika. Their escape came at a time of hysteria about the underground and was greeted with blaring newspaper headlines. It was an embarrassment to the government and a boost to our morale.

Our judge in the Rivonia Trial was Mr Quartus de Wet, judge-president of the Transvaal, who sat in his flowing red robes beneath a wooden canopy. De Wet was one of the last judges appointed by the United Party before the Nationalists came to power and was not considered a government lackey. He was a poker-faced judge who did not suffer fools gladly. The prosecutor was Dr Percy Yutar, deputy attorney general of the Transvaal, whose ambition was to become attorney general of South Africa. He was a small, bald, dapper fellow, whose voice squeaked when he became angry or emotional. He had a flair for the dramatic and for high-flown if imprecise language.

Yutar rose and addressed the court, 'My Lord, I call the case of the state against the National High Command and others.' I was accused No. 1. Yutar handed in the indictment and authorized that we be charged immediately and tried summarily. This was the first time we were given a copy of the indictment. The prosecution had kept it from us, though they gave it to the *Rand Daily Mail*, which had splashed it all over that day's edition of the paper. The indictment charged eleven of us with complicity in over two hundred acts of sabotage

31

aimed at facilitating violent revolution and an armed invasion of the country. The state contended that we were actors in a conspiracy to overthrow the government.

We were charged with sabotage and conspiracy rather than high treason because the law does not require a long preparatory examination (which is highly useful to the defence) for sabotage and conspiracy as it does for treason. Yet the supreme penalty—death by hanging—is the same. With high treason, the state must prove its case beyond a reasonable doubt and needs two witnesses to testify to each charge. Under the Sabotage Law, the onus was on the defence to prove the accused innocent.

Bram Fischer stood up and asked the court for a remand on the grounds that the defence had not had time to prepare its case. He noted that a number of the accused had been held in solitary confinement for unconscionable lengths of time. The state had been preparing for three months, but we had only received the indictment that day. Justice de Wet gave us a three-week adjournment until 29 October.

I was disturbed to discover that first day that Winnie was unable to attend. Because of her banning and her restriction to Johannesburg, she needed police permission to come to court. She had applied and been refused. I also learned that our house had been raided and the police had detained a young relative of Winnie's. Winnie was not the only wife being harassed. Albertina Sisulu and Caroline Motsoaledi were detained under the Ninety-Day Detention Act, and Walter's young son Max was also arrested. This was one of the state's most barbarous techniques of applying pressure:

imprisoning the wives and children of freedom fighters. Many men in prison were able to handle anything the authorities did to them, but the thought of the state doing the same thing to their families was almost impossible to bear.

Winnie subsequently appealed to the minister of justice, who granted her permission to attend the trial on condition that she did not wear traditional dress. Ironically, the same government that was telling us to embrace our culture in the homelands forbade Winnie to wear a Xhosa gown into court.

*   *   *

During the next three weeks, we were permitted to spend our days together preparing our case. I was now among my fellow accused, and the company of my colleagues was a tonic. As awaiting-trial prisoners we were entitled to two half-hour visits a week, and one meal a day could be sent in from the outside. I soon gained back my lost weight with Mrs Pillay's delicious dinners.

While we were preparing our defence, the government was trying the case in the newspapers. Normally, a case that is *sub judice* cannot be commented upon in public or in the press. But since the men arrested at Rivonia were Ninety-Day detainees, and therefore not technically charged with a crime, this judicial principle went by the wayside. We were publicly branded as violent revolutionaries by everyone from the minister of justice on down. Newspapers regularly featured headlines like 'REVOLUTION ON MILITARY BASIS'.

On 29 October, we again entered the Palace of

Justice; again the crowds were large and excited; again the security was extremely tight; again the court was filled with dignitaries from many foreign embassies. After three weeks with my comrades I felt rejuvenated, and I was far more comfortable in court this time in a suit. Our attorneys had objected to our having to come to court in prison garb and we had won the right to wear our own clothes. We raised clenched fists to the gallery, and we were warned by the authorities that if we did it again, we would be forced to come to court in our prison khakis. To prevent such outbursts, the authorities reversed the normal order of the prisoners preceding the judge into the courtroom. After that first day, the judge entered first so that court would already be in session when we entered.

We went on the attack immediately—Bram Fischer criticized the state's indictment as shoddy, poorly drawn and containing absurdities such as the allegation that I had participated in certain acts of sabotage on dates when I was in Pretoria Local. Yutar was flummoxed. Judge de Wet looked to him to reply to Bram's argument, and instead of offering particulars he began to give what the judge derided as 'a political speech'. De Wet was impatient with Yutar's fumbling and told him so. 'The whole basis of your argument as I understand it, Mr Yutar, is that you are satisfied that the accused are guilty.' De Wet then quashed the indictment and gavelled the session to a close.

For that moment we were technically free, and there was pandemonium in the court. But we were rearrested even before Judge de Wet left his seat. Lieutenant Swanepoel clapped each of us on the shoulder and said, 'I am arresting you on a charge

34

of sabotage', and we were herded back to our cells. Even so, this was a blow to the government, for it now had to go back to the drawing-board in the case it was calling the trial to end all trials.

*   *   *

The state redrew its indictment and we were back in court in early December. We all sensed that in the interim Justice de Wet had grown more hostile to us. We suspected his previous independence had brought down the wrath of the government and that pressure had been applied. The new charges were read: we were alleged to have recruited persons for sabotage and guerrilla warfare for the purpose of starting a violent revolution; we had allegedly conspired to aid foreign military units to invade the republic in order to support a communist revolution; and we had solicited and received funds from foreign countries for this purpose. The orders for munitions on the part of the accused, said Yutar melodramatically, were enough to blow up Johannesburg.

The registrar then requested our pleas. We had agreed not to plead in the traditional manner but to use the moment to show our disdain for the proceedings.

'Accused No. 1, Nelson Mandela, do you plead guilty or not guilty?'

I rose and said, 'My Lord, it is not I, but the government that should be in the dock. I plead not guilty.'

'Accused No. 2, Walter Sisulu, do you plead guilty or not guilty?'

Sisulu: 'The government is responsible for what

35

has happened in this country. I plead not guilty.'

Justice de Wet said he was not interested in hearing political speeches, but that we should merely plead not guilty or guilty. His direction was ignored. Each of the accused suggested that it was the government that was criminal before pleading not guilty.

To enhance the drama of the proceedings, the state had made arrangements for a live broadcast of Yutar's speech on the South African Broadcasting System. Microphones had been placed on the prosecution table as well as in front of the judge. But just as Yutar was clearing his throat, Bram Fischer rose and made an application to the court for the removal of the microphones on the grounds that the broadcasts would unfairly prejudice the case and were not in keeping with the dignity of the court. Despite Yutar's shrill plea for their retention, Justice de Wet ordered them removed.

In his address, Yutar argued that from the time the ANC had been driven underground, the organization had embarked on a policy of violence designed to lead from sabotage through guerrilla warfare to an armed invasion of the country. He asserted that we planned to deploy thousands of trained guerrilla units throughout the country, and these units were to spearhead an uprising that would be followed by an armed invasion by military units of a foreign power. 'In the midst of the resulting chaos, turmoil and disorder,' Yutar proclaimed, 'it was planned by the accused to set up a Provisional Revolutionary Government to take over the administration and control of the country.' The engine of this grand plan was

36

Umkhonto we Sizwe, under the political direction of the ANC and the Communist Party, and the headquarters of Umkhonto was Rivonia.

In his orotund prose, Yutar described how we recruited members for MK, how we planned our national uprising for 1963 (here he was confusing us with the PAC), how we erected a powerful radio transmitter at Rivonia, and how we were collectively responsible for 222 acts of sabotage. He said Elias Motsoaledi and Andrew Mlangeni were in charge of recruiting members and that Dennis Goldberg ran a special school for recruits in the Cape. He detailed the production of various bombs, as well as the solicitation of money abroad.

Over the next three months, the state produced 173 witnesses and entered into the record thousands of documents and photographs, including standard works on Marxism, histories of guerrilla warfare, maps, blueprints, and a passport made out to one David Motsamayi. The first witness was a police photographer who had taken pictures of Rivonia, and the next witnesses were domestic workers for the Goldreich family, who had been held in detention all this time even though they had no connection with the politics of the household. These servants identified most of us by pointing to us in the dock, but old Mr Jelliman, in a brave attempt to help me, pretended that he did not see me when he was asked to point to accused No. 1. Look again, the prosecutor said, go over all the faces carefully. 'I do not think he is here,' Jelliman said quietly.

We wondered what evidence the state had to prove my guilt. I had been out of the country and in prison while much of the planning at Rivonia had taken place. When I saw Walter in Pretoria Local just after my sentencing, I urged him to make sure that all my books and notes were removed from the farm. But during the first week of the trial, when Rusty Bernstein applied for bail, Percy Yutar dramatically produced the sketch of the Fort and the accompanying note about escape that I had made while detained there. Yutar exclaimed that this was evidence that all of the accused meant to escape. It was a sign that nothing of mine had been removed from Rivonia. Later, I was told that my colleagues at Rivonia had decided to preserve my escape note because they thought it would be historic in the future. But in the present, it cost Rusty Bernstein his bail.

The state's star witness was Bruno Mtolo, or 'Mr X' as he was known in court. In introducing 'Mr X', Yutar informed the court that the interrogation would take three days and then, in theatrical tones, he added that the witness was 'in mortal danger'. Yutar asked that the evidence be given *in camera*, but that the press be included provided that they not identify the witness.

Mtolo was a tall, well-built man with an excellent memory. A Zulu from Durban, he had become the leader of the Natal region of MK. He was an experienced saboteur, and had been to Rivonia. I had met him only once, when I addressed his group of MK cadres in Natal after my return from the continent. His evidence concerning me in particular made me realize that the state would certainly be able to convict me.

He began by saying that he was an MK saboteur who had blown up a municipal office, a power pylon and an electricity line. With impressive

38

precision, he explained the operation of bombs, land mines and grenades, and how MK worked from underground. Mtolo said that while he had never lost faith in the ideals of the ANC, he did lose faith in the organization when he realized that it and MK were instruments of the Communist Party.

His testimony was given with simplicity and what seemed like candour, but Mtolo had gone out of his way to embellish his evidence. This was undoubtedly done on police instructions. He told the court that during my remarks to the Natal Regional Command I had stated that all MK cadres ought to be good communists but not to disclose their views publicly. In fact, I never said anything of the sort, but his testimony was meant to link me and MK to the Communist Party. His memory appeared so precise that the ordinary person would assume that it was accurate in all instances. But this was not so.

I was bewildered by Mtolo's betrayal. I never ruled out the possibility of even senior ANC men breaking down under police torture. But by all accounts, Mtolo was never touched. On the stand, he went out of his way to implicate people who were not even mentioned in the case. It is possible, I know, to have a change of heart, but to betray so many others, many of whom were quite innocent, seemed to me inexcusable.

During cross-examination we learned that Mtolo had been a petty criminal before joining MK and had been imprisoned three previous times for theft. But despite these revelations, he was an extremely damaging witness, for the judge found him reliable and believable, and his testimony incriminated nearly all of us.

The keystone of the state's case was the six-page Plan of Action confiscated in the Rivonia raid. The leaders of the High Command had had this very document before them on the table when the police stormed the farm. Operation Mayibuye sketches out in general form the plan for the possible commencement of guerrilla operations, and how it might spark a mass armed uprising against the government. It envisions an initial landing of small guerrilla forces in four different areas of South Africa and the attacking of preselected targets. The document set a goal of some 7,000 MK recruits in the country who would meet the initial outside force of 120 trained guerrillas.

The prosecution's case rested in large part on their contention that Operation Mayibuye had been approved by the ANC Executive and had become the operating plan of MK. We insisted that Operation Mayibuye had not yet been formally adopted and was still under discussion at the time of the arrests. As far as I was concerned, Operation Mayibuye was a draft document that was not only not approved, but was entirely unrealistic in its goals and plans. I did not believe that guerrilla warfare was a viable option at that stage.

The plan had been drafted in my absence, so I had very little knowledge of it. Even among the Rivonia Trialists there was disagreement as to whether the plan had been adopted as ANC policy. Govan, who had drafted the document with Joe Slovo, insisted that it had been agreed upon and felt that it was wrong for us to argue in court that it was still under discussion. But all the other accused contended that the document, while drawn up by the High Command, had not been approved by the ANC Executive or even seen by Chief Luthuli.

*   *   *

Although a capital trial can be quite grim, our spirits were generally high. There was a good deal of gallows humour among us. Dennis Goldberg, the youngest of the accused, had an irrepressible sense of humour and often had us laughing when we should not have been. When one of the prosecution witnesses described how Raymond Mhlaba had worn a clerical collar as a disguise, Dennis took to calling him Reverend Mhlaba.

In our consulting room downstairs, we often communicated through notes, which we would then burn and throw in the wastebasket. One of the Special Branch officers who looked after us was Lieutenant Swanepoel, a burly, red-faced fellow who was convinced we were always putting one over on him. One day, while Swanepoel was observing us from the door, Govan Mbeki began to write a note in a conspicuously secretive manner. With similar drama he handed me the note. I read it, nodded my head sagely, and passed it to Kathy, who ostentatiously took out his matches as if to burn the note when Swanepoel swooped into the room, grabbed the paper out of Kathy's hands, and said something about the dangers of lighting matches indoors. He then left the room to read his prize; a few seconds later, he stormed back saying, 'I will get all of you for this!' Govan had written in capital letters: 'ISN'T SWANEPOEL A FINE-LOOKING CHAP?'

41

We were locked up in prison and on trial for our lives but, outside, new life was blossoming. Jimmy Kantor's wife was to give birth any day. Jimmy was an attorney who had been roped into the trial by the state for no other reason than that he was Harold Wolpe's brother-in-law.

One morning, when we were sitting in the dock, a note was passed down to me from the other end.

Barbara and I have discussed godfathers at length and we have come to the conclusion that, whether the baby is a girl or boy, we would consider it an honour if you would agree to accept this office as an adjunct to the more disreputable positions you have held in the past.

By return mail I sent Jimmy back a note.

I would be more than delighted, and the honour is mine, not the baby's. Now they dare not hang me.

56

The state case continued during the Christmas season of 1963, ending on 29 February 1964. We had a little over a month to examine the evidence and prepare our defence. We were not all equally affected by the evidence. There was no evidence against James Kantor; he was not even a member of our organization and should not have been on trial at all. For Rusty Bernstein, Raymond Mhlaba and Ahmed Kathrada, the evidence of involvement in conspiracy was slight and we decided they should not incriminate themselves. In Rusty's case, the evidence was negligible; he had merely been found at Rivonia with the others. The remaining six of us would make admissions of guilt on certain charges.

Bram was deeply pessimistic. He avowed that even if we proved that guerrilla war had not been approved and our policy of sabotage was designed not to sacrifice human life, the state could still impose the death sentence. The defence team was divided on whether or not we should testify. Some asserted that it would hurt our case if we testified. George Bizos, though, suggested that unless we gave evidence and convinced the judge that we had not decided on guerrilla warfare, he would certainly impose the supreme penalty.

Right from the start we had made it clear that we intended to use the trial not as a test of the law but as a platform for our beliefs. We would not deny, for example, that we had been responsible for acts of sabotage. We would not deny that a group of us had turned away from non-violence. We were not concerned with getting off or lessening our punishment, but with making the trial strengthen the cause for which we were all struggling—at whatever cost to ourselves. We would not defend ourselves in a legal sense so much as in a moral sense. We saw the trial as a continuation of the struggle by other means. We would readily admit what was known by the state to be true but refuse to give away any information we thought might implicate others.

We would dispute the state's central contention that we had embarked on guerrilla warfare. We would admit that we had made contingency plans to undertake guerrilla warfare in the event of sabotage failing. But we would claim it had not yet failed, for it had not been sufficiently attempted. We would deny the claims of murder and damage to innocent bystanders that the state alleged; either these claims were outright lies, or the incidents were the work of someone else. We had never contemplated the intervention of foreign military forces. In order to make these claims, we believed we would have to explain Operation Mayibuye to the court.

In my own case, the court had sufficient evidence for a conviction. Documents in my handwriting showed that I had left the country illegally, had arranged for military training for our men and had been behind the formation of Umkhonto we Sizwe. There was also a document in my handwriting called 'How to be a good communist', which the state suggested was proof that I was a card-carrying communist. In fact the document's title was taken from the work of a Chinese theoretician named Liu Shao Chi, and was written by me to prove a point to Moses Kotane. We had been engaged in a running debate about the appeal of communism to ordinary South Africans. I had long argued that communist literature was, for the most part, dull, esoteric and Western-centred, but ought to be simple, clear and relevant to the African masses. Moses insisted it could not be done. To prove my point, I had taken Liu's essay and rewritten it for an African audience.

*   *   *

44

I would be the first witness and therefore set the tone for the defence. In South African courts, evidence from the witness box can be given only in the form of an answer to a question. I did not want to be limited to that format. We decided that instead of giving testimony, I would read a statement from the dock, while the others would testify and go through cross-examination.

Because a witness making a statement from the dock does not submit to cross-examination or questions from the bench, the statement does not have the same legal weight as ordinary testimony. Those who choose to make such a statement usually do so to avoid cross-examination. Our attorneys warned me that it would put me in a more precarious legal situation; anything I said in my statement regarding my own innocence would be discounted by the judge. But that was not our highest priority. We believed it was important to open the defence with a statement of our politics and ideals, which would establish the context for all that followed. I wanted very much to cross swords with Percy Yutar, but it was more important that I use the platform to highlight our grievances.

All of this was agreed upon in consultation, mainly through notes because the consultation room was bugged. We even used the state's eavesdropping to our advantage by supplying them with disinformation. We gave every indication that I was going to testify so that they would spend their time planning their cross-examination. In a staged conversation, I told our attorney Joel Joffe that I would need the Treason Trial record to prepare my testimony. We smiled at the notion of Yutar poring over the hundred or so volumes of Treason Trial transcripts.

*   *   *

I spent about a fortnight drafting my address, working mainly in my cell in the evenings. When I was finished, I read it first to my comrades and fellow accused. They approved of it, suggesting a few changes, and then I asked Bram Fischer to look it over. Bram became concerned after reading it and got a respected advocate named Hal Hanson to read it. Hanson told Bram, 'If Mandela reads this in court they will take him straight out to the back of the courthouse and string him up.' That confirmed Bram's anxieties and he came to me the next day and urged me to modify the speech. I felt we were likely to hang no matter what we said, so we might as well say what we truly believed. The atmosphere at the time was extremely grim, with newspapers routinely speculating that we would receive the death sentence. Bram begged me not to read the final paragraph, but I was adamant.

*   *   *

On Monday 20 April, under the tightest of security, we were taken to the Palace of Justice, this time to begin our defence. Winnie was there with my mother, and I nodded to them as we entered the court, which was again full.

Bram announced that certain parts of the state's evidence would be conceded by the accused, and there was a buzz in the court. But he went on to say that the defence would deny a number of the

46

state's assertions, including the contention that Umkhonto we Sizwe was the military wing of the ANC. He said that the leaders of MK and the ANC 'endeavoured to keep these two organizations entirely separate. They did not always succeed in this', he said, 'but . . . every effort was made to achieve that object'. He emphatically denied that the ANC took orders from the Communist Party. He said the defence would challenge the allegation that Goldberg, Kathrada, Bernstein and Mhlaba were members of Umkhonto. He stated that the defence would show that Umkhonto had not in fact adopted Operation Mayibuye, and that MK had not embarked on preparations for guerrilla warfare.

'That will be denied?' asked Justice de Wet incredulously.

'That will be denied,' replied Bram. 'The evidence will show that while preparations for guerrilla warfare were being made, no plan was ever adopted. It was hoped throughout that such a step could be avoided.'

Then, in his soft voice, Bram said, 'The defence case, My Lord, will commence with a statement from the dock by accused No. 1, who personally took part in the establishment of Umkhonto, and who will be able to inform the court of the beginnings of that organization.'

At this, Yutar popped up from the table and cried, 'My Lord! My Lord!' He was distressed that I would not be testifying, for he had undoubtedly prepared for my cross-examination. 'My Lord,' he said rather despondently, 'a statement from the dock does not carry the same weight as evidence under oath.'

47

'I think, Dr Yutar,' Justice de Wet responded drily, 'that counsel for the defence have sufficient experience to advise their clients without your assistance.' Yutar sat down.

'Neither we nor our clients are unaware of the provisions of the criminal code,' replied Bram. 'I call on Nelson Mandela.'

I rose and faced the courtroom and read slowly.

I am the first accused.

I hold a bachelor's degree in Arts, and practised as an attorney in Johannesburg for a number of years in partnership with Mr Oliver Tambo. I am a convicted prisoner, serving five years for leaving the country without a permit and for inciting people to go on strike at the end of May 1961.

I admit immediately that I was one of the persons who helped to form Umkhonto we Sizwe and that I played a prominent role in its affairs until I was arrested in August 1962.

At the outset, I want to say that the suggestion made by the state in its opening that the struggle in South Africa is under the influence of foreigners or communists is wholly incorrect. I have done whatever I did, both as an individual and as a leader of my people, because of my experience in South Africa, and my own proudly felt African background, and not because of what any outsider might have said.

In my youth in the Transkei, I listened to the elders of my tribe telling stories of the old days. Amongst the tales they related to me were those of wars fought by our ancestors in defence of the fatherland. The names of Dingane and Bambatha, Hintsa and Makanna, Squngthi and Dalasile, Moshoeshoe and Sekhukhuni were praised as the pride and glory of the entire African nation. I hoped then that life might offer me the opportunity to serve my people and make my own humble contribution to their freedom struggle. This is what has motivated me in all that I have done in relation to the charges made against me in this case.

Having said this, I must deal immediately and at some length with the question of violence. Some of the things so far told the court are true and some are untrue. I do not, however, deny that I planned sabotage. I did not plan it in a spirit of recklessness or because I have any love of violence. I planned it as a result of a calm and sober assessment of the political situation that had arisen after many years of tyranny, exploitation, and oppression of my people by whites.

I wanted to impress upon the court that we had not acted irresponsibly or without thought to the ramifications of taking up violent action. I laid particular emphasis on our resolve to cause no harm to human life.

We of the ANC have always stood for a non-racial democracy, and we shrank from any action which might drive the races further apart than they already were. But the hard facts were that fifty years of non-violence had brought the African people nothing but more repressive legislation, and fewer and fewer rights. It may not be easy for this court to understand, but it is a fact that for a long time the people had been talking of violence—of the day when they would fight the white man and win back their country, and we, the leaders of the ANC, had nevertheless always prevailed upon them to avoid violence and to use peaceful methods. While some of us discussed this in May and June 1961, it could not be denied that our policy to achieve a non-racial state by non-violence had achieved nothing, and that our followers were beginning to lose confidence in this policy and were developing disturbing ideas of terrorism . . .

Umkhonto was formed in November 1961. When we took this decision, and subsequently formulated our plans, the ANC heritage of non-violence and racial harmony was very much with us. We felt that the country was drifting towards a civil war in which blacks and whites would fight each other. We viewed the situation with alarm. Civil war would mean the destruction of what the ANC stood for; with civil war racial peace would be more difficult than ever to achieve. We already have examples in South African history of the results of war. It has taken more than fifty years for the scars of the South African [Anglo-Boer] War to disappear. How much longer would it take to eradicate the scars of inter-racial civil war, which could not be fought without a great loss of life on both sides?

50

Sabotage, I said, offered the best hope for future race relations. The reaction of the white rulers to our first efforts were swift and brutal: sabotage was declared to be a crime punishable by death. We did not want civil war, I said, but we needed to be prepared for it.

Experience convinced us that rebellion would offer the government limitless opportunities for the indiscriminate slaughter of our people. But it was precisely because the soil of South Africa is already drenched with the blood of innocent Africans that we felt it our duty to make preparations as a long-term undertaking to use force in order to defend ourselves against force. If war were inevitable, we wanted the fight to be conducted on terms most favourable to our people. The fight which held out prospects best for us and the least risk of life to both sides was guerrilla warfare. We decided, therefore, in our preparations for the future, to make provision for the possibility of guerrilla warfare.

All whites undergo compulsory military training, but no such training was given to Africans. It was in our view essential to build up a nucleus of trained men who would be able to provide the leadership which would be required if guerrilla warfare started. We had to prepare for such a situation before it became too late to make proper preparations.

I explained that at this stage in our discussions I left the country to attend the PAFMECSA conference and undergo military training. I said that I underwent training because if there was to be a guerrilla war, I wanted to be able to stand and fight beside my own people. Even so, I believed that the possibilities of sabotage were far from exhausted and should be pursued with vigour.

I told the court of the dividing line between the ANC and MK, and how we made good-faith attempts to keep the two separate. This was our policy, but in practice it was not so simple. Because of bannings and imprisonment, people often had to work in both organizations. Though this might have sometimes blurred the distinction, it did not abolish it. I disputed the allegations of the state that the aims and objects of the ANC and the Communist Party were one and the same.

The ideological creed of the ANC is, and always has been, the creed of African Nationalism. It is not the concept of African Nationalism expressed in the cry, 'Drive the white man into the sea.' The African Nationalism for which the ANC stands is the concept of freedom and fulfilment for the African people in their own land. The most important political document ever adopted by the ANC is the Freedom Charter. It is by no means a blueprint for a socialist state . . . The ANC has never at any period of its history advocated a revolutionary change in the economic structure of the country, nor has it, to the best of my recollection, ever condemned capitalist society . . .

The ANC, unlike the Communist Party, admitted Africans only as members. Its chief

52

goal was, and is, for the African people to win unity and full political rights. The Communist Party's main aim, on the other hand, was to remove the capitalists and to replace them with a working-class government. The Communist Party sought to emphasize class distinctions whilst the ANC seeks to harmonize them.

It is true that there has often been close cooperation between the ANC and the Communist Party. But cooperation is merely proof of a common goal—in this case the removal of white supremacy—and is not proof of a complete community of interests. The history of the world is full of similar examples. Perhaps the most striking illustration is to be found in the cooperation between Great Britain, the United States of America and the Soviet Union in the fight against Hitler. Nobody but Hitler would have dared to suggest that such cooperation turned Churchill or Roosevelt into communists or communist tools, or that Britain and America were working to bring about a communist world.

It is perhaps difficult for white South Africans, with an ingrained prejudice against communism, to understand why experienced African politicians so readily accepted communists as their friends. But to us the reason is obvious. Theoretical differences amongst those fighting against oppression are a luxury we cannot afford at this stage. What is more, for many decades communists were the only political group in South Africa who were prepared to treat Africans as human beings and their equals; who were prepared to eat with us; talk with us, live with and work with us. Because of this, there are many Africans who, today, tend to equate freedom with communism.

I told the court that I was not a communist and had always regarded myself as an African patriot. I did not deny that I was attracted by the idea of a classless society, or that I had been influenced by Marxist thought. This was true of many leaders of the newly independent states of Africa, who accepted the need for some form of socialism to enable their people to catch up with the advanced countries of the West.

From my reading of Marxist literature and from conversations with Marxists, I have gained the impression that communists regard the parliamentary system of the West as undemocratic and reactionary. But, on the contrary, I am an admirer of such a system.

The Magna Carta, the Petition of Rights and the Bill of Rights are documents which are held in veneration by democrats throughout the world. I have great respect for British political institutions, and for the country's system of justice. I regard the British Parliament as the most democratic institution in the world, and the independence and impartiality of its judiciary never fail to arouse my admiration. The American Congress, the country's doctrine of separation of powers, as well as the independence of its judiciary, arouse in me similar sentiments.

I detailed the terrible disparities between black and white life in South Africa. In education, health, income, every aspect of life, blacks were barely at a subsistence level while whites had the highest standards in the world—and aimed to keep it that way. Whites, I said, often claimed that Africans in South Africa were better off than Africans in the rest of the continent. Our complaint, I said, was not that we were poor by comparison with the people in the rest of Africa, but that we were poor by comparison with the whites in our country, and that we were prevented by legislation from righting that imbalance.

> The lack of human dignity experienced by Africans is the direct result of the policy of white supremacy. White supremacy implies black inferiority. Legislation designed to preserve white supremacy entrenches this notion. Menial tasks in South Africa are invariably performed by Africans. When anything has to be carried or cleaned the white man looks around for an African to do it for him, whether the African is employed by him or not . . .
> Poverty and the breakdown of family life have secondary effects. Children wander about the streets of the townships because they have no schools to go to, or no money to enable them to go to school, or no parents at home to see that they go to school, because both parents (if there be two) have to work to keep the family alive. This leads to a

breakdown in moral standards, to an alarming rise in illegitimacy and to growing violence which erupts, not only politically, but everywhere . . .

Africans want a just share in the whole of South Africa; they want security and a stake in society. Above all, we want equal political rights, because without them our disabilities will be permanent. I know this sounds revolutionary to the whites in this country, because the majority of voters will be Africans. This makes the white man fear democracy . . .

This then is what the ANC is fighting for. Their struggle is a truly national one. It is a struggle of the African people, inspired by their own suffering and their own experience. It is a struggle for the right to live.

I had been reading my speech, and at this point I placed my papers on the defence table, and turned to face the judge. The courtroom became extremely quiet. I did not take my eyes off Justice de Wet as I spoke from memory the final words.

During my lifetime I have dedicated myself to this struggle of the African people. I have fought against white domination, and I have fought against black domination. I have cherished the ideal of a democratic and free society in which all persons live together in harmony and with equal opportunities. It is an ideal which I hope to live for and to achieve. But if needs be, it is an ideal for which I am prepared to die.

The silence in the courtroom was now complete. At the end of the address, I simply sat down. I did not turn and face the gallery, though I felt all their eyes on me. The silence seemed to stretch for many minutes. But in fact it lasted probably no more than thirty seconds, and then from the gallery I heard what sounded like a great sigh, a deep, collective 'ummmm', followed by the cries of women.

I had read for over four hours. It was a little after 4 in the afternoon, the time court normally adjourned. But Justice de Wet, as soon as there was order in the courtroom, asked for the next witness. He was determined to lessen the impact of my statement. He did not want it to be the last and only testimony of the day. But nothing he did could weaken its effect. When I finished my address and sat down, it was the last time that Justice de Wet ever looked me in the eye.

The speech received wide publicity in both the local and foreign press, and was printed, virtually word for word, in the *Rand Daily Mail*. This despite the fact that all my words were banned. The speech both indicated our line of defence and disarmed the prosecution, which had prepared its entire case based on the expectation that I would be giving evidence denying responsibility for sabotage. It was now plain that we would not attempt to use legal niceties to avoid accepting responsibility for actions we had taken with pride and premeditation.

*   *   *

Accused No. 2, Walter Sisulu, was next. Walter had

to bear the brunt of the cross-examination that Yutar had prepared for me. Walter withstood a barrage of hostile questions and rose above Yutar's petty machinations to explain our policy in clear and simple terms. He asserted that Operation Mayibuye and the policy of guerrilla warfare had not been adopted as ANC policy. In fact, Walter told the court that he had personally opposed its adoption on the grounds that it was premature.

Govan followed Walter into the witness box and proudly related to the court his longtime membership of the Communist Party. The prosecutor asked Govan why, if he admitted many of the actions in the four counts against him, he did not simply plead guilty to the four counts? 'First,' Govan said, 'I felt I should come and explain under oath some of the reasons that led me to join these organizations. There was a sense of moral duty attached to it. Secondly, for the simple reason that to plead guilty would to my mind indicate a sense of moral guilt. I do not accept there is moral guilt attached to my answers.'

Like Govan, Ahmed Kathrada and Rusty Bernstein testified to their membership of the Communist Party as well as the ANC. Although Rusty was captured at Rivonia during the raid, the only direct evidence that the state had against him was that he had assisted in the erection of a radio aerial at the farm. Kathy, in his sharp-witted testimony, denied committing acts of sabotage or inciting others to do so, but he said he supported such acts if they advanced the struggle.

We had all been surprised when accused No. 8, James Kantor, had been arrested and grouped with us. Apart from being the brother-in-law and legal

58

partner of Harold Wolpe, who performed a number of transactions for us through his office, he had no involvement whatsoever with the ANC or MK. There was virtually no evidence against him, and I assumed the only reason the state kept up the charade of prosecuting him in prison was to intimidate progressive lawyers.

On the day that Justice de Wet was to rule on Jimmy's case, we were waiting in the cells underneath the court and I said to Jimmy, 'Let us exchange ties for good luck.' But when he saw the wide, old-fashioned tie I gave him compared to the lovely silk tie he gave me, he probably thought I was merely trying to improve my wardrobe. Jimmy was something of a clothes-horse, but he wore the tie to court and when Justice de Wet dismissed the charges against him, he lifted the tie up to me as a kind of salute and farewell.

Raymond Mhlaba was one of the leading ANC and MK figures in the eastern Cape, but because the state did not have much evidence against him, he denied he was a member of MK and that he knew anything about sabotage. We all decided that neither Elias Motsoaledi, accused No. 9, nor Andrew Mlangeni, accused No. 10, should testify. They were low-level members of MK, and could not add much to what had already been said. Elias Motsoaledi, despite having been beaten and tortured in prison, never broke down. Andrew Mlangeni, the last accused, made an unsworn statement admitting that he carried messages and instructions for MK and had disguised himself as a priest to facilitate this work. He, too, informed the court that he had been assaulted while in prison, and subjected to electric shock treatment. Andrew was the last witness. The defence rested. All that remained were the final arguments and then judgment.

*   *   *

On 20 May, Yutar handed out a dozen blue leather-bound volumes of his final speech to the press and one to the defence. Despite its handsome packaging, Yutar's address was a garbled summary of the prosecution's case and did not explain the indictment or assess the evidence. It was filled with *ad hominem* insults. 'The deceit of the accused is amazing,' he said at one point. 'Although they represented scarcely 1 per cent of the Bantu population they took it upon themselves to tell the world that the Africans in South Africa are suppressed, oppressed and depressed.' Even Judge de Wet seemed mystified by Yutar's speech, and at one point interrupted him to say, 'Mr Yutar, you do concede that you failed to prove guerrilla warfare was ever decided upon, do you not?'

Yutar was stunned. He had assumed precisely the opposite. We were surprised as well, for the judge's question gave us hope. Yutar haltingly told the court that preparations for guerrilla warfare were indeed made.

'Yes, I know that,' de Wet replied impatiently, 'the defence concedes that. But they say that prior to their arrest they took no decision to engage in guerrilla warfare. I take it that you have no evidence contradicting that and that you accept it?'

'As Your Worship wishes,' Yutar said in a strangled voice.

Yutar finished by saying that the case was not

only one of high treason *par excellence*, but of murder and attempted murder—neither of which was mentioned in the indictment. In a fit of bluster, he proclaimed, 'I make bold to say that every particular allegation in the indictment has been proved.' He knew, even as he uttered those words, that they were patently false.

*   *   *

Defence counsel Arthur Chaskalson rose first to deal with some of the legal questions raised by the prosecution. He rejected Yutar's statement that the trial had anything to do with murder, and reminded the court that MK's express policy was that there should be no loss of life. When Arthur began to explain that other organizations committed acts of sabotage for which the accused were blamed, de Wet interrupted to say he already accepted that as a fact. This was another unexpected victory.

Bram Fischer spoke next and was prepared to tackle the state's two most serious contentions: that we had undertaken guerrilla warfare and that the ANC and MK were the same. Though de Wet had said he believed that guerrilla warfare had not yet begun, we were taking no chances. But as Bram launched into his first point, de Wet interjected somewhat testily, 'I thought I made my attitude clear. I accept that no decision or date was fixed upon for guerrilla warfare.'

When Bram began his second point, de Wet again interrupted him to say that he also conceded the fact that the two organizations were separate. Bram, who was usually prepared for anything, was hardly prepared for de Wet's response. He then sat

61

down; the judge had accepted his arguments even before he had made them. We were jubilant—that is, if men facing the death sentence can be said to be jubilant. Court was adjourned for three weeks while de Wet considered the verdict.

57

The world had been paying attention to the Rivonia Trial. Night-long vigils were held for us at St Paul's Cathedral in London. The students of the University of London elected me president of their Students' Union, *in absentia*. A group of experts at the UN pressed for a national convention for South Africa that would lead to a truly representative parliament, and recommended an amnesty for all opponents of apartheid. Two days before Judge de Wet was due to give his decision, the UN Security Council (with four abstentions, including Great Britain and the United States) urged the South African government to end the trial and grant amnesty to the defendants.

In the days before we were due to reconvene, I wrote papers for a set of University of London examinations for my LLB. It might seem odd that I was taking law exams a few days before the verdict. It certainly seemed bizarre to my guards, who said I would not need a law degree where I was going. But I had continued my studies throughout the trial and I wanted to take the examination. I was single-minded about it, and I later realized that it was a way to keep myself from thinking negatively. I knew I would not be practising law again very soon, but I did not want to consider the alternative. I passed the exams.

* * *

On Thursday 11 June we reassembled in the Palace of Justice for the verdict. We knew that for at least six of us there could be no verdict but guilty. The question was the sentence.

De Wet wasted no time in getting down to business. He spoke in low, rapid tones. 'I have recorded the reasons for the conclusions I have come to. I do not propose to read them out.

'Accused No. 1 is found guilty on all four counts. Accused No. 2 is found guilty on all four counts. Accused No. 3 is found guilty on all four counts . . .'

De Wet pronounced each of the main accused guilty on all counts. Kathy was found guilty on only one of four counts, and Rusty Bernstein was found not guilty and discharged.

'I do not propose to deal with the question of sentence today,' de Wet said. 'The state and the defence will be given opportunities to make any submission they want tomorrow morning at ten o'clock.' Court was then adjourned.

We had hoped that Kathy and Mhlaba might escape conviction, but it was another sign, if one was necessary, that the state was taking a harsh line. If he could convict Mhlaba on all four counts with little evidence, could the death sentence be far behind for those of us against whom the evidence was overwhelming?

* * *

63

That night, after a discussion among ourselves, Walter, Govan and I informed counsel that whatever sentences we received, even the death sentence, we would not appeal. Our decision stunned our lawyers. Walter, Govan and I believed an appeal would undermine the moral stance we had taken. We had from the first maintained that what we had done, we had done proudly and for moral reasons. We were not now going to suggest otherwise in an appeal. If a death sentence was passed, we did not want to hamper the mass campaign that would surely spring up. In light of the bold and defiant line we had taken all along, an appeal would seem anti-climactic and even disillusioning. Our message was that no sacrifice was too great in the struggle for freedom.

Counsel were unhappy about our decision, and wanted to talk about an appeal. But Walter, Govan and I wanted to discuss the mechanics of the sentencing procedure the next day. If we were sentenced to death, what would then happen? We were told that after de Wet pronounced the death sentence, he would ask me, as the first accused, 'Have you any reason to advance why the sentence of death should not be passed?' I told Bram, Joel and Vernon that in that case I would have quite a lot to say. I would tell de Wet that I was prepared to die secure in the knowledge that my death would be an inspiration to the cause for which I was giving my life. My death—our deaths—would not be in vain; if anything we might serve the cause better in death as martyrs than we ever could in life. Counsel said that such a speech would not be very helpful for an appeal, and I reaffirmed that we would not be appealing.

Even if—especially if—we did not receive the death penalty, there were practical reasons not to appeal. For one thing, we might lose. An appellate court might decide that de Wet had been too lenient and that we deserved the death penalty. An appeal would forestall international pressure to release us.

For the state, a death sentence would be the most practical verdict. We had heard that John Vorster, the minister of justice, had told friends that Prime Minister Smuts's greatest blunder during the Second World War was not hanging him for his treason. The Nationalists, he said, would not make the same mistake.

I was prepared for the death penalty. To be truly prepared for something, one must actually expect it. One cannot be prepared for something while secretly believing it will not happen. We were all prepared, not because we were brave but because we were realistic. I thought of the line from Shakespeare: 'Be absolute for death; for either death or life shall be the sweeter.'

58

On Friday 12 June 1964 we entered court for the last time. Nearly a year had passed since the fateful arrests at Rivonia. Security was extraordinarily high. Our convoy raced through the streets with sirens wailing. All the roads leading to the courthouse had been blocked off to normal traffic. The police checked the identification of anyone attempting to go near the Palace of Justice. They had even set up checkpoints at the local bus and railway stations. Despite the intimidation, as many as two thousand people assembled in front of the courthouse holding banners and signs such as 'WE STAND BY OUR LEADERS'. Inside, the spectators' gallery was full, and it was standing room only for the local and foreign press.

I waved hello to Winnie and my mother. It was heartening to see them there; my mother had journeyed all the way from the Transkei. It must be a very odd sensation to come to a courtroom to see whether or not your son will be sentenced to death. Though I suspect my mother did not understand all that was going on, her support never wavered. Winnie was equally stalwart, and her strength gave me strength.

The registrar called out the case: 'The State against Nelson Mandela and others.' Before sentence was passed, there were two pleas in mitigation. One was delivered by Harold Hanson and the other by the author Alan Paton, who was also national president of the Liberal Party. Hanson spoke eloquently, saying that a nation's grievances cannot be suppressed, that people will always find a way to give voice to those grievances. 'It was not their aims which had been criminal,' said Hanson, 'only the means to which they had resorted.' Hanson said the judge would do well to recall that his own people, the Afrikaners, had struggled violently for their freedom.

Though Paton did not himself support violence, he said the accused had had only two alternatives: 'to bow their heads and submit, or to resist by force'. The defendants should receive clemency, he said, otherwise the future of South Africa would be bleak.

But de Wet did not seem to be listening to either man. He neither looked up nor took any notes while they spoke. He seemed absorbed in his own thoughts. He had obviously already decided; he was merely waiting for the moment to reveal his decision.

*   *   *

He nodded for us to rise. I tried to catch his eye, but he was not even looking in our direction. His eyes were focused on the middle distance. His face was very pale, and he was breathing heavily. We looked at each other and seemed to know: it would be death, otherwise why was this normally calm man so nervous? And then he began to speak.

> I have heard a great deal during the course of this case about the grievances of the non-European population. The accused have told me and their counsel have told me that the accused who were all leaders of the non-European population were motivated entirely by a desire to ameliorate these grievances. I am by no means convinced that the motives of the accused were as altruistic as they wish the court to believe. People who organize a revolution usually take over the government and personal ambition cannot be excluded as a motive.

De Wet paused for a moment as if to catch his breath. His voice, which was muted before, was now barely audible.

The function of this court, as is the function of the court in any other country, is to enforce law and order and to enforce the laws of the state within which it functions. The crime of which the accused have been convicted, that is the main crime, the crime of conspiracy, is in essence one of high treason. The state has decided not to charge the crime in this form. Bearing this in mind and giving the matter very serious consideration I have decided not to impose the supreme penalty which in a case like this would usually be the proper penalty for the crime, but consistent with my duty that is the only leniency which I can show. The sentence in the case of all the accused will be one of life imprisonment.

We looked at each other and smiled. There had been a great collective gasp in the courtroom when de Wet announced that he was not sentencing us to death. But there was consternation among some spectators because they had been unable to hear de Wet's sentence. Dennis Goldberg's wife called to him, 'Dennis, what is it?'

'Life!' he yelled back, grinning. 'Life! To live!'

I turned and smiled broadly to the gallery, searching out Winnie's face and that of my mother, but it was extremely confused in the court, with people shouting, police pushing the crowd this way and that. I could not see them. I flashed the thumbs-up ANC salute as many of the spectators were dashing outside to tell the crowd the verdict. Our police guardians began to hustle us out of the dock and towards the door leading underground, but although I looked again for Winnie's face, I was not able to see her before I ducked through the door leading to the cells below.

* * *

We were kept handcuffed in the cells underneath the courthouse. The police were extremely nervous about the crowd outside. They kept us underground for more than half an hour, hoping people would disperse. We were taken through the back of the building and entered the black van. We could hear the motorcycle escort revving up beside us. To avoid the crowd, the van took a different route, but even so, we could hear the crowd shouting *'Amandla!'*, and the slow beautiful rhythms of *'Nkosi Sikelel' iAfrika'*. We made clenched fists through the bars of the window, hoping the crowd could see us, not knowing if they could.

All of us were now convicted prisoners. We were separated from Dennis Goldberg because he was white and was taken to a different facility. The rest of us were locked up in cells in Pretoria Local away from all the other prisoners. Instead of shouts and songs, we now heard only the clanging of doors and gates.

* * *

That night, as I lay on my mat on the floor of my cell, I ran over the reasons for de Wet's decision. The demonstrations throughout South Africa and the international pressure undoubtedly weighed on his mind. International trade unions had protested

69

the trial. Dock-workers' unions around the world threatened not to handle South African goods. The Russian prime minister, Leonid Brezhnev, wrote to Dr Verwoerd asking for leniency. Members of the United States Congress protested. Fifty members of the British Parliament had staged a march in London. Alec Douglas-Home, the British foreign secretary, was rumoured to be working behind the scenes to help our cause. Adlai Stevenson, the US representative at the UN, wrote a letter saying that his government would do everything it could to prevent a death sentence. I thought that once de Wet had accepted that we had not yet initiated guerrilla warfare and that the ANC and MK were separate entities, it would have been difficult to impose the death penalty; it would have seemed excessive.

Verwoerd told Parliament that the judgment had not been influenced by the telegrams of protest and representations that had come in from around the world. He boasted that he had tossed into the waste-basket all the telegrams from socialist nations.

Towards the end of the proceedings, Judge de Wet had remarked in passing to Bram Fischer that the defence had generated a great deal of worldwide propaganda in the case. This was perhaps his own way of acknowledging the pressure. He knew that if we were executed, the great majority of the people would regard him as our killer.

Yet he was under even greater pressure from his own people. He was a white Afrikaner, a creature of the South African system and mind-set. He had no inclination to go against the belief system that had formed him. He had succumbed to these pressures by sentencing us to life and resisted them by not giving us death.

I was surprised and displeased by the sentences de Wet imposed on Kathrada, Motsoaledi and Mlangeni. I had expected him to discharge Kathy, and to give Elias and Andrew lighter sentences. The latter two were comparatively junior members of MK, and the combined offences of the three of them could hardly be compared with those of the rest of us. But by not appealing, we undoubtedly cost Kathy, Andrew and Elias: an appeals court might have cut down their sentences.

Every evening, in Pretoria Local, before lights were out, the jail would echo to African prisoners singing freedom songs. We too would sing in this great swelling chorus. But, each evening, seconds before the lights were dimmed, as if in obedience to some silent command, the hum of voices would stop and the entire jail would become silent. Then, from a dozen places throughout the prison, men would yell *'Amandla!'* This would be met by hundreds of voices replying *'Ngawethu!'* Often we would start this call-and-response ourselves, but that night other, nameless, prisoners took the initiative, and the voices from around the prison seemed uncommonly strong as though steeling us for what lay ahead.

PART EIGHT

Robben Island:
The Dark Years

At midnight, I was awake and staring at the ceiling—images from the trial were still rattling around in my head—when I heard steps coming down the corridor. I was locked in my own cell, away from the others. There was a knock at my door and I could see Colonel Aucamp's face at the bars. 'Mandela,' he said in a husky whisper, 'are you awake?'

I told him I was. 'You are a lucky man,' he said. 'We are taking you to a place where you will have your freedom. You will be able to move around; you'll see the ocean and the sky, not just grey walls.'

He intended no sarcasm, but I well knew that the place he was referring to would not afford me the freedom I longed for. He then remarked rather cryptically, 'As long as you don't make trouble, you'll get everything you want.'

Aucamp then woke the others, all of whom were in a single cell, ordering them to pack their things. Fifteen minutes later we were making our way through the iron labyrinth of Pretoria Local, with its endless series of clanging metal doors echoing in our ears.

Once outside, the seven of us—Walter, Raymond, Govan, Kathy, Andrew, Elias and I— were handcuffed and piled into the back of a police van. It was well after midnight, but none of us was tired, and the atmosphere was not at all sombre. We sat on the dusty floor, singing and chanting, reliving the final moments of the trial. The warders provided us with sandwiches and cold drinks and Lieutenant van Wyck was perched in the back with us. He was a pleasant fellow and, during a lull in the singing, he offered his unsolicited opinion on our future. 'Well,' he said, 'you chaps won't be in prison long. The demand for your release is too strong. In a year or two, you will get out and you will return as national heroes. Crowds will cheer you, everyone will want to be your friend, women will want you. Ag, you fellows have it made.' We listened without comment, but I confess his speech cheered me considerably. Unfortunately, his prediction proved to be out by nearly three decades.

*   *   *

We were departing quietly, secretly, under a heavy police escort, in the middle of the night, and in less than half an hour we found ourselves at a small military airport outside the city. We were hustled on to a Dakota, a large military transport plane that had seen better days. There was no heat, and we shivered in the belly of the plane. Some of the others had never flown before and they seemed more anxious about our voyage than our destination; bumping up and down in a plane at fifteen thousand feet seemed far more perilous than being locked in a cell behind high walls.

After about an hour in the air, dawn lightened the terrain below. The plane had portholes, and as soon as we could see in the half-light, my comrades pressed their faces to the glass. We flew southeast, over the dry, flat plains of the Orange Free State and the green and mountainous Cape peninsula. I, too, craned to see out of the portholes, examining the scenery not as a tourist but as a strategist, looking for areas where a guerrilla army might hide itself.

There had been a running argument since the formation of MK as to whether the countryside of South Africa could support a guerrilla army. Most of the High Command thought that it could not. When we flew over a wooded, mountainous area called Matroosberg in the Cape, I yelled to my colleagues that here was terrain where we could fight. The men became excited and craned to get a better look, and indeed, the heavily forested area appeared as though it could shelter a nascent guerrilla force.

Minutes later we approached the outskirts of Cape Town. Soon, we could see the little matchbox houses of the Cape Flats, the gleaming towers of downtown, and the horizontal top of Table Mountain. Then, out in Table Bay, in the dark blue waters of the Atlantic, we could make out the misty outline of Robben Island.

* * *

We landed at an airstrip on one end of the island. It was a grim, overcast day, and when I stepped out of the plane, the cold winter wind whipped through our thin prison uniforms. We were met by guards with automatic weapons; the atmosphere was tense but quiet, unlike the boisterous reception I had received on my arrival on the island two years before.

We were driven to the old jail, an isolated stone building, where we were ordered to strip while standing outside. One of the ritual indignities of prison life is that when you are transferred from one prison to another, the first thing that happens is that you change from the garb of the old prison to that of the new. When we were undressed, we were thrown the plain khaki uniforms of Robben Island.

Apartheid's regulations extended even to clothing. All of us, except Kathy, received short trousers, an insubstantial jersey and a canvas jacket. Kathy, the one Indian among us, was given long trousers. Normally Africans would receive sandals made from car tyres, but in this instance we were given shoes. Kathy, alone, received socks. Short trousers for Africans were meant to remind us that we were 'boys'. I put on the short trousers that day, but I vowed that I would not put up with them for long.

The warders pointed with their guns to where they wanted us to go, and barked their orders in simple one-word commands: 'Move!' 'Silence!' 'Halt!' They did not threaten us in the swaggering way that I recalled from my previous stay, and betrayed no emotion.

The old jail was only temporary quarters for us. The authorities were in the process of finishing an entirely separate maximum-security structure for political prisoners. While there, we were not permitted to go outside or have any contact with other prisoners.

*　　*　　*

The fourth morning we were handcuffed and taken in a covered truck to a prison within a prison. This

78

new structure was a one-storey rectangular stone fortress with a flat cement courtyard in the centre, about one hundred feet by thirty feet. It had cells on three of the four sides. The fourth side was a twenty-foot-high wall with a catwalk patrolled by guards with German shepherds.

The three lines of cells were known as sections A, B and C, and we were put in section B, on the easternmost side of the quadrangle. We were each given individual cells on either side of a long corridor, with half the cells facing the courtyard. There were about thirty cells in all. The total number of prisoners in the single cells was usually about twenty-four. Each cell had one window, about a foot square, covered with iron bars. The cell had two doors: a metal gate or grille with iron bars on the inside and a thick wooden door outside that. During the day, only the grille was locked; at night, the wooden door was locked as well.

The cells had been constructed hurriedly, and the walls were perpetually damp. When I mentioned this to the commanding officer, he told me our bodies would absorb the moisture. We were each issued with three blankets so flimsy and worn they were practically transparent. Our bedding consisted of a single sisal or straw mat. Later we were given a felt mat, and one placed the felt mat on top of the sisal one to provide some softness. At that time of year, the cells were so cold and the blankets provided so little warmth that we always slept fully dressed.

I was assigned a cell at the head of the corridor. It overlooked the courtyard and had a small eye-level window. I could walk the length of my cell in three paces. When I lay down, I could feel the wall with my feet and my head grazed the concrete at the other side. The width was about six feet, and the walls were at least two feet thick. Each cell had a white card posted outside it with our name and our prison service number. Mine read, 'N. Mandela 466/64', which meant I was the 466th prisoner admitted to the island in 1964. I was forty-six years old, a political prisoner with a life sentence, and that small cramped space was to be my home for I knew not how long.

*　　*　　*

We were immediately joined by a number of prisoners who had been held in the general section of the prison, a squat brick building not far from section B. The general prison, known as sections F and G, contained about a thousand mostly common-law prisoners. As many as a quarter of them were political prisoners, and a handful of those men were put with us in section B. We were isolated from the general prisoners for two reasons: we were considered risky from a security perspective, but even more dangerous from a political standpoint. The authorities were concerned that we might 'infect' the other prisoners with our political views.

Among the men put with us was George Peake, one of the founders of the South African Coloured People's Organization, a Treason Trialist, and most recently a member of the Cape Town City Council. He had been sentenced for planting explosives outside a Cape Town prison. Dennis Brutus, another Coloured political activist, was a poet and writer from Port Elizabeth imprisoned for violating his bans. We were also joined by Billy Nair, a long-time member of the Natal Indian Congress, sentenced for sabotage as a member of Umkhonto we Sizwe.

Within a few days we had more company, including Neville Alexander, a prominent Coloured intellectual and member of the Non-European Unity Movement, who had formed a tiny radical offshoot called the Yu Chi Chan Club in Cape Town which studied guerrilla warfare. Neville had a BA from the University of Cape Town and a doctorate in German literature from Tubingen University in Germany. Along with Neville, there was Fikile Bam, a law student from the University of Cape Town and another member of the Yu Chi Chan Club, and Zephania Mothopeng, a member of the PAC National Executive. Zeph had been a teacher in Orlando, and was a staunch opponent of Bantu Education, and one of the most level-headed of the PAC's leaders. Three aged peasants from the Transkei, sentenced for plotting to assassinate K. D. Matanzima, now the chief minister of the 'self-governing' Transkei, were also imprisoned with us.

This became our core group of about twenty prisoners. Some I knew, some I had heard of, while others I did not know at all. Normally in prison one of the few festive times is seeing old friends and new faces, but the atmosphere in those first few weeks was so oppressive that we were not even able to greet each other. There were as many guards as prisoners, and they enforced every regulation with threats and intimidation.

*   *   *

That first week we began the work that would occupy us for the next few months. Each morning, a load of stones about the size of volleyballs was dumped by the entrance to the courtyard. Using wheelbarrows, we moved the stones to the centre of the yard. We were given either four-pound hammers, or fourteen-pound hammers for the larger stones. Our job was to crush the stones into gravel. We were divided into four rows, about a yard-and-a-half apart, and sat cross-legged on the ground. We were each given a thick rubber ring, made from tyres, in which to place the stones. The ring was meant to catch flying chips of stone, but hardly ever did so. We wore makeshift wire masks to protect our eyes.

Warders walked among us to enforce the silence. During those first few weeks, warders from other sections and even other prisons came to stare at us as if we were a collection of rare caged animals. The work was tedious and difficult; it was not strenuous enough to keep us warm but demanding enough to make all our muscles ache.

June and July were the bleakest months on Robben Island. Winter was in the air, and the rains were just beginning. It never seemed to go above 40 degrees Fahrenheit. Even in the sun, I shivered in my light khaki shirt. It was then that I first understood the cliché of feeling the cold in one's bones. At noon we would break for lunch. That first week all we were given was soup, which stank horribly. In the afternoons we were permitted to exercise for half an hour under strict supervision. We walked briskly around the courtyard in single file.

On one of our first days pounding rocks, a warder commanded Kathy to take a wheelbarrow filled with gravel to the truck parked by the entrance. Kathy was a slender fellow unused to hard physical labour. He could not shift the wheelbarrow. The warders yelled: '*Laat daardie kruiwa loop!*' ('Make that wheelbarrow move!') As Kathy managed to nudge it forward, the wheelbarrow looked as if it would tip over, and the warders began to laugh. Kathy, I could see, was determined not to give them cause for mirth. I knew how to manoeuvre the wheelbarrows, and I jumped up to help him. Before being ordered to sit down, I managed to tell Kathy to wheel it slowly, that it was a matter of balance not strength. He nodded and then carefully moved the wheelbarrow across the courtyard. The warders stopped smiling.

The next morning, the authorities placed an enormous skip in the courtyard and announced that it had to be half full by the end of the week. We worked hard, and succeeded. The following week, the warder in charge announced that we must now fill the skip three-quarters of the way. We worked with great diligence, and succeeded. The next week we were ordered to fill the skip to the top. We knew we could not tolerate this much longer, but said nothing. We even managed to fill the skip all the way, but the warders had provoked us. In stolen whispers we resolved on a policy: no quotas. The next week we initiated our first go-slow strike on the island: we would work at less than half the speed we had before to protest at the excessive and unfair demands. The guards immediately saw this and threatened us, but we would not increase our pace, and we continued this go-slow strategy for as long as we worked in the courtyard.

*　　*　　*

Robben Island had changed since I had been there for a fortnight in 1962. In 1962 there were few prisoners; the place seemed more like an experiment than a fully-fledged prison. Two years later, Robben Island was without question the harshest, most iron-fisted outpost in the South African penal system. It was a hardship station not only for the prisoners but for the prison staff. Gone were the Coloured warders who had supplied cigarettes and sympathy. The warders, now white and overwhelmingly Afrikaans-speaking, demanded a master–servant relationship. They ordered us to call them *baas*, which we refused to do. The racial divide on Robben Island was absolute: there were no black warders, and no white prisoners.

Moving from one prison to another always requires a period of adjustment. But journeying to Robben Island was like going to another country. Its isolation made it not simply another prison, but a world of its own, far removed from the one we had come from. The high spirits with which we left Pretoria had been snuffed out by its stern atmosphere; we were face to face with the realization that our life would be unredeemably grim. In Pretoria we felt connected to our supporters and our families; on the island we felt cut off, and indeed we were. We had the consolation of being with each other, but that was the only consolation. My dismay was quickly

84

replaced by a sense that a new and different fight had begun.

From the first day, I had protested about being forced to wear short trousers. I demanded to see the head of the prison and made a list of complaints. The warders ignored my protests, but by the end of the second week, I found a pair of old khaki trousers unceremoniously dumped on the floor of my cell. No pin-striped three-piece suit has ever pleased me as much. But before putting them on I checked to see if my comrades had also been issued with trousers.

They had not, and I told the warder to take the trousers back. I insisted that all African prisoners must have long trousers. The warder grumbled, 'Mandela, you say you want long pants and then you don't want them when we give them to you.' The warder baulked at touching trousers worn by a black man, and finally the commanding officer himself came to my cell to pick them up. 'Very well, Mandela,' he said, 'you are going to have the same clothing as everyone else.' I replied that if he was willing to give me long trousers, why couldn't everyone else have them? He did not have an answer.

60

At the end of our first two weeks on the island, we were informed that our lawyers, Bram Fischer and Joel Joffe, were going to be visiting the following day. When they arrived, we were escorted to the visiting area to meet them. The purpose of their visit was twofold: to see how we had settled in, and to verify that we still did not want to appeal against our sentences. It had only been a few weeks since I had seen them, but it felt like an eternity. They seemed like visitors from another world.

We sat in an empty room, a major just outside to supervise the consultation. I felt like hugging them, but I was restrained by the presence of the major. I told them that all of us were well, and explained that we were still opposed to an appeal for all the reasons we had previously enunciated, including the fact that we did not want our appeal to interfere with the cases of other ANC defendants. Bram and Joel seemed resigned to this, though I knew Bram believed we should mount an appeal.

When we were winding up our conversation, I briefly asked Bram about Molly, his wife. No sooner had I pronounced Molly's name than Bram stood up, turned away, and abruptly walked out of the room. A few minutes later he returned, once again composed, and resumed the conversation, but without answering my question.

Our meeting ended shortly afterwards, and when we were walking back to our cells with the major, he said to me, 'Mandela, were you struck by the behaviour of Bram Fischer?' I said that I had been. He told me that Molly had died in a car accident the previous week. Bram, he said, had been driving and had swerved to avoid an animal in the road, and the car had plunged into a river. Molly had drowned.

We were devastated by the news. Molly was a wonderful woman, generous and unselfish, utterly without prejudice. She had supported Bram in more ways than it was possible to know. She had been wife, colleague and comrade. Bram had already experienced disaster in his life: his son had died of cystic fibrosis in adolescence.

The act of turning away when I asked about Molly was typical of Bram's character. He was a stoic, a man who never burdened his friends with his own pain and troubles. As an Afrikaner whose conscience forced him to reject his own heritage and be ostracized by his own people, he showed a level of courage and sacrifice that was in a class by itself. I fought only against injustice, not my own people.

I informed the major that I intended to write Bram a letter of condolence, and he responded that I could. The rules governing letter-writing were then extremely strict. We were permitted to write only to our immediate families, and just one letter of five hundred words every six months. I was therefore surprised and pleased when the major did not oppose my writing to Bram. But he didn't live up to his agreement. I wrote the letter and handed it over, but it was never posted.

*　　　*　　　*

Within a few months our life settled into a pattern. Prison life is about routine: each day like the one before; each week like the one before it, so that the months and years blend into each other. Anything that departs from this pattern upsets the authorities, for routine is the sign of a well-run prison.

Routine is also comforting for the prisoner, which is why it can be a trap. Routine can be a pleasant mistress whom it is hard to resist, for routine makes the time go faster. Watches and timepieces of any kind were barred on Robben Island, so we never knew precisely what time it was. We were dependent on bells and warders' whistles and shouts. With each week resembling the one before, one must make an effort to recall what day and month it is. One of the first things I did was to make a calendar on the wall of my cell. Losing a sense of time is an easy way to lose one's grip and even one's sanity.

Time slows down in prison; the days seem endless. The cliché of time passing slowly usually has to do with idleness and inactivity. But this was not the case on Robben Island. We were busy almost all the time with work, study, resolving disputes. Yet time nevertheless moved glacially. This is partially because things that took a few hours or days outside would take months or years in prison. A request for a new toothbrush might take six months or a year to be fulfilled. Ahmed Kathrada once said that in prison the minutes can seem like years, but the years go by like minutes. An afternoon pounding rocks in the courtyard might seem like forever, but suddenly it is the end of the year, and you do not know where all the months went.

The challenge for every prisoner, particularly every political prisoner, is how to survive prison intact, how to emerge from prison undiminished, how to conserve and even replenish one's beliefs. The first task in accomplishing that is learning exactly what one must do to survive. To that end, one must know the enemy's purpose before adopting a strategy to undermine it. Prison is designed to break one's spirit and destroy one's resolve. To do this, the authorities attempt to exploit every weakness, demolish every initiative, negate all signs of individuality—all with the idea of stamping out that spark that makes each of us human and each of us who we are.

Our survival depended on understanding what the authorities were attempting to do to us, and sharing that understanding with each other. It would be very hard, if not impossible, for one man alone to resist. I do not know that I could have done it had I been alone. But the authorities' greatest mistake was to keep us together, for together our determination was reinforced. We supported each other and gained strength from each other. Whatever we knew, whatever we learned, we shared, and by sharing we multiplied whatever courage we had individually. That is not to say that we were all alike in our responses to the hardships we suffered. Men have different capacities and react differently to stress. But the stronger ones raised up the weaker ones, and both became stronger in the process. Ultimately, we had to create our own lives in prison. In a way that even the authorities acknowledged, order in prison was preserved not by the warders but by ourselves.

As a leader, one must sometimes take actions that are unpopular, or whose results will not be known for years to come. There are victories whose glory lies only in the fact that they are known to those who win them. This is particularly true of prison, where you must find consolation in being true to your ideals, even if no one else knows of it.

I was now on the sidelines, but I also knew that I would not give up the fight. I was in a different and smaller arena, an arena for whom the only audience was ourselves and our oppressors. We regarded the struggle in prison as a microcosm of the struggle as a whole. We would fight inside as we had fought outside. The racism and repression were the same; I would simply have to fight on different terms.

Prison and the authorities conspire to rob each man of his dignity. In and of itself, that assured that I would survive, for any man or institution that tries to rob me of my dignity will lose because I will not part with it at any price or under any pressure. I never seriously considered the possibility that I would not emerge from prison one day. I never thought that a life sentence truly meant life and that I would die behind bars. Perhaps I was denying this prospect because it was too unpleasant to contemplate. But I always knew that someday I would once again feel the grass under my feet and walk in the sunshine as a free man.

I am fundamentally an optimist. Whether that comes from nature or nurture, I cannot say. Part of being optimistic is keeping one's head pointed towards the sun, one's feet moving forward. There were many dark moments when my faith in humanity was sorely tested, but I would not and could not give myself up to despair. That way lay defeat and death.

61

We were awakened at 5.30 each morning by the night warder, who clanged a brass bell at the head of our corridor and yelled, *'Word wakker! Staan op!'*

90

('Wake up! Get up!') I have always been an early riser and this hour was not a burden to me. Although we were roused at 5.30, we were not let out of our cells until 6.45, by which time we were meant to have cleaned our cells and rolled up our mats and blankets. We had no running water in our cells and instead of toilets had iron sanitary buckets known as 'ballies'. The ballies had a diameter of ten inches with a concave porcelain lid on the top that could contain water. The water in this lid was meant to be used for shaving and to clean our hands and faces.

At 6.45, when we were let out of our cells, the first thing we did was to empty our ballies. The ballies had to be thoroughly cleansed in the sinks at the end of the corridor or they created a stench. The only pleasant thing about cleaning one's ballie was that this was the one moment in those early days when we could have a whispered word with our colleagues. The warders did not like to linger when we cleaned them, so it was a chance to talk softly.

During those first few months, breakfast was delivered to us in our cells by prisoners from the general section. Breakfast consisted of mealie pap porridge, cereal made from maize or corn, which the general prisoners would slop in a bowl and then spin through the bars of our cells. It was a clever trick and required a deft hand so as not to spill any of the porridge.

After a few months, breakfast was delivered to us in the courtyard in old metal drums. We would help ourselves to pap using simple metal bowls. We each received a mug of what was described as coffee, but which was in fact ground-up maize, baked until it was black, and then brewed with hot water. Later, when we were able to go into the courtyard to serve ourselves, I would go out there and jog around the perimeter until breakfast arrived.

Like everything else in prison, diet is discriminatory. In general, Coloureds and Indians received a slightly better diet than Africans, but it was not much of a distinction. The authorities liked to say that we received a balanced diet; it was indeed balanced—between the unpalatable and the inedible. Food was the source of many of our protests, but in those early days, the warders would say, 'Ag, you kaffirs are eating better in prison than you ever ate at home!'

*   *   *

In the midst of breakfast, the guards would yell, *'Val in! Val in!'* ('Fall in! Fall in!'), and we would stand outside our cells for inspection. Each prisoner was required to have the three buttons of his khaki jacket properly buttoned. We were required to doff our hats as the warder walked by. If our buttons were undone, our hats unremoved, or our cells untidy, we were charged with a violation of the prison code and punished with either solitary confinement or the loss of meals.

After inspection we would work in the courtyard hammering stones until noon. There were no breaks; if we slowed down, the warders would yell at us to speed up. At noon, the bell would clang for lunch and another metal drum of food would be wheeled into the courtyard. For Africans, lunch consisted of boiled mealies, that is, coarse kernels of corn. The Indians and Coloured prisoners received samp, or mealie rice, which consisted of ground mealies in a soup-like mixture. The samp was sometimes served with vegetables, whereas our mealies were served straight.

For lunch we often received *phuzamandla*, which means 'drink of strength', a powder made from mealies and a bit of yeast. It is meant to be stirred into water or milk, and when it is thick it can be tasty, but the prison authorities gave us so little of the powder that it barely coloured the water. I would usually try to save my powder for several days until I had enough to make a proper drink, but if the authorities discovered that you were hoarding food, the powder was confiscated and you were punished.

After lunch we worked until 4, when the guards blew shrill whistles and we once again lined up to be counted and inspected. We were then permitted half an hour to clean up. The bathroom at the end of our corridor had two seawater showers, a saltwater tap and three large galvanized metal buckets, which were used as bathtubs. There was no hot water. We would stand or squat in these buckets, soaping ourselves with the brackish water, rinsing off the dust from the day. To wash yourself with cold water when it is cold outside is not pleasant, but we made the best of it. We would sometimes sing while washing, which made the water seem less icy. In those early days, this was one of the only times when we could converse.

Precisely at 4.30 there would be a loud knock on the wooden door at the end of our corridor, which meant that supper had been delivered. Common-law prisoners used to dish out the food to us and we would return to our cells to eat it. We again received mealie pap porridge, sometimes with the odd carrot or piece of cabbage or beetroot thrown in—but one usually had to search for it. If we did get a vegetable, we would usually have the same one for weeks on end, until the carrots or cabbages were old and mouldy and we were thoroughly sick of them. Every other day we received a small piece of meat with our porridge. The meat was usually mostly gristle.

For supper, Coloured and Indian prisoners received a quarter loaf of bread (known as a *katkop*, that is, a cat's head, after the shape of the bread) and a slab of margarine. Africans, it was presumed, did not care for bread as it was a 'European' type of food.

Typically, we received even less than the scanty amounts stipulated in the regulations. This was because the kitchen was rife with smuggling. The cooks—all of whom were common-law prisoners—kept the best food for themselves or their friends. Often they would lay aside the tastiest morsels for the warders in exchange for favours or preferential treatment.

At 8 p.m. the night warder would lock himself in the corridor with us, passing the key through a small hole in the door to another warder outside. The warder would then walk up and down the corridor, ordering us to go to sleep. No cry of 'lights out' was ever given on Robben Island because the single mesh-covered bulb in our cell burned day and night. Later, those studying for higher degrees were permitted to read until 10 or 11 p.m.

The acoustics along the corridor were quite

good, and we would try to chat a bit to each other before going to sleep. But if we could hear a whisper quite clearly, so could the warder, who would yell, *'Stilte in die gang!'* ('Quiet in the passage!') The warder would walk up and down a few times to make sure we were not reading or writing. After a few months, we would sprinkle a handful of sand along the corridor so that we could hear the warder's footsteps and have time to stop talking or hide any contraband. Only when we were quiet did he take a seat in the small office at the end of the passage where he dozed until morning.

62

One morning, several days after my meeting with Bram and Joel, we were taken to the head office. This was only about a quarter of a mile away and was a simple stone structure that resembled our own section. Once there, we were lined up to have our fingerprints taken, which was routine prison service business. But, while waiting, I noticed a warder with a camera. After our fingerprints had been taken, the chief warder ordered us to line up for photographs. I motioned to my colleagues not to move, and I addressed the warder: 'I would like you to produce the document from the commissioner of prisons authorizing our pictures to be taken.' Photographs of prisoners required such authorization.

It was always valuable to be familiar with regulation, because the warders themselves were often ignorant of them and could be intimidated by one's superior knowledge. The warder was taken aback by my request and unable to offer any explanation or produce anything in writing from the commissioner of prisons. He threatened to charge us if we did not consent to have our photographs taken, but I said that if there was no authorization, there would be no pictures, and that was where the matter remained.

As a rule, we objected to having our pictures taken in prison on the ground that it is generally demeaning to be seen as a prisoner. But there was one photograph I did consent to, the only one I ever agreed to while on Robben Island.

*   *   *

One morning a few weeks later, the chief warder, instead of handing us hammers for our work in the courtyard, gave us each needles and thread and a pile of worn prison jerseys. We were instructed to repair the garments, but we discovered that most of these jerseys were frayed beyond repair. This struck us as a curious task, and we wondered what had provoked the change. Later that morning, at about eleven o'clock, the front gate swung open to reveal the commanding officer with two men in suits. The CO announced that the two visitors were a reporter and photographer from the *Daily Telegraph* in London. He related this as if visiting members of the international press were a regular diversion for us.

Although these men were our first official visitors, we regarded them sceptically. First, they were brought in under the auspices of the government, and second, we were aware that the

Telegraph was a conservative newspaper unlikely to be sympathetic to our cause. We well knew that there was great concern in the outside world about our situation and that it was in the government's interest to show that we were not being mistreated.

The two journalists walked slowly around the courtyard, surveying us. We kept our heads down, concentrating on our work. After they had made one circuit, one of the guards plucked me by the shoulder and said, 'Mandela, come, you will talk now.' In those early days I often spoke on behalf of my fellow prisoners. The prison service regulations were explicit that each prisoner was permitted to speak only for himself. This was done to negate the power of organization and to neutralize our collective strength. We objected to this rule, but made little headway. We were not even permitted to use the word *we* when we made complaints. But during the first few years, when the authorities needed one prisoner to speak on behalf of others, that individual would be me.

I talked to the reporter, whose name was Mr Newman, for about twenty minutes, and was candid about both prison and the Rivonia Trial. He was an agreeable fellow, and at the end of our talk he said he would like the photographer to take my picture. I was reluctant, but in this case relented because I knew the photograph would be published only overseas, and might serve to help our cause if the article were even the least bit friendly. I told him I would agree, provided Mr Sisulu could join me. The image shows the two of us talking in the courtyard about some matter that I can no longer remember. I never saw the article or heard anything about it. The reporters were barely out of sight when the warders removed the jerseys and gave us back our hammers.

* * *

The men from the *Telegraph* were the first of a small stream of visitors during those early months. While the Rivonia Trial still resonated in people's minds, the government was eager to show the international community that we were being treated properly. There were stories in the press about the inhuman conditions on the island, about how we were being assaulted and tortured. These allegations embarrassed the government, and to combat them they brought in a string of outsiders meant to rebut these critical stories.

We were briefly visited by a British lawyer who had argued for Namibian independence before the World Court, after which we were informed that a Mr Hynning, a representative of the American Bar Association, would be coming to see us. Americans were then a novelty in South Africa, and I was curious to meet a representative of so august a legal organization.

On the day of Mr Hynning's visit we were called into the courtyard. The American arrived in the company of General Steyn, the commissioner of prisons, who rarely made appearances on the island. General Steyn was that unusual thing in the prison service, a polished and sophisticated man. His suits were always of a fine quality and a fashionable cut. He was courtly, and referred to us as 'gentlemen', even doffing his hat to us, something no one else in the prison service ever did. Yet General Steyn oppressed us by omission

98

rather than commission. He basically turned a blind eye to what was happening on the island. His habitual absence emboldened the more brutal prison officials and gave them carte blanche to do whatever they wanted. In his most gracious manner, the general introduced our guest and said, 'Gentlemen, please select your spokesman.' A number of the prisoners called out my name.

General Steyn nodded in my direction, and I stood up. In contrast to General Steyn, Mr Hynning was a heavyset, unkempt man. I thanked him for visiting us and said we were honoured by his presence. I then summarized our complaints, beginning with the central and most important one, that we were political prisoners, not criminals, and that we should be treated as such. I enumerated our grievances about the food, our living conditions and the work detail. But as I was speaking, Mr Hynning kept interrupting me. When I made a point about the long hours of mindless work, he declared that as prisoners we had to work and were probably lazy to boot.

When I started to explain the problems with our cells, he interjected that the conditions in backward American prisons were far worse than on Robben Island, which was a paradise by comparison. He added that we had been justly convicted and were lucky not to have received the death penalty, which we probably deserved.

Mr Hynning perspired a great deal and there were those among us who thought he was not altogether sober. He spoke in what I assumed was a southern American accent, and had a curious habit of spitting when he talked, something none of us had ever seen before.

Finally, I had heard enough, and I interrupted him, 'No, sir, you misunderstand the points that I am making.' Hynning took offence that I was now contradicting him, while General Steyn watched and listened without comment. Under the circumstances, it was difficult to keep tempers down. The men were angered by Mr Hynning's remarks and annoyed that he had been permitted to see us at all. Normally a visit of any kind lifted our spirits, but the visit of Mr Hynning was demoralizing. Perhaps that is what the authorities wanted. To meet someone with so impressive an affiliation and so little understanding was depressing. Hynning finally just turned and walked away without so much as a good-bye. We were not sorry to see him go.

We discussed Mr Hynning for years afterwards and many of the men imitated the way he spoke to comic effect. We never heard about him again, and he certainly did not win any friends on Robben Island for the American Bar Association.

63

In jail, all prisoners are classified by the authorities as one of four categories: A, B, C or D. A is the highest classification and confers the most privileges; D is the lowest and confers the least. All political prisoners, or what the authorities called 'security prisoners', were automatically classified as D on admission. The privileges affected by these classifications included visits and letters, studies, and the opportunity to buy groceries and incidentals—all of which are the lifeblood of any prisoner. It normally took years for a political prisoner to raise his status from D to C.

We despised the classification system. It was corrupt and demeaning, another way of repressing prisoners in general and political prisoners in particular. We demanded that all political prisoners be in one category. Although we criticized it, we could not ignore it: the classification system was an inflexible feature of prison life. If you protested that, as a D group prisoner, you could receive only one letter every six months, the authorities would say, 'Improve your behaviour, become a C group prisoner, and you will be able to receive two letters every six months.' If you complained that you did not receive enough food, the authorities would remind you that if you were in A group, you would be able to receive money orders from the outside and purchase extra food at the prison tuckshop. Even a freedom fighter benefits from the ability to buy groceries and books.

The classifications generally ran parallel to the length of one's sentence. If you were sentenced to eight years, you would generally be classified as D for the first two years, C for the next two, B for the following two and A for the last two. But the prison authorities wielded the classification system as a weapon against political prisoners, threatening to lower our hard-won classifications in order to control our behaviour.

Though I had been in prison for nearly two years before I was taken to Robben Island, I was still in D group when I arrived. While I desired the privileges that came with higher classifications, I refused to compromise my conduct. The fastest way to raise one's classification was to be docile and not complain. 'Ag, Mandela, you are a troublemaker,' the warders would say. 'You will be in D group for the rest of your life.'

Every six months, prisoners were called before the prison board to have their classifications evaluated. The board was meant to assess our behaviour in terms of prison regulations, but we found that it preferred to act as a political tribunal rather than a mere evaluator of behaviour. During my first meeting with the board, the officials asked me questions about the ANC and my beliefs. Although this had nothing to do with the classification system, I was vain enough to answer and think that I might convert them to my beliefs. It was one of the few times we were treated as human beings, and I for one responded. Later I realized that this was simply a technique on the part of the authorities to glean information from us, and I had fallen for it. Shortly afterwards, we agreed among ourselves not to discuss politics with the prison board.

*   *   *

As a D group prisoner, I was entitled to have only one visitor, and write and receive only one letter every six months. I found this one of the most inhumane restrictions of the prison system. Communication with one's family is a human right; it should not be restricted by the artificial gradations of a prison system. But it was one of the facts of prison life.

Visits and letters were restricted to 'first degree' relatives. This was a restriction we not only found irksome but racist. The African sense of immediate family is very different from that of the European or Westerner. Our family structures are larger and more inclusive; anyone who claims descent from a common ancestor is deemed part of the same family.

In prison, the only thing worse than bad news about one's family is no news at all. It is always harder to cope with the disasters and tragedies one imagines than with the reality, however grim or disagreeable. A letter with ill tidings was always preferable to no letter at all.

But even this miserable restriction was abused by the authorities. The anticipation of mail was overwhelming. Mail-call took place once a month, and sometimes six months would go by without a letter. To be allowed one letter in six months and then not to receive it is a great blow. One wonders: What has happened to my wife and children, to my mother and my sisters? When I did not receive a letter I felt as dry and barren as the Great Karroo desert. Often the authorities would withhold mail out of spite. I can remember warders saying, 'Mandela, we have received a letter for you, but we cannot give it to you.' No explanation of why, or who the letter is from. It required all my self-discipline not to explode at such times. Afterwards, I would protest through the proper channels, and sometimes get it.

When letters did arrive, they were cherished. A letter was like the summer rain that could make even the desert bloom. When I was handed a letter by the authorities, I would not rush forward and grab it as I felt like doing, but take it in a leisurely manner. Though I yearned to tear it open and read it on the spot, I would not give the authorities the satisfaction of seeing my eagerness, and I would return slowly to my cell as though I had many things to occupy me before opening a letter from my family.

During the first few months, I received one letter from Winnie, but it was so heavily censored that not much more than the salutation was left. The island's censors would black out the offending passages in ink, but they later changed this when they realized we could wash away the ink and see what was underneath. They began to use razors to slice out whole paragraphs. Since most letters were written on both sides of a single piece of paper, the material on the other side would also be excised. They seemed to relish delivering letters in tatters. The censorship delayed the delivery of mail because the warders, some of whom were not proficient in English, might take as long as a month to censor a letter. The letters we wrote were censored as well; they were often as cut up as those we received.

* * *

At the end of August, after I had been on the island less than three months, I was informed by the authorities that I would have a visitor the following day. They would not tell me who it was. Walter was informed that he, too, would have a visitor, and I suspected, I hoped, I wished—I believed—that it would be a visit from Winnie and Albertina.

From the moment Winnie learned we had been brought to the island, she had been trying to arrange a visit. As a banned person, she had to

104

receive a special dispensation from the minister of justice, for she was technically not permitted to communicate with me.

Even with the help of the authorities, visiting Robben Island was not an easy proposition. Visits were a maximum of thirty minutes long, and political prisoners were not permitted contact visits, in which the visitor and prisoner were in the same room.

Visits did not seem to be planned in advance by the authorities. One day, they would contact your wife and say, 'You have permission to visit your husband tomorrow.' This was enormously inconvenient, and often had the effect of making visits impossible. If a family member was able to plan a visit in advance, the authorities would sometimes deliberately delay issuing a permit until after the plane had departed. Since most of the men's families lived far from the Cape and had very little money, visits by family members were often far beyond their means. Some men who came from poor families did not see their wives for many years at a time, if at all. I knew of men who spent a decade or more on Robben Island without a single visit.

The visiting room for non-contact visits was cramped and windowless. On the prisoner's side was a row of five cubicles with small square pieces of glass that looked out on identical cubicles on the other side. One sat in a chair and looked through the thick, smudged glass that had a few small holes drilled into it to permit conversation. One had to talk very loudly to be heard. Later the authorities installed microphones and speakers in front of the glass, a marginal improvement.

Walter and I were called to the visitors' office in the late morning and took seats at the far end of the room. I waited with some anxiety, and suddenly, filling the glass on the other side of the window was Winnie's lovely face. Winnie always dressed up for prison visits, and tried to wear something new and elegant. It was tremendously frustrating not to be able to touch my wife, to speak tenderly to her, to have a private moment together. We had to conduct our relationship at a distance under the eyes of people we despised.

I could see immediately that Winnie was under tremendous strain. Seeing me in such circumstances must have been trying. Just getting to the island itself was difficult, and added to that were the harsh rituals of the prison, the undoubted indignities of the warders and the impersonality of the contact.

Winnie, I later discovered, had recently received a second banning order and had been dismissed from her job at the Child Welfare Office as a result. Her office was searched by the police shortly before she was sacked. The authorities were convinced that she was in secret communication with me. Winnie loved her job as a social worker. It was the hands-on end of the struggle: placing babies with adoptive parents, finding work for the unemployed and medical help for the uninsured. The banning and harassment of my wife greatly troubled me: I could not look after her and the children, and the state was making it difficult for her to look after herself. My powerlessness gnawed at me.

Our conversation was awkward at first, and was not made easier by the presence of two warders standing directly behind her and three behind me. Their role was not only to monitor but to intimidate. Regulations dictated that conversation had to be in either English or Afrikaans—African languages were forbidden—and could involve family matters only. Any line of talk that departed from the family and verged on the political might mean the abrupt termination of the visit. If one mentioned a name unfamiliar to the warders, they would interrupt the conversation, and ask who the person was and the nature of the relationship. This happened often, as the warders were generally unfamiliar with the variety and nature of African names. It was frustrating to spend precious minutes of one's visit explaining to a warder the different branches of one's family tree. But their ignorance also worked in our favour: it allowed us to invent code names for people we wanted to talk about and pretend that we were referring to family members.

That first visit was important, for I knew that Winnie was anxious about my health: she had heard stories that we were being physically abused. I quickly informed her that I was fine and she could see that I was fit, though a bit thinner than before. She, too, was thinner, something I always attributed to stress. After a visit in which Winnie's face looked drawn or tense, I would urge her to put on a bit of weight. She was always dieting, and I was always telling her not to. I inquired one by one about all the children, about my mother and sisters and Winnie's own family.

Suddenly, I heard the warder behind me say, 'Time up! Time up!' I turned and looked at him with incredulity. It was impossible that half an hour had passed. But, in fact, he was right; visits always

107

seemed to go by in the blinking of an eye. For all the years that I was in prison, I never failed to be surprised when the warder called, 'Time up!' Winnie and I were both hustled from our chairs and we waved a quick farewell. I always felt like lingering after Winnie left, just to retain the sense of her presence, but I would not let the warders see such emotion. As I walked back to the cell, I reviewed in my head what we had talked about. Over the next days, weeks and months, I would return to that one visit again and again. I knew I would not be able to see my wife again for at least six months. As it turned out, Winnie was not able to visit me for another two years.

64

One morning in early January, as we lined up to be counted before beginning work in the courtyard, we were instead marched outside and ordered into a covered truck. It was the first time that we had left our compound. No announcement was made as to our destination, but I had an idea of where we were headed. A few minutes later we emerged from the truck in a place that I had first seen when I was on the island in 1962: the lime quarry.

The lime quarry looked like an enormous white crater cut into a rocky hillside. The cliffs and the base of the hillside were blindingly white. At the top of the quarry were grass and palm trees, and at the base was a clearing with a few old metal sheds.

We were met by the commanding officer, Colonel Wessels, a rather colourless fellow who cared only about strict adherence to prison regulations. We stood at attention as he told us that the work we would be doing would last six months and afterwards we would be given light tasks for the duration of our terms. His timing was considerably off. We remained at the quarry for the next thirteen years.

After the CO's speech, we were handed picks and shovels and given rudimentary instructions as to the mining of lime. Mining lime is not a simple task. That first day, we were clumsy with our new tools and extracted little. The lime itself, which is the soft, calcified residue of seashells and coral, is buried in layers of rock, and one had to break through to it with a pick, and then extract the seam of lime with a shovel. This was far more strenuous than the work in the courtyard, and after our first few days on the quarry we fell asleep immediately after our supper at 4.30 in the afternoon. We woke the next morning aching and still tired.

The authorities never explained why we had been taken from the courtyard to the quarry. They may simply have needed extra lime for the island's roads. But when we later discussed the transfer, we assumed it was another way of enforcing discipline, of showing us that we were no different from the general prisoners—who worked in the island's stone quarry—and that we had to pay for our crimes just as they did. It was an attempt to crush our spirits.

But those first few weeks at the quarry had the opposite effect on us. Despite blistered and bleeding hands, we were invigorated. I much preferred being outside in nature, being able to see grass and trees, to observe birds flitting overhead, to feel the wind blowing in from the sea. It felt good to use all one's muscles, with the sun at one's back, and there was simple gratification in building up mounds of stone and lime.

Within a few days we were walking to the quarry, rather than going by truck, and this too was a tonic. During our twenty-minute march we got a better sense of the island, and could see the dense brush and tall trees that covered our home, and smell the eucalyptus blossoms, spot the occasional springbok or kudu grazing in the distance. Although some of the men regarded the march as drudgery, I never did.

*   *   *

Although our work at the quarry was meant to show us that we were no different from the other prisoners, the authorities still treated us like the lepers who once populated the island. Sometimes we would see a group of common-law prisoners working by the side of the road, and their warders would order them into the bushes so they would not see us as we marched past. It was as if the mere sight of us might somehow affect their discipline. Sometimes out of the corner of an eye we could see a prisoner raise his fist in the ANC salute.

Near the quarry the dirt road diverged, and to the right the general prisoners trooped off to the rock quarry. This crossroads was later to become an important site of communication with them. Where the road branched, we could see in the brush the small white cottage where Robert Sobukwe lived. The house had been built for a black warder years before, and now Sobukwe lived in it by himself. It was a tiny plot, unkempt and overgrown, and one would not even know that anyone lived there, except for the guard who stood in front.

Sobukwe's sentence had ended in 1963, but under what became known as the Sobukwe clause of the General Law Amendment Act of 1963, the minister of justice could hold political prisoners indefinitely without charge. That is precisely what they did with Bob. For six years, Sobukwe lived a kind of half-life on the island; he was a free man who was denied his liberty. Sometimes we were able to get a glimpse of him in his garden, but that was all.

*   *   *

After arriving in the morning, we would fetch our picks, shovels, hammers and wheelbarrows from a zinc shed at the top of the quarry. Then we would assemble along the quarry face, usually in groups of three or four. Warders with automatic weapons stood on raised platforms watching us. Unarmed warders walked among us, urging us to work harder. *'Gaan aan! Gaan aan!'* ('Go on! Go on!'), they would shout, as if we were oxen.

By eleven, when the sun was high in the sky, we would begin to flag. By that time I would already be drenched in sweat. The warders would then drive us even harder. *'Nee, man! Kom aan! Kom aan!'* ('No, man! Come on! Come on!') they would shout. Just before noon, when we would break for lunch, we would pile the lime into wheelbarrows and cart it over to the truck that would take it away.

At midday, a whistle would blow, and we would make our way to the bottom of the hill. We sat on makeshift seats under a simple zinc shed shielding us from the sun. The warders ate at a larger shed with tables and benches. Drums of boiled mealies were delivered to us. Hundreds of seagulls, screaming and swooping, circled above us as we ate, and a well-aimed dropping could sometimes spoil a man's lunch.

We worked until four, when we again carted the lime to the waiting truck. By the end of the day, our faces and bodies were caked with white dust. We looked like pale ghosts except where rivulets of sweat had washed away the lime. When we returned to our cells, we would scrub ourselves in the cold water, which never seemed to rinse away the dust completely.

*　　　*　　　*

Worse than the heat at the quarry was the light. Our backs were protected from the sun by our shirts, but the sun's rays would be reflected into our eyes by the lime itself. The glare hurt our eyes and, along with the dust, made it difficult to see. Our eyes streamed and our faces became fixed in a permanent squint. It would take a long time after each day's work for our eyes to adjust to the diminished light.

After our first few days at the quarry, we made an official request for sunglasses. The authorities refused. This was not unexpected, for we were then not even permitted reading glasses. I had previously pointed out to the commanding officer that it did not make sense to permit us to read books but not to permit us glasses to read them with.

During the following weeks and months we requested sunglasses again and again. But it was to take us almost three years before we were allowed to have them, and that was only after a sympathetic physician agreed that the glasses were necessary to preserve our eyesight. Even then, we had to purchase the glasses ourselves.

For us, such struggles—for sunglasses, long trousers, study privileges, equalized food—were corollaries to the struggle we waged outside prison. The campaign to improve conditions in prison was part of the apartheid struggle. It was, in that sense, all the same; we fought injustice wherever we found it, no matter how large or how small, and we fought injustice to preserve our own humanity.

*   *   *

Shortly after we started working at the quarry, we were joined in section B by a number of other prominent political prisoners. Several were MK men who had been arrested in July 1964 and convicted of more than fifty acts of sabotage in what became known as the 'little Rivonia Trial'. These included Mac Maharaj, a member of the SACP and one of the sharpest minds in the struggle; Laloo Chiba, also a member of the MK high command and a stalwart colleague who proved a great asset in prison; and Wilton Mkwayi, the Treason Trialist who had been mistakenly let go during a moment of confusion when the State of Emergency was declared in 1960. He had left South Africa secretly, received military training and became commander-in-chief of MK after the Rivonia Trial. We were also joined by Eddie Daniels, a Coloured member of the Liberal Party, who had been convicted for sabotage operations undertaken by the African Resistance Movement, a small sabotage group composed of members of the Liberal Party. Eddie was to become one of my greatest friends in prison.

To counterbalance the effect of these new political allies, the authorities also put a handful of common-law prisoners in our section. These men were hardened criminals, convicted of murder, rape and armed robbery. They were members of the island's notorious criminal gangs, either the Big Fives or the Twenty-Eights, which terrorized other prisoners. They were brawny and surly, and their faces bore the scars of the knife fights that were common among gang members. Their role was to act as *agents provocateurs*, and they would attempt to push us around, take our food and inhibit any political discussions we tried to have. One of these fellows was known as Bogart, after the American tough-guy movie actor. He had a cell opposite Walter's and Walter used to complain that he would demand Walter's breakfast from him each morning, and that he was too scared to refuse.

The gang members worked in their own group apart from us at the quarry. One day, they began singing what sounded like a work song. In fact, it was a famous work song, with their own adapted lyrics: *'Benifunani eRivonia?'* which means 'What did you want at Rivonia?' The next line was something like 'Did you think that you would become the government?' They sang exuberantly and with a mocking tone. They had obviously been encouraged by the warders, who were hoping that the song would provoke us.

Although the more hotheaded among us wanted to confront them, we decided to fight fire with fire. We had far more and better singers among us than they had, and we huddled together and planned our response. Within a few minutes, we were all singing the song 'Stimela', a rousing anthem about a train making its way down from Southern Rhodesia. 'Stimela' is not a political song but, in the context, it became one, for the implication was that the train contained guerrillas coming down to fight the South African army.

For a number of weeks our two groups sang as we worked, adding songs and changing lyrics. Our repertoire increased, and we were soon singing overt political songs, such as 'Amajoni', a song about guerrilla soldiers, the title of which was a corruption of the English slang word for soldier, Johnny, and 'Tshotsholoza', a song that compares the struggle to the motion of an oncoming train. (If you say the title over and over, it mimics the sound of the train.) We sang a song about the Freedom Charter, and another about the Transkei, with the lyrics, 'There are two roads, one road is the Matanzima road, and one road is the Mandela road, which one will you take?'

The singing made the work lighter. A few of the fellows had extraordinary voices, and I often felt like putting my pick down and simply listening. The gang members were no competition for us; they soon became quiet while we continued singing. But one of the warders was fluent in Xhosa and understood the content of our songs, and we were soon ordered to stop singing. (Whistling was also

115

banned.) From that day on we worked in silence.

* * *

I saw the gang members not as rivals but as raw material to be converted. There was a non-political prisoner among us nicknamed 'Joe My Baby' who later joined the ANC and proved invaluable in helping us smuggle material in and out of prison.

One day we heard that Bogart had been savagely beaten by a warder at the quarry. I did not see the assault, but I saw the results. His face was cut and badly bruised. Bogart approached me in our corridor and asked for help. I immediately agreed to take up his case.

We were always looking for ways to stand up to the authorities, and the report of a beating was the kind of incident we could raise with head office. Shortly before this, we had learned that a certain PAC man named Ganya had been beaten by a warder. In my role as an attorney, I wrote a letter to the commissioner of prisons protesting on behalf of Ganya. I was brought to head office, where I was confronted by prison officials. In the same breath they denied that the beating had occurred and wanted to know how I had heard about it. I insisted that the warder who had beaten Ganya be removed from the island. They refused, saying there was no evidence against him. But shortly afterwards the warder in question was transferred off the island.

I had been emboldened by this case, so when Bogart asked for help I immediately demanded to see the commanding officer. The next day I was summoned to head office, where the commander blandly informed me that the case had been investigated and dismissed. 'That's a violation of regulations,' I said. 'The case must be tried.'

'No,' he said, 'we have attempted to interview the so-called complainant and he denies that he was ever assaulted.'

'That's impossible,' I said. 'I spoke to him only yesterday.'

The commander gestured to a lieutenant and said, 'Then see for yourself.' The lieutenant led Bogart into the room. His face was covered with bandages. The commander asked him whether or not he had been beaten. 'No, *baas*,' he said quietly, without meeting my gaze, 'I was never assaulted.' He was then dismissed.

'Well, Mandela,' the commander said, 'the case is closed.' The commander had succeeded in humiliating me. He had obviously bribed Bogart with extra food and tobacco to drop his charges. From that point on, I demanded a signed and written statement from a prisoner before I agreed to take up his case.

65

One day in the summer of 1965 we discovered some fat glistening on our porridge at breakfast and chunks of fresh meat with our pap at supper. The next day some of the men received new shirts. The guards at the quarry and the warders in our section seemed a bit more deferential. All of us were suspicious; in prison, no improvement happens without a reason. A day later we were notified that the International Red Cross would be arriving the following day.

This was a crucial occasion, more important than that of any of our previous visitors. The International Red Cross was responsible and independent, an international organization to whom the Western powers and the United Nations paid attention. The prison authorities respected the International Red Cross—and by respected, I mean feared, for the authorities respected only what they were afraid of. The prison service distrusted all organizations that could affect world opinion, and regarded them not as legitimate investigators to be dealt with honestly but as meddling interlopers to be hoodwinked if possible. Avoiding international condemnation was the authorities' principal goal.

In those early years, the International Red Cross was the only organization that both listened to our complaints and responded to them. This was vital, because the authorities ignored us. Regulations required that the authorities provide some official procedure for acknowledging our complaints. They did so, but only in the most perfunctory manner. Every Saturday morning, the chief warder would come into our section and call out, *'Klagtes en Versoeke! Klagtes en Versoeke!'* ('Complaints and requests! Complaints and requests!') Those of us with *klagtes* and *versoeke*—which was nearly everyone—lined up to see the chief warder. One by one, we would make formal complaints about food, or clothing, or visits. To each, the chief warder would nod his head and simply say, *'Ja, ja,'* and then, 'Next!' He did not even write down what we said. If we tried to speak for our organizations, the warders would yell, 'No ANC or PAC here!

118

Verstaan?' ('Understand?')

* * *

Shortly before the International Red Cross visit we had submitted a formal list of complaints to the commissioner of prisons. At the time we were permitted paper and pencil only to write letters. We had secretly consulted with each other at the quarry and in the lavatory, and put together a list. We submitted it to our chief warder, who did not want to take it and accused us of violating regulations by making such a list. One of our complaints to the International Red Cross would be that the authorities did not listen to our grievances.

On the day of their visit, I was called to head office to meet the International Red Cross representative. That year, and for the following few years, the representative was a Mr Senn, a former director of prisons in his native Sweden who had emigrated to Rhodesia. Senn was a quiet, rather nervous man in his mid-fifties who did not seem at all comfortable in his surroundings.

The meeting was not monitored, a critical difference from nearly all of our other visitors. He asked to hear all of our complaints and grievances, and listened very carefully, taking extensive notes. He was very courteous and thanked me for all that I told him. Even so, that first visit was rather tense. Neither of us yet knew what to expect from the other.

I complained quite vociferously about our clothing, affirming that we did not want to wear short trousers and needed proper clothing

119

including socks and underwear, which we were not then given. I recounted our grievances regarding food, visits, letters, studies, exercise, hard labour and the behaviour of the warders. I made certain requests I knew the authorities would never satisfy, such as our desire to be transferred to prisons nearer our homes.

After our session, Senn met the commissioner of prisons and his staff while I waited. I assumed that he relayed our complaints to the authorities, indicating the ones he thought were reasonable. Not long after Senn's visit our clothing did improve and we were given long trousers. But Senn was not a progressive fellow by any means; his years in Rhodesia seemed to have acclimatized him to racism. Before I returned to my cell, I reminded him of our complaint that African prisoners did not receive bread. Mr Senn appeared flustered, and glanced over at the colonel, who was head of the prison. 'Bread is very bad for your teeth, you know, Mandela,' Mr Senn said. 'Mealies are much better for you. They make your teeth strong.'

In later years, the International Red Cross sent more liberal men who wholeheartedly fought for improvements. The organization also played a critical role in an area that was less obvious but no less important to us. They often provided money to wives and relatives who would not otherwise have been able to visit us on the island.

*   *   *

After we had been sent to Robben Island, there was concern among our supporters that we would not be permitted to study. Within a few months of

120

our arrival, the authorities announced that those who wanted to study could apply for permission. Most of the men did so, and even though they were D group prisoners, permission was granted. The state, after the Rivonia Trial, was feeling confident and thought giving us study privileges would be harmless. Later, they came to regret it. Postgraduate study was not permitted, but they made an exception in my case because I had established a precedent when I was in Pretoria.

Very few of the men in our section had BAs and many registered for university-level courses. Quite a few did not have high school certificates and chose courses to qualify for them. Some of the men were already well educated, like Govan Mbeki and Neville Alexander, but others had not gone past Standard V or VI. Within months, virtually all of us were studying for one qualification or another. At night, our cell block seemed more like a study hall than a prison.

But the privilege of studying came with a host of conditions. Certain subjects, such as politics or military history, were prohibited. For years, we were not permitted to receive funds except from our families, so that poor prisoners rarely had money for books or tuition. This made the opportunity to study a function of how much money one had. Nor were we permitted to lend books to other prisoners, which would have enabled our poorer colleagues to study.

There was always controversy about whether or not we should accept study privileges. Some members of the Unity Movement at first felt that we were accepting a handout from the government, which compromised our integrity. They argued that studying should not be a conditional privilege but an unfettered right. While I agreed, I could not accept that we should therefore refuse studying. As freedom fighters and political prisoners, we had an obligation to improve and strengthen ourselves, and study was one of the few opportunities to do so.

Prisoners were permitted to enrol at either the University of South Africa (UNISA) or the Rapid Results College, which was for those studying for their high school qualification. In my own case, studying under the auspices of the University of London was a mixed blessing. On the one hand I was assigned the sort of stimulating books that would not have been on a South African reading list; on the other, the authorities inevitably regarded many of them as unsuitable and thus banned them.

Receiving books at all was often a challenge. You might make an application to a South African library for a book on contract law. They would process your request and then send you the book by post. But because of the vagaries of the mail system, the remoteness of the island and the often deliberate slowness of the censors, the book would reach you after the date by which it needed to be returned. If the date had passed, the warders would typically send the book back without even showing it to you. Given the nature of the system, you might receive a late fine without ever having received the book.

In addition to books, we were permitted to order publications necessary to our studies. The authorities were extremely strict about this and the only kind of publication that would pass muster might be a quarterly on actuarial science for a prisoner studying accounting. But one day Mac Maharaj told a comrade who was studying economics to request the *Economist*. We laughed and said we might as well ask for *Time* magazine, because the *Economist* was also a newsweekly. But Mac simply smiled and said the authorities wouldn't know that; they judged a book by its title. Within a month, we were receiving the *Economist* and reading the news we hungered for. But the authorities soon discovered their mistake and ended the subscription.

Once most of the men began to study, we complained that we did not even have the minimum facilities necessary for studying, such as desks and chairs. I made this complaint to the International Red Cross. Finally, the authorities built in each cell a kind of stand-up desk, a simple wooden board that jutted out from the wall at about chest-level.

This was not precisely what we had envisaged. After a tedious day at the quarry, one did not much feel like working at a stand-up desk. A number of us complained about the desks, and Kathy was the most vociferous. He informed the commanding officer that not only was it an imposition to have stand-up desks, but that they sloped so steeply that the books fell off. The commanding officer made a surprise visit to Kathy's cell, asked for a book, and plonked it on his desk. It did not move. He asked Kathy for another and placed it on top of the first one; again, nothing happened. Finally, after placing four books on the desk, he turned to a sheepish Kathy and said, 'Ag, there's nothing wrong with these desks,' and walked out. But about six months later the authorities relented and we were given three-legged wooden stools and the stand-up desks were lowered.

*   *   *

One complaint I voiced to the International Red Cross concerned the arbitrary way in which we were charged by the warders. To be 'charged' meant that a warder claimed that a prisoner had violated a specific regulation, which could be punished by isolation or by loss of meals and privileges. Warders generally did not treat this lightly, for when a prisoner was charged he was allowed a judicial hearing and, depending on the seriousness of the offence, a magistrate was brought in from Cape Town. At the time, the authorities were refusing to permit hearings. When I complained to the International Red Cross about this, I had yet to experience the problem myself. But that situation was soon altered.

At weekends, during our first year on the island, we were kept inside our cells all day except for half an hour of exercise. One Saturday, after returning from exercise in the courtyard, I noticed that a warder had left a newspaper on the bench at the end of the corridor. He had become rather friendly to us, and I assumed that he had not left the newspaper there by accident.

Newspapers are more valuable to political prisoners than gold or diamonds, more hungered for than food or tobacco; they were the most precious contraband on Robben Island. News was the intellectual raw material of the struggle. We were not allowed any news at all, and we craved it.

Walter, even more than myself, seemed bereft without news. The authorities attempted to impose a complete blackout; they did not want us to learn anything that might raise our morale or reassure us that people on the outside were still thinking about us.

We regarded it as our duty to keep ourselves up to date with the politics of the country and fought long and hard for the right to have newspapers. Over the years we devised many ways of obtaining them, but at that time we were not so adept. One of the advantages of going to the quarry was that warders' sandwiches were wrapped in newspaper and they would often discard these newsprint wrappers in the rubbish, where we secretly retrieved them. We would distract the warders' attention, pluck the papers out of the bin and slide them into our shirts.

One of the most reliable ways to acquire papers was through bribery, and this was the only area where I tolerated what were often unethical means of obtaining information. The warders always seemed to be short of money, and their poverty was our opportunity.

When we did get hold of a paper, it was far too risky to pass around. Possession of a newspaper was a serious charge. Instead, one person would read the paper, usually Kathy or, later, Mac Maharaj. Kathy was in charge of communications, and he had thought of ingenious ways for us to pass information. Kathy would go through the paper and make cuttings of relevant stories, which were then secretly distributed to the rest of us. Each of us would write out a summary of the story we were given; these summaries were then passed among

125

us, and later smuggled to the general section. When the authorities were particularly vigilant, Kathy or Mac would write out his summary of the news and then destroy the paper, usually by tearing it into small pieces and placing it in his ballie, which the warders never inspected.

*   *   *

When I noticed the newspaper lying on the bench, I quickly left my cell, walked to the end of the corridor, looked in both directions and then plucked it off the bench and slipped it into my shirt. Normally, I would have hidden the newspaper somewhere in my cell and taken it out only after bedtime. But like a child who eats his pudding before his main course, I was so eager for news that I opened the paper in my cell immediately.

I don't know how long I was reading; I was so engrossed in the paper that I did not hear any footsteps. Suddenly an officer and two other warders appeared, and I did not even have time to slide the paper under my bed. I was caught black-and-white-handed, so to speak. 'Mandela,' the officer said, 'we are charging you for possession of contraband, and you will pay for this.' The two warders then began a thorough search of my cell to see if they could turn up anything else.

Within a day or two a magistrate was brought in from Cape Town and I was taken to the room at headquarters that was used as the island's court. In this instance, the authorities were willing to call in an outside magistrate because they knew they had an open-and-shut case. I offered no defence, and

126

was sentenced to three days in isolation and deprivation of meals.

I do not think that I was set up by the warder who left the newspaper on the bench, though some assumed I had been. At the hearing, the authorities grilled me as to how I got the newspaper, and I refused to answer. If I had been railroaded, the authorities would have known how I'd got it.

*   *   *

The isolation cells were in our same complex, but in another wing. Although just across the courtyard, they felt enormously distant. In isolation, one was deprived of company, exercise and even food: one received only rice water three times a day for three days. (Rice water is simply water in which rice has been boiled.) By comparison, our normal ration of pap seemed like a feast.

The first day in isolation was always the most painful. One grows accustomed to eating regularly and the body is not used to being deprived. I found that by the second day I had more or less adjusted to the absence of food, and the third passed without much craving at all. Such deprivation was not uncommon among Africans in everyday life. I myself had gone without food for days at a time in my early years in Johannesburg.

As I have already mentioned, I found solitary confinement the most forbidding aspect of prison life. There was no end and no beginning; there is only one's own mind, which can begin to play tricks. Was that a dream or did it really happen? One begins to question everything. Did I make the right decision, was my sacrifice worth it? In solitary, there is no distraction from these haunting questions.

But the human body has an enormous capacity for adjusting to trying circumstances. I have found that one can bear the unbearable if one can keep one's spirits strong even when one's body is being tested. Strong convictions are the secret of surviving deprivation; your spirit can be full even when your stomach is empty.

*   *   *

In those early years, isolation became a habit. We were routinely charged for the smallest infractions and sentenced to isolation. A man might lose his meals for a sidelong glance or be sentenced for failing to stand when a warder entered the room. Some PAC prisoners, who often flouted the rules simply for the sake of doing so, spent a great deal of time in isolation. The authorities believed that isolation was the cure for our defiance and rebelliousness.

The second time I was charged and spent time in isolation occurred shortly after the first. As I have mentioned, we were having great difficulty making our complaints heard. The remoteness of the prison made the authorities feel they could ignore us with impunity. They believed that if they turned a deaf ear, we would give up in frustration and the people on the outside would forget about us.

One day we were working at the lime quarry when the commanding officer came to observe us, accompanied by a gentleman whom we at first did not recognize. One of my colleagues whispered to me that it was Brigadier Aucamp [He is not to be confused with the officer with the same name at Pretoria Local, who looked after us during the Rivonia Trial.] from Head Office, our commanding officer's commanding officer. The two men stood at a distance, watching us.

Aucamp was a short, heavyset fellow in a suit rather than a military uniform. He normally came to the island on biannual inspections. On those occasions we were ordered to stand to attention at the grille of our cells and hold up our prison cards as he walked by.

I decided that Aucamp's unexpected appearance was a singular opportunity to present our grievances to the man who had the power to remedy them. I put down my pick and began to walk over to them. The warders immediately became alarmed and moved towards me. I knew that I was violating regulations, but I hoped the warders would be so surprised by the novelty of my action that they would do nothing to stop me. That proved to be the case.

When I reached the two men, the commanding officer said bluntly, 'Mandela, go back to your place. No one called you.' I disregarded him and addressed Aucamp, saying I had taken this extraordinary action because our complaints were being ignored. The CO interrupted me: 'Mandela, I order you back to your place.' I turned to him and said in a measured tone, 'I am here already, I will not go back.' I was hoping that Aucamp would agree to hear me out, but he studied me coldly and then turned to the warders and said calmly, 'Charge him.'

I continued to speak as the guards led me away.

'Take him back to the cells,' the CO said. I was charged and, once again, I had no defence. The punishment this time was four days in isolation. There was a lesson in what I had done, a lesson I already knew but had disobeyed out of desperation. No one, least of all a prison official, ever likes to have his authority publicly challenged. In order to respond to me, Aucamp would have had to humiliate his subordinate. Prison officials responded much better to private overtures. The best way to effect change on Robben Island was to attempt to influence officials privately rather than publicly. I was sometimes condemned for appearing to be too accommodating to prison officials, but I was willing to accept the criticism in exchange for the improvement.

66

The most important person in any prisoner's life is not the minister of justice, not the commissioner of prisons, not even the head of prison, but the warder in one's section. If you are cold and want an extra blanket, you might petition the minister of justice, but you will get no response. If you go to the commissioner of prisons, he will say, 'Sorry, it is against regulations.' The head of prison will say, 'If I give you an extra blanket, I must give one to everyone.' But if you approach the warder in your corridor, and you are on good terms with him, he will simply go to the stockroom and fetch a blanket.

I always tried to be decent to the warders in my section; hostility was usually self-defeating. There was no point in having a permanent enemy among the warders. It was ANC policy to try to educate all people, even our enemies: we believed that all men, even prison service warders, were capable of change, and we did our utmost to try to sway them.

In general we treated the warders as they treated us. If a man was considerate, we were considerate in return. Not all of our warders were ogres. We noticed right from the start that there were some among them who believed in fairness. Yet being friendly with warders was not an easy proposition, for they generally found the idea of being courteous to a black man abhorrent. Because it was useful to have warders who were well disposed towards us, I often asked certain men to make overtures to selected warders. No one liked to take on such a job.

We had one warder at the quarry who seemed particularly hostile to us. This was troublesome, for at the quarry we would hold discussions among ourselves, and a warder who did not permit us to talk was a great hindrance. I asked a certain comrade to befriend this fellow so that he would not interrupt our talks. The warder was quite crude, but he soon began to relax a bit around this one prisoner. One day, the warder asked this comrade for his jacket so that he could lay it on the grass and sit on it. Even though I knew it went against the comrade's grain, I nodded to him to do it.

A few days later, we were having our lunch under the shed when this warder wandered over. The warder had an extra sandwich, and he threw it on the grass near us and said, 'Here.' That was his way of showing friendship.

This presented us with a dilemma. On the one hand, he was treating us as animals to whom he could toss a bit of slop, and I felt it would undermine our dignity to take the sandwich. On the other hand, we were hungry, and to reject the gesture altogether would humiliate the warder we were trying to befriend. I could see that the comrade who had befriended the warder wanted the sandwich, and I nodded for him to take it.

The strategy worked, for this warder became less wary around us. He even began to ask questions about the ANC. By definition, if a man worked for the prison service he was probably brainwashed by the government's propaganda. He would have believed that we were terrorists and communists who wanted to drive the white man into the sea. But as we quietly explained to him our non-racialism, our desire for equal rights and our plans for the redistribution of wealth, he scratched his head and said, 'It makes more bloody sense than the Nats.'

*　　　　*　　　　*

Having sympathetic warders facilitated one of our most vital tasks on Robben Island: communication. We regarded it as our duty to stay in touch with our men in groups F and G, which was where the general prisoners were kept. As politicians, we were just as intent on fortifying our organization in prison as we had been outside. Communication was essential if we were to coordinate our protests and complaints. Because of the greater numbers of prisoners coming and going in the general section, the men in F and G tended to have more recent information about not only what was happening in the movement, but about our friends and families.

Communication between sections was a serious violation of regulations. We found many effective ways around the ban. The men who delivered our drums of food were from the general section, and in the early months we managed to have whispered conversations with them in which we conveyed brief messages. We formed a clandestine communications committee, composed of Kathy, Mac Maharaj, Laloo Chiba and several others, and their job was to organize all such practices.

One of the first techniques was engineered by Kathy and Mac, who had noticed that, on our walks to the quarry, the warders often tossed away empty matchboxes. They began secretly collecting them, and Mac had the idea of constructing a false bottom to the box and placing in it a tiny written message. Laloo Chiba, who once trained as a tailor, wrote out minuscule coded messages that would be placed in the converted matchbox. Joe Gqabi, another MK soldier who was with us, would carry the matchboxes on our walks to the quarry and drop them at a strategic crossing where we knew the general prisoners would pass. Through whispered conversations at food deliveries, we explained the plan. Designated prisoners from F and G would pick up the matchboxes on their walks, and we retrieved messages in the same fashion. It was far from perfect, and we could easily be foiled by something as simple as the rain. We soon evolved more efficient methods.

We looked for moments when the warders were inattentive. One such time was during and after meals. We helped ourselves to our food, and we worked out a scheme whereby comrades from the general section who worked in the kitchen began placing letters and notes wrapped in plastic at the bottom of the food drums. We sent return communications in a similar way, wrapping notes in the same plastic and placing them at the bottom of the mounds of dirty dishes that were routed back to the kitchen. We would do our best to create a mess, scattering food all over the plates. The warders even complained about the disarray, but never bothered to investigate.

Our toilets and showers were adjacent to the isolation section. Prisoners from the general section were often sentenced to isolation there and would use the same set of toilets we did, though at different times. Mac devised a method of wrapping notes in plastic and then taping them inside the rim of the toilet bowl. We encouraged our political comrades in the general section to be charged and placed in isolation so that they could retrieve these notes and send replies. The warders never bothered to search there.

In order not to have our notes read or understood by the authorities if they were found, we devised ways of writing that could not easily be seen or deciphered. One way was to write messages with milk. The milk would dry almost immediately, and the paper would look blank. But the disinfectant we were given to clean our cells, when sprayed on the dried milk, made the writing reappear. Unfortunately we did not regularly receive milk. After one of us was diagnosed with an ulcer, we used his.

Another technique was to write in tiny coded script on toilet paper. The paper was so small and easily hidden that this became a popular way of smuggling out messages. When the authorities discovered a number of these communications, they took the extraordinary measure of rationing toilet paper. Govan was then ill and not going to the quarry, and he was given the task of counting out eight squares of toilet paper for each prisoner per day.

But even with all these ingenious methods, one of the best ways was also the easiest: getting sent to the prison hospital. The island had one hospital, and it was difficult to segregate us from the general prisoners while we were there. Sometimes prisoners from the different sections even shared the same wards, and men from section B and prisoners from F and G mingled and exchanged information about political organizations, strikes, go-slows, whatever the current prison issues were.

Communication with the outside world was accomplished in two ways: through prisoners whose sentences were completed and who were leaving the island, and through contact with visitors. Prisoners who were leaving would smuggle out letters in their clothes or baggage. With outside visitors, the situation was even more dangerous, because the risks were also borne by the visitor. When lawyers visited us, warders were not permitted in the room and we would sometimes pass a letter to the lawyer to be taken out. Lawyers were not searched. In these meetings, we could also communicate by writing as we had during the Rivonia Trial. Because the room was bugged, we might say, 'Please tell . . .' and then pause and write 'O.T.,' meaning Oliver Tambo, on a piece of paper, 'that we approve of his plan to cut down the size

135

of the . . .' and then write 'National Executive'.

* * *

Through a plastic-wrapped note hidden in our food drum, we learned in July 1966 that the men in the general section had embarked on a hunger strike to protest at the poor conditions. The note was imprecise, and we did not know exactly when the strike had started or exactly what it was about. But we would support any strike of prisoners for whatever reason they were striking. Word was passed among us, and we resolved to initiate a sympathetic strike beginning with our next meal. A hunger strike consists of one thing: not eating.

Because of the time-lag in communication, the general prisoners probably did not learn of our participation for a day or so. But we knew that the news would hearten them. The authorities would be telling them that we were not participating in the strike, that we were gorging ourselves on gourmet meals. This was standard operating procedure; in a crisis, the authorities inevitably started a disinformation campaign to play off one section against the other. In this case, while the ANC unanimously supported the strike, some PAC men in the general section did not.

During the first day of our strike, we were served our normal rations and refused to take them. On the second day, we noticed that our portions were larger and a few more vegetables accompanied our pap. On the third day, juicy pieces of meat were served with supper. By the fourth day, the porridge was glistening with fat, and great hunks of meat and colourful vegetables were steaming on top.

136

The food was positively mouthwatering. The warders smiled when we refused the food. The temptation was great, but we resisted, even though we were being driven especially hard at the quarry. We heard that in the main section, prisoners were collapsing and being taken away in wheelbarrows.

I was called to head office for an interview with Colonel Wessels. Such sessions were delicate, as my fellow prisoners knew that the authorities would attempt to influence me to call off the strike. Wessels was a direct man and demanded to know why we were on hunger strike. I explained that as political prisoners we saw protest to alter prison conditions as an extension of the anti-apartheid struggle. 'But you don't even know why they are striking in F and G,' he said. I said that did not matter, that the men in F and G were our brothers and that our struggle was indivisible. He snorted, and dismissed me.

The following day we learned of an extraordinary course of events: the warders had gone on their own food boycott, refusing to go to their own cafeteria. They were not striking in support of us, but had decided that if we could do such a thing, why couldn't they? They were demanding better food and improved living conditions. The combination of the two strikes was too much for the authorities. They settled with the warders and then, a day or two later, we learned the authorities had gone to the general section and asked for three representatives to negotiate changes. The general prisoners declared victory and called off the hunger strike. We followed suit a day later.

That was the first and most successful of the hunger strikes on the island. As a form of protest, they did not have a high success rate and the rationale behind them always struck me as quixotic. In order for a hunger strike to succeed, the outside world must learn of it. Otherwise, prisoners will simply starve themselves to death and no one will know. Smuggled-out information that we were on a hunger strike would elicit newspaper stories, which in turn would generate pressure from support groups. The problem, particularly in the early years, was that it was next to impossible to alert people on the outside that we were waging a hunger strike inside.

For me, hunger strikes were altogether too passive. We who were already suffering were threatening our health, even courting death. I have always favoured a more active, militant style of protest such as work strikes, go-slow strikes, or refusing to clean up; actions that punished the authorities, not ourselves. They wanted gravel and we produced no gravel. They wanted the prison yard clean, and it was untidy. This kind of behaviour distressed and exasperated them, whereas I think they secretly enjoyed watching us go hungry.

But when it came to a decision, I was often outvoted. My colleagues even jokingly accused me of not wanting to miss a meal. The advocates of hunger strikes argued that it was a traditionally accepted form of protest that had been waged all over the world by such prominent leaders as Mahatma Gandhi. Once the decision was taken,

138

however, I would support it as wholeheartedly as any of its advocates. In fact, during the strikes I was often in the position of remonstrating with some of my more wayward colleagues who did not want to abide by our agreement. 'Madiba, I want my food,' I remember one man saying. 'I don't see why I should go without. I have served the struggle for many years.'

Comrades would sometimes eat on the sly. We knew this for a simple reason: by the second day of a hunger strike, no one needs to use the toilet. Yet one morning you might see a fellow going to the toilet. We had our own internal intelligence service because we knew that certain men were weak in this regard.

67

In the midst of the July 1966 hunger strike I had my second visit from my wife. It was almost exactly two years after the first, and it nearly did not happen at all. Winnie had been under constant harassment since her first visit in 1964. Her sisters and brother were persecuted by the police, and the authorities attempted to forbid anyone in her family from living with her. Some of this I learned at the time, much of it I found out later. Some of the nastiest items were known to me because when I would return from the quarry, I would often find neatly cut clippings about Winnie that had been anonymously placed on my bed by the warders.

In small and spiteful ways, the authorities did their best to make Winnie's journeys as unpleasant as possible. For the previous two years, her visits had been stymied by local magistrates and by the repeated bannings that prevented her from travelling. I had recently heard through counsel that Winnie had been informed by the police that she could visit me only if she carried a pass. Winnie, who had been protesting against the government's policy regarding women's passes since the 1950s, rightly refused to carry the hated document. The authorities were clearly attempting to humiliate her and me. But I thought it was more important that we see each other than to resist the petty machinations of the authorities, and Winnie consented to carry a pass. I missed her enormously and needed the reassurance of seeing her, and we also had vital family matters to discuss.

The regulations governing each of Winnie's visits were long and complicated. She was barred from taking a train or car and had to fly, making the trip much more expensive. She was required to take the shortest route from the airport to Caledon Square, the Cape Town police station, where she was required to sign various documents. She had to report to the same station on the way back and sign more documents.

I had also learned from a newspaper clipping that a Special Branch officer broke into our Orlando house while Winnie was dressing and she reacted angrily, pushing the officer out of the bedroom. The lieutenant laid a charge of assault against her, and I asked my friend and colleague George Bizos to defend her, which he ably did. We had seen stories about this in the newspapers, and some of the men even joked with me about Winnie's bellicosity. 'You are not the only boxer in the family, Madiba,' they said.

This second visit was for only half an hour, and we had much to discuss. Winnie was a bit agitated from the rough treatment in Cape Town and the fact that, as always, she had to travel in the hold of the ferry where the fumes from the engine made her ill. She had taken pains to dress up for me, but she looked thin and drawn.

We reviewed the education of the children, the health of my mother, which was not very good, and our finances. A critical issue was the education of Zeni and Zindzi. Winnie had placed the girls in a school designated as Indian, and the authorities were harassing the principal on the grounds that it was a violation of the law for the school to accept 'African' pupils. We made the difficult decision to send Zeni and Zindzi to boarding school in Swaziland. This was hard on Winnie, who found her greatest support in the two girls. I was consoled by the fact that their education would probably be superior there, but I worried about Winnie. She would be lonely and a prey for people who sought to undermine her under the guise of being her friends. If anything, Winnie was too trusting of people's motives.

To get around the restrictions on discussing non-family matters, we used names whose meaning was clear to us, but not to the warders. If I wanted to know how Winnie was really doing, I might say, 'Have you heard about Ngutyana recently; is she all right?' Ngutyana is one of Winnie's clan names, but the authorities were unaware of that. Then Winnie could talk about how and what Ngutyana was doing. If the warder asked who Ngutyana was, we would say she was a cousin. If I wanted to know

141

about how the external mission of the ANC was faring, I would ask, 'How is the church?' Winnie would discuss 'the church' in appropriate terms, and I might then ask, 'How are the priests? Are there any new sermons?' We improvised and managed to exchange a great deal of information that way.

As always, when the warder yelled 'Time up!', I thought only a few minutes had passed. I wanted to kiss the glass barrier good-bye, but restrained myself. I always preferred Winnie to leave first so that she would not have to see me led away, and I watched as she whispered a good-bye, hiding her pain from the warders.

After the visit I replayed all the details in my mind, what Winnie wore, what she said, what I said. I then wrote her a letter going over some of what we had discussed, and reminding her of how much I cared for her, how unshakable our bond was, how courageous she was. I saw my letters to her both as love letters and as the only way I could give her the emotional support she needed.

Soon after the visit, I learned that Winnie had been charged for failing to report to the police on her arrival in Cape Town as well as refusing to furnish the police with her address when she left. Having already given her address at the ferry, she was asked again when she returned, and refused, saying she had done so earlier.

Winnie was arrested and released on bail. She was tried and sentenced to a year's imprisonment, which was suspended except for four days. Winnie was subsequently dismissed from her second job as a social worker because of the incident, and lost her main source of income.

The state did its utmost to harass me in ways they thought I would be powerless to resist. Towards the end of 1966 the Transvaal Law Society, at the instigation of the minister of justice, made a motion to strike me off the roll of practising attorneys as a result of my conviction in the Rivonia Trial. Apparently they were not discouraged by the earlier unsuccessful attempt to remove my name from the roll because of my conviction in the Defiance Campaign.

I found out about the Law Society's action only after it had been initiated. The Transvaal Law Society was an extremely conservative organization, and it was seeking to punish me at a time when it assumed I would be unable to defend myself. It is not easy for a prisoner on Robben Island to defend himself in court, but that is precisely what I intended to do.

I informed the authorities that I planned to contest the action and would prepare my own defence. I told prison officials that in order to prepare adequately, I would need to be exempt from going to the quarry and would also require a proper table, chair and reading light to work on my brief. I said I needed access to a law library and demanded to be taken to Pretoria.

My strategy was to overwhelm the prison authorities and the courts with legitimate requests, which I knew they would have a difficult time satisfying. The authorities always found it distressing when I wanted to defend myself in court because the accompanying publicity would show that I was still fighting for the same values I always had.

Their first response was 'Mandela, why don't you retain a lawyer to defend you? He will be able to handle the case properly. Why put yourself out?' I went ahead and applied to the registrar of the Supreme Court for the records, documents and books that I would need. I also requested a list of the state's witnesses and summaries of their prospective testimony.

I received a letter stating that before the registrar would grant my requests he would need to know the nature of my defence. This was extraordinary. To ask the nature of a lawyer's defence before the trial? No defendant can be compelled to reveal his defence before he is actually in court. I wrote back to tell him that the nature of my defence would become clear when I filed my papers—and not until then.

This was the beginning of a flurry of correspondence between me and the registrar as well as the state attorney, who was representing the Law Society. I would not back down on any of my requests. The authorities were equally intransigent: I could not be taken off quarry detail, I could not have a table and chair, and under no circumstances would I be able to go to Pretoria to use the law library.

I continued to bedevil the Law Society and registrar with demands, which they continued to deflect. Finally, several months and many letters later, without any fanfare and with just a cursory notification to me, they dropped the entire matter. The case was becoming more than they had bargained for. They had reckoned I would not have the initiative or wherewithal to defend myself; they were mistaken.

*　　　　*　　　　*

I was able to read in detail about the official reactions to my opposition to the Law Society's actions because we were receiving a daily newspaper just as if it were delivered to our door. In effect, it was.

The warder who supervised us at night was a quiet, elderly Jehovah's Witness whom Mac Maharaj had befriended. One night he wandered over to Mac's cell and told him that he wanted to enter a newspaper contest that required an essay. Would Mac, he wondered, be willing to assist him in writing it? The old warder hinted that if Mac helped him, there would be a reward. Mac agreed, and duly wrote the essay. A fortnight later, the old man came to Mac very excited. He was now a finalist in the competition; would Mac write him another essay? The warder promised Mac a cooked chicken in return. Mac told the old warder that he would think about it.

The next day Mac came to Walter and me and explained the situation. While Walter encouraged Mac to accept the food, I appreciated his reluctance to do so, because it would appear that he was getting special treatment. That night, he told the warder he would write the essay in exchange for a pack of cigarettes. The old warder agreed, and the following evening presented Mac with a newly bought pack of cigarettes.

The next day Mac told us that he now had the leverage he wanted over the old warder. How? we asked. 'Because I have his fingerprints on the cigarette pack,' Mac said, 'and I can blackmail him.' Walter exclaimed that that was immoral. I did not criticize Mac, but asked what he would blackmail him for. Mac raised his eyebrows. 'Newspapers,' he said. Walter and I looked at each other. I think Walter was the only man on Robben Island who relished newspapers as much as I did. Mac had already discussed his plan with the communications committee, and although we both had reservations about Mac's technique, we did not stop him.

That night Mac told the warder that he had his fingerprints on the pack of cigarettes and that if he did not cooperate, he would expose him to the commanding officer. Terrified of being sacked and losing his pension, the warder agreed to do whatever Mac wanted. For the next six months, until the warder was transferred, the old man would smuggle that day's newspaper to Mac. Mac would then summarize the news and reduce it to a single small piece of paper, which would circulate among us. The unfortunate warder did not win the contest, either.

*　　　*　　　*

It would be hard to say what we did more of at the quarry: mine lime or talk. By 1966, the warders had adopted a laissez-faire attitude: we could talk as much as we wanted as long as we worked. We would cluster in small groups, four or five men in a rough circle, and talk all day long, about every subject under the sun. We were in a perpetual conversation with each other on topics both solemn and trifling.

There is no prospect about prison which pleases—with the possible exception of one. One has time to think. In the vortex of the struggle, when one is constantly reacting to changing circumstances, one rarely has the chance to consider carefully all the ramifications of one's decisions or policies. Prison provided the time—much more than enough time—to reflect on what one had done and not done.

We were constantly engaged in political debates. Some were dispatched in a day; others were disputed for years. I have always enjoyed the cut-and-thrust of debating, and was a ready participant. One of our earliest and longest debates concerned the relationship between the ANC and the Communist Party. Some of the men, especially those MK soldiers who had been trained in socialist countries, believed that the ANC and the party were one and the same. Even some very senior ANC colleagues, such as Govan Mbeki and Harry Gwala, subscribed to this theory.

The party did not exist as a separate entity on Robben Island. In prison, there was no point in making the distinction between the ANC and the party that existed on the outside. My own views on the subject had not altered in many years. The ANC was a mass liberation movement that welcomed all those with the same objectives.

Over time, the debate concerning the ANC and the party grew progressively acrimonious. A number of us proposed one way to resolve it: we would write to the ANC in exile in Lusaka. We prepared a secret twenty-two-page document on the subject with a covering letter from myself to be sent to Lusaka. It was a risky manoeuvre to prepare and smuggle out such a document. In the end, Lusaka confirmed the separation of the ANC and the party and the argument eventually withered away.

Another recurrent political discussion was whether or not the ANC leadership should come exclusively from the working class. Some argued that because the ANC was a mass organization made up mainly of ordinary workers, the leadership should come from those same ranks. My argument was that it was as undemocratic to specify that the leaders had to be from the working class as to declare that they should be bourgeois intellectuals. If the movement had insisted on such a rule, most of its leaders, men such as Chief Luthuli, Moses Kotane, Dr Dadoo, would have been ineligible. Revolutionaries are drawn from every class.

*   *   *

Not all debates were political. One issue that provoked much discussion was circumcision. Some among us maintained that circumcision as practised by the Xhosa and other tribes was not only an unnecessary mutilation of the body but a reversion to the type of tribalism that the ANC was seeking to overthrow. It was not an unreasonable argument, but the prevailing view, with which I agreed, was that circumcision was a cultural ritual that had not only a salutary health benefit but an important psychological effect. It was a rite that strengthened group identification and inculcated positive values.

148

The debate continued for years, and a number of men voted in favour of circumcision in a very direct way. A prisoner working in the hospital who had formerly practised as an *ingcibi* set up a secret circumcision school, and a number of the younger prisoners from our section were circumcised there. Afterwards, we would organize a small party of tea and biscuits for the men, and they would spend a day or two walking around in blankets, as was the custom.

*　　　*　　　*

One subject we harkened back to again and again was whether there were tigers in Africa. Some argued that although it was popularly assumed that tigers lived in Africa, this was a myth and that they were native to Asia and the Indian subcontinent. Africa had leopards in abundance, but no tigers. The other side argued that tigers were native to Africa and some still lived there. Some claimed to have seen with their own eyes this most powerful and beautiful of cats in the jungles of Africa.

I maintained that while there were no tigers to be found in contemporary Africa, there was a Xhosa word for tiger, a word different from the one for leopard, and that if the word existed in our language, the creature must have once existed in Africa. Otherwise, why would there be a name for it? This argument went round and round, and I remember Mac retorting that hundreds of years ago there was a Hindi word for a craft that flew in the air, long before the aeroplane was invented, but that did not mean that aeroplanes existed in ancient India.

149

68

'Zithulele', the Quiet One, was what we called the tolerant, soft-spoken warder in charge of us at the quarry. He routinely stood a great distance from us while we worked and did not appear to care what we did as long as we were orderly. He never berated us when he found us leaning on our spades and talking.

We responded in kind. One day in 1966 he came to us and said, 'Gentlemen, the rains have washed away the lines on the roads; we need twenty kilos of lime today. Can you help?' Although we were working very little at the time, he had approached us as human beings, and we agreed to assist him.

That spring, we had felt a certain thawing on the part of the authorities, a relaxation of the iron-fisted discipline that had prevailed on the island. The tension between prisoners and warders had lessened somewhat.

But this lull proved to be short-lived and it came to an abrupt end one morning in September. We had just put down our picks and shovels on the quarry face and were walking to the shed for lunch. As one of the general prisoners wheeled a drum of food towards us, he whispered, 'Verwoerd is dead.' That was all. The news quickly passed among us. We looked at each other in disbelief and glanced over at the warders, who seemed unaware that anything momentous had occurred. We did not know how the prime minister had died. Later, we heard about the obscure white parliamentary messenger who stabbed Verwoerd to death, and we wondered at his motives. Although Verwoerd thought Africans were lower than animals, his death did not yield us any pleasure. Political assassination is not something I or the ANC have ever supported. It is a primitive way of contending with an opponent.

Verwoerd had proved to be both the chief theorist and master builder of grand apartheid. He had championed the creation of the Bantustans and Bantu Education. Shortly before his death he had led the Nationalists in the general election of 1966, in which the party of apartheid had increased its majority, winning 126 seats to the 39 achieved by the United Party, and the single seat won by the Progressive Party.

As often happened on the island, we had learned significant political news before our own guards. But by the following day it was obvious the warders knew, for they took out their anger on us. The tension that had taken months to abate was suddenly at full force. The authorities began a crackdown against political prisoners as though we had held the knife that stabbed Verwoerd.

The authorities always imagined that we were secretly linked with all kinds of powerful forces on the outside. The spate of successful guerrilla attacks against the South African police forces in Namibia by the South West African People's Organization (SWAPO)—an ally of the ANC—had also unnerved them. I suppose we should have been flattered that the government thought our nascent military ability was sophisticated enough to eliminate successfully their head of state. But their suspicions merely reflected the insecurities of narrow, shortsighted men who blamed their problems not on their own misguided policies but on an opponent by the name of the ANC.

The punishment against us was never spelled out as an official policy, but it was a renewal of the harsh atmosphere that had prevailed upon our arrival on the island. The Quiet One was replaced by a man who was a vicious martinet. His name was van Rensburg and he had been flown to the island at twenty-four hours' notice after the assassination. His reputation preceded him, for his name was a byword among prisoners for brutality.

Van Rensburg was a big, clumsy, brutish fellow who did not speak but shouted. During his first day on the job we noticed he had a small swastika tattooed on his wrist. But he did not need this offensive symbol to prove his cruelty. His job was to make our lives as wretched as possible, and he pursued that goal with great enthusiasm.

*   *   *

Each day over the next few months, van Rensburg would charge one of us for insubordination or malingering. Each morning, he and the other warders would discuss who would be charged that afternoon. It was a policy of selective intimidation, and the decision on who would be charged was taken regardless of how hard that prisoner had worked that day. When we were trudging back to our cells, van Rensburg would read from a list, 'Mandela [or Sisulu or Kathrada], I want to see you immediately in front of the head of prison.'

The island's administrative court began working overtime. In response, we formed our own legal committee made up of myself, Fikile Bam and Mac

152

Maharaj. Mac had studied law and was adept at putting the authorities on the defensive. Fiks, who was working towards a law degree, was a vigilant, resourceful fellow who had become the head of the prisoners' committee in our section. The job of our legal committee was to advise our comrades on how to conduct themselves in the island's administrative court. Van Rensburg was not a clever fellow, and while he would lord it over us at the quarry, we could outwit him in court. Our strategy was not to argue with him in the field, but to contest the charges in court where we would have a chance to make our case before slightly more enlightened officers. In the administrative court, the charge would be read by the presiding magistrate. 'Malingering at the quarry,' he might say, at which van Rensburg would look smug. After the charge had been read in full, I always advised my colleagues to do one thing and one thing only: ask the court for 'further particulars'. This was one's right as a defendant, and though the request became a regular occurrence, van Rensburg would almost always be stumped. Court would then have to be adjourned while van Rensburg went out to gather 'further particulars'.

* * *

Van Rensburg was vindictive in large ways and small. When our lunch arrived at the quarry and we would sit down to eat—we now had a simple wooden table—van Rensburg would inevitably choose that moment to urinate next to our food. I suppose we should have been grateful that he did not urinate directly on our food, but we lodged a

153

protest against the practice anyway.

One of the few ways prisoners can take their revenge on warders is through humour, and van Rensburg became the butt of many of our jokes. Among ourselves we called him 'Suitcase'. Warders' lunch boxes were known as 'suitcases' and normally a warder would designate a prisoner, usually his favourite, to carry his 'suitcase' and then reward him with half a sandwich. But we always refused to carry van Rensburg's 'suitcase', hence the nickname. It was humiliating for a warder to carry his own lunch box. One day Wilton Mkwayi inadvertently referred to 'Suitcase' within van Rensburg's hearing. 'Who is Suitcase?' van Rensburg bellowed. Wilton paused for a moment and then blurted out, 'It's you!'

'Why do you call me Suitcase?' van Rensburg asked. Wilton paused. 'Come, man,' van Rensburg said. 'Because you carry your own "suitcase",' Wilton replied tentatively. 'The general prisoners carry the "suitcases" of their warders, but we won't carry yours—so we call you Suitcase.'

Van Rensburg considered this for a moment and, instead of getting angry, announced, 'My name is not Suitcase, it's Dik Nek.' There was silence for a moment, and then all of us burst into laughter. In Afrikaans, 'Dik Nek' literally means 'thick neck'; it suggests someone who is stubborn and unyielding. Suitcase, I suspect, was too thick to know that he had been insulted.

*　　*　　*

One day at the quarry, we resumed our discussion of whether the tiger was native to Africa. We were

154

not able to talk as freely during van Rensburg's tenure as we had been before, but we were able to talk nonetheless while we worked.

The principal advocate of those who argued that the tiger was not native to Africa was Andrew Masondo, an ANC leader from the Cape who had also been a lecturer at Fort Hare. Masondo could be a volatile fellow, and he was vehement in his assertion that no tigers had ever been found in Africa. The argument was going back and forth and the men had put down their picks and shovels in the heat of the debate. This attracted the attention of the warders, and they shouted at us to get back to work. But we were so absorbed in the argument that we ignored them. A few of the lower-ranking warders ordered us to go back to work, but we paid them no attention. Finally, Suitcase marched over and bellowed at us in English, a language in which he was not expert: 'You talk too much, but you work too few!'

The men now did not pick up their tools because they were bent over in laughter. Suitcase's grammatical mistake struck everyone as extremely comical. But Suitcase was not at all amused. He immediately sent for Major Kellerman, the commanding officer.

Kellerman arrived on the scene a few minutes later to find us in much the same state as we had been before. He was relatively new to the island, and was determined to set the right tone. One of the warders then reported to Kellerman that Andrew Masondo and I had not been working, and we were to be charged with malingering and insubordination. Under Kellerman's authority, we were then led away handcuffed and put in isolation.

From that point on, Suitcase seemed to hold a special grudge against me. One day, while he was supervising us, I was working next to Fikile Bam. We were by ourselves, on the far side of the quarry. We worked diligently, but since we were both studying law at the time, we were discussing what we had read the night before. At the end of the day, van Rensburg stood in front of us and said, 'Fikile Bam and Nelson Mandela, I want to see you in front of the head of prison.'

We were brought before the lieutenant who was the head of prison, and van Rensburg announced, 'These men did not work the whole day. I'm charging them with defying orders.' The lieutenant asked if we had anything to say. 'Lieutenant,' I responded, 'we dispute the charge. We have been working and, in fact, we have evidence that we have been working, and it is essential to our defence.' The lieutenant scoffed at this. 'All you men work in the same area,' he said. 'How is it possible to have evidence?' I explained that Fiks and I had been working apart from the others and that we could show exactly how much work we had done. Suitcase naively confirmed that we had been off by ourselves, and the lieutenant agreed to have a look. We drove back to the quarry.

Once there, Fiks and I walked to the area where we had been working. I pointed to the considerable pile of rocks and lime that we had built up, and said, 'There, that is what we have done today.' Suitcase had never even bothered to examine our work and was rattled by the quantity of it. 'No,' he said to the lieutenant, 'that is the result of a week's work.' The lieutenant was sceptical. 'All right, then,' he said to Suitcase, 'show me the small pile that Mandela and Bam put together today.' Suitcase had no reply, and the lieutenant did something I have rarely seen a superior officer do: he chastised his subordinate in the presence of prisoners. 'You are telling lies,' he said, and dismissed the charges on the spot.

*   *   *

One morning in early 1967, during Suitcase's tenure, we were preparing to walk to the quarry when Suitcase informed us that an order had come down from Major Kellerman forbidding us to talk. Not only was conversation banned on our walks; henceforth, there would be no conversation permitted at the quarry. 'From now on, silence!' he yelled.

This command was greeted by profound dismay and outrage. Talking and discussing issues were the only things that made the work at the quarry tolerable. Of course we could not discuss this problem on the way to the quarry because we were ordered not to talk, but during our lunch break the ANC leadership and the heads of the other political groups managed secretly to work out a plan.

While we were surreptitiously hatching our plan, Major Kellerman himself appeared and walked into our lunch shed. This was highly unusual; we had never had such a high-ranking visitor in our lowly shed. With a cough of embarrassment, he announced that his order had been a mistake and that we could resume talking at the quarry, just as long as we did it quietly. He then told us to carry on, and turned on his heel and was gone. We were glad the order was rescinded, but suspicious as to why.

For the remainder of the day, we were not forced to work very hard. Suitcase did his best to be friendly, and said that as a gesture of goodwill he had decided to withdraw all pending charges against us.

That afternoon, I discovered that my cell had been moved from No. 4, near the entrance of the passage, to No. 18, at the back. All my belongings had been dumped in the new cell. As always, there was no explanation.

We guessed that we were to have a visitor and I had been moved because the authorities did not want me to be the first among the prisoners to talk to whoever was coming. If each prisoner in turn voiced his complaints, the authorities could yell 'Time up!' before a visitor reached cell No. 18. We resolved that in the interest of unity, each individual along the passage would inform any visitor that while everyone had individual complaints, the prisoner in No. 18 would speak for all.

The following morning after breakfast, we were informed by Suitcase that we would not be going to the quarry. Then Major Kellerman appeared to say that Mrs Helen Suzman, the only member of the liberal Progressive Party in Parliament and the lone parliamentary voice of true opposition to the Nationalists, would be arriving shortly. In less than fifteen minutes, Mrs Suzman—all five feet two inches of her—came through the door of our corridor, accompanied by General Steyn, the commissioner of prisons. As she was introduced to each prisoner, she asked him whether he had any complaints. Each man replied in the same way: 'I have many complaints, but our spokesman is Mr Nelson Mandela at the end of the corridor.' To General Steyn's dismay, Mrs Suzman was soon at my cell. She firmly shook my hand and cordially introduced herself.

Unlike judges and magistrates, who were automatically permitted access to prisons, members of Parliament had to request permission to visit a prison. Mrs Suzman was one of the few, if not the only, member of Parliament who took an interest in the plight of political prisoners. Many stories were circulating about Robben Island, and Mrs Suzman had come to investigate for herself.

As this was Mrs Suzman's first visit to Robben Island, I attempted to put her at ease. But she was remarkably confident and utterly unfazed by her surroundings, and proposed that we get down to business right away. General Steyn and the commanding officer stood by her, but I did not mince words. I told her of our desire to have the food improved and equalized and to have better clothing, the need for facilities for studying, our lack of rights to information such as newspapers and many more things. I told her of the harshness of the warders, and mentioned van Rensburg in particular. I pointed out that he had a swastika tattooed on his forearm. Helen reacted like a lawyer. 'Well, Mr Mandela,' she said, 'we must not take that too far because we don't know when it was done. Perhaps, for example, his parents had it tattooed on him?' I assured her that was not the case.

Normally I would not complain about an individual warder. One learns in prison that it is better to fight for general principles than to battle each individual case. However callous a warder may be, he is usually just carrying out prison policy. But van Rensburg was in a class by himself, and we believed that if he were gone, it would make a disproportionate difference to all of us.

Mrs Suzman listened attentively, jotting down what I said in a small notebook, and promised to take these matters up with the minister of justice. She then made an inspection of our cells, and talked a bit with some of the other men. It was an odd and wonderful sight to see this courageous woman peering into our cells and strolling around our courtyard. She was the first and only woman ever to grace our cells.

Van Rensburg was exceedingly nervous during Mrs Suzman's visit. According to Kathy, while Mrs Suzman and I were talking, van Rensburg apologized for all his past actions. But his contrition did not last long, for the next day he informed us that he was reinstating all the charges against us. We later learned that Mrs Suzman had taken up our case in Parliament, and within a few weeks of her visit, Suitcase was transferred off the island.

69

I never imagined the struggle would be either short or easy. The first few years on the island were

160

difficult times both for the organization outside and those of us in prison. After Rivonia, much of the movement's underground machinery had been destroyed. Our structures had been discovered and uprooted; those who were not captured were scrambling to stay one step ahead of the enemy. Virtually every one of the ANC's senior leaders was either in jail or in exile.

In the years after Rivonia, the ANC's External Mission, formerly responsible for fund-raising, diplomacy and establishing a military training programme, took up the reins of the organization as a whole. The External Mission not only had to create an organization in exile, but had the even more formidable task of trying to revitalize the underground ANC inside South Africa.

The state had grown stronger. The police had become more powerful, their methods more ruthless, their techniques more sophisticated. The South African Defence Force was expanding. The economy was stable, the white electorate untroubled. The South African government had powerful allies in Great Britain and the United States who were content to maintain the status quo.

But elsewhere the struggle against imperialism was on the march. In the middle to late 1960s armed struggles were being fought throughout southern Africa. In Namibia (then South West Africa), SWAPO was making its first incursions into the Caprivi Strip; in Mozambique and Angola the guerrilla movement was growing and spreading. In Zimbabwe (then Rhodesia), the battle against white minority rule was advancing. Ian Smith's white government was bolstered by the South

161

African Defence Force, and the ANC regarded the battle in Zimbabwe as an extension of our struggle at home. In 1967 we learned that the ANC had forged an alliance with the Zimbabwe African People's Union (ZAPU), which had been formed by Joshua Nkomo.

That year, a group of MK soldiers who had been training in Tanzania and Zambia crossed the Zambezi River into Rhodesia with the intention of making their way home. This first group of MK soldiers was christened the Luthuli Detachment and they were the spearhead of the armed struggle. In August, as the Luthuli Detachment, accompanied by ZAPU troops, moved southward, they were spotted by the Rhodesian army. Over the next few weeks, fierce battles were fought and both sides sustained casualties. Finally, our troops were overpowered by the superior numbers of the Rhodesian forces. Some were captured, and others retreated into Bechuanaland—which had become independent Botswana. By the beginning of 1968 another, larger, ANC detachment had entered Rhodesia and fought not only the Rhodesian army but South African policemen who had been posted to Rhodesia.

We heard of this months later by rumour, but did not learn the full story until some of the men who had fought there were imprisoned with us. Though our forces were not victorious, we quietly celebrated the fact that our MK cadres had engaged the enemy in combat on their own terms. It was a milestone in the struggle. 'Justice' Panza, one of the commanders of the Luthuli Detachment, was later imprisoned with us. He briefed us on the detachment's military training, political education and valour in the field. As a former commander-in-chief of MK, I was terribly proud of our soldiers.

*   *   *

Before receiving the news of MK's battles abroad, we also learned of Chief Luthuli's death at home in July 1967. The circumstances were curious: he had been hit by a train in an area near his farm where he often walked. I was granted permission to write a letter to his widow. Luthuli's death left a great vacuum in the organization; the chief was a Nobel Prize winner, a distinguished, internationally known figure, a man who commanded respect from both black and white. For these reasons, he was irreplaceable. Yet in Oliver Tambo, who was acting president-general of the ANC, the organization found a man who could fill the chief's shoes. Like Luthuli, he was articulate yet not showy, confident but humble. He too epitomized Chief Luthuli's precept: 'Let your courage rise with danger.'

We organized a small memorial service for the chief in section B and permitted everyone who wanted to say something to do so. It was a quiet, respectful service with only one sour note. When Neville Alexander of the Non-European Unity Movement rose to speak, it was apparent that he had come not to praise the chief but to bury him. Without even perfunctory regrets at the man's passing, he accused Luthuli of being a stooge of the white man, mainly on the ground that the chief had accepted the Nobel Peace Prize.

Apart from its wrong-headedness, Neville's speech was entirely contrary to the climate of cooperation between organizations we were trying to create on the island. From the moment I had arrived, I had made it my mission to seek some accommodation with our rivals in the struggle. I saw Robben Island as an opportunity to patch up the long and often bitter differences between the PAC and the ANC. If we could unite the two organizations on the island, that could set a precedent for uniting them in the liberation struggle as a whole.

Yet, from the beginning, relations with the PAC had been more competitive than cooperative. Some of the PAC men were already on the island, and saw our arrival as an encroachment on their territory. We heard from some of our men that the most senior PAC prisoners had expressed regret that we had not been hanged.

In 1962, on my first stay on the island, the PAC had greatly outnumbered the ANC. In 1967 the numbers were reversed. Yet this seemed to harden the PAC in their positions. They were unashamedly anti-communist and anti-Indian. In the early years, I had talks with Zeph Mothopeng, who had been on the PAC's National Executive Committee. Zeph argued that the PAC was more militant than the ANC, and that in prison, the ANC should follow the PAC's lead. The PAC maintained that negotiations with the authorities were a betrayal, but that did not stop them from taking advantage of the benefits that resulted from negotiations. In 1967 I held talks with Selby Ngendane on the question of unity. Outside prison, Ngendane had been violently opposed to the Freedom Charter, but in prison, particularly when sent to our section, Selby mellowed. We eventually wrote separate letters to our respective organizations in the general section advocating the idea of unity. The ANC also worked well with Clarence Makwetu, who later became president of the PAC. Makwetu, who had once been a member of the ANC Youth League, was in our section and was a balanced, sensible man. We had many fruitful discussions about the unity of our two organizations, but after Makwetu was released and was succeeded in the PAC leadership on Robben Island by John Pokela, the talks foundered.

The PAC's insecurity occasionally had comical results. At one point, an order came from Pretoria that I was to be isolated from all other prisoners at the quarry. I would work separately, eat separately and have my own guard. We noticed that this new ruling caused some agitation among the PAC. Several days later, the PAC decided that their leader, Zeph Mothopeng, would also be isolated, and on their own they made him work and eat separately for as long as I did.

The PAC often refused to participate in meetings that had no overt party affiliation. When we called meetings to discuss our grievances and later had news sessions to discuss what we had learned from the paper, the PAC boycotted these gatherings. I found this greatly annoying. The PAC, we learned, were ignorant of changes in their own organization on the outside. At the time, the PAC members on the island refused to believe our claims that the PAC in exile had opened its doors to whites and Indians as members. That was heresy. Yet we had read in the paper that the white activist Patrick Duncan had become a member of the PAC Executive. The PAC members derided this at the time as ANC propaganda.

*   *   *

The ANC formed its own internal organization on Robben Island. Known as the High Command or, more officially, the High Organ, it consisted of the most senior ANC leaders on the island, the men who had been members of the National Executive: Walter Sisulu, Govan Mbeki, Raymond Mhlaba and me. I served as the head of the High Organ.

From its inception, we decided the High Organ would not try to influence external ANC policy. We had no reliable way of evaluating the situation in the country, and concluded it would be neither fair nor wise for us to offer guidance on matters about which we were uninformed. Instead, we made decisions about such matters as prisoners' complaints, strikes, mail, food—all the day-to-day concerns of prison life. We would, when possible, convene a general members' meeting, which we regarded as vital to the health of our organization. But as these meetings were extremely dangerous and thus infrequent, the High Organ would often take decisions that were then communicated to all the other members. The High Organ also operated a cell system, with each cell consisting of three members.

In the first few years on the island, the High Organ also acted as a representative committee for all the political prisoners in our section. In 1967 we organized a petition demanding better treatment that was signed by virtually everyone, including members of the PAC, the Unity Movement and the Liberal Party, represented by Eddie Daniels. This

166

arrangement was acceptable to all until Neville Alexander complained that the High Organ was neither democratic nor truly representative, and that some other body ought to be created.

Neville's original suggestion eventually turned into a prisoners' committee composed of people from all political parties. There was fear among the other organizations that the ANC would attempt to dominate it, and the committee's rules were crafted so that its powers were purely consultative and its decisions not binding. Even so, it was still difficult to agree on a common approach to problems. We suggested that Fikile Bam, a member of the Yu Chi Chan Club, preside over meetings. Later, the committee leadership would rotate. Eventually the committee became known as Ulundi, and acted as a disciplinary committee for all political prisoners.

The High Organ was the source of some controversy because of its ethnic composition: all four permanent members were from Xhosa backgrounds. This was a matter of coincidence rather than design; the senior ANC leadership on the island, the only four to have served on the National Executive Committee, happened to be Xhosa. It would not have been proper to take a less senior comrade and put him on the High Organ simply because he was not a Xhosa. But the fact that the High Organ was Xhosa-dominated disturbed me because it seemed to reinforce the mistaken perception that we were a Xhosa organization.

I have always found this criticism to be vexing and based on both ignorance of ANC history and maliciousness. I would refute it by noting that the presidents of the ANC have been Zulus, Mosothos,

Pedis and Tswanas, and the Executive has always been a mixture of tribal groups. I recall once working in our courtyard on a sunny afternoon while some men from the general section were working on the roof above me. They shouted at me, 'Mdala! [Old man!], why do you talk only to Xhosas?' The accusation stung me. I looked up and said, 'How can you accuse me of discrimination? We are one people.' They seemed satisfied by that, but their perception stuck in my mind. From then on, whenever I knew I would be walking in front of men from the general section, I would try to converse with Kathy or Eddie Daniels, or someone who was not a Xhosa.

We subsequently decided that there should be a fifth, rotating, member of the High Organ. He was usually not a Xhosa: Kathy, for example, was the fifth member of the High Organ for more than five years. Laloo Chiba also served for a time and, in the end, the criticism died a slow and unremarkable death.

I did not by any means dominate the High Organ, and in fact, a number of proposals that I felt strongly about were rejected. This was as it should be, but I sometimes found it frustrating. There were two issues regarding the authorities about which I could never persuade my colleagues. Prison regulations stated that prisoners must stand in the presence of a senior officer. I advocated that we should remain seated, as it was demeaning to have to recognize the enemy when he did not recognize us as political prisoners. My comrades believed this was a trivial matter and the negative consequences of resistance would outweigh any benefits.

The second issue was rejected by the High Organ on similar grounds. The warders either called us by our surnames or our Christian names. Each, I felt, was degrading, and I thought we should insist on the honorific 'Mr'. I pressed for this for many years, without success. Later, it even became a source of humour as my colleagues would occasionally call me 'Mr' Mandela.

70

Time may seem to stand still for those of us in prison, but it did not halt for those outside. I was reminded of this when I was visited by my mother in spring 1968. I had not seen her since the end of the Rivonia Trial. Change is gradual and incremental, and when one lives in the midst of one's family, one rarely notices differences in them. But when one doesn't see one's family for many years at a time, the transformation can be striking. My mother suddenly seemed very old.

She had journeyed all the way from the Transkei, accompanied by my son Makgatho, my daughter Makaziwe and my sister Mabel. Because I had four visitors and they had come a great distance, the authorities extended the visiting time from half an hour to forty-five minutes.

I had not seen my son and daughter since before the trial and they had become adults in the interim, growing up without me. I looked at them with amazement and pride. But though they had grown up, I am afraid I still treated them more or less as the children they had been when I went to prison.

They may have changed, but I hadn't.

My mother had lost a great deal of weight, which concerned me. Her face appeared haggard. Only my sister Mabel seemed unchanged. While it was a great pleasure to see all of them and to discuss family issues, I was uneasy about my mother's health.

I spoke to Makgatho and Maki about my desire for them both to pursue further schooling and asked Mabel about relatives in the Transkei. The time passed far too quickly. As with most visits, the greatest pleasure often lies in the recollection of it, but this time, I could not stop worrying about my mother. I feared that it would be the last time I would ever see her.

Several weeks later, after returning from the quarry, I was told to go to head office to collect a telegram. It was from Makgatho, informing me that my mother had died of a heart attack. I immediately made a request to the commanding officer to be permitted to attend her funeral in the Transkei, which he turned down. 'Mandela,' he said, 'while I know you are a man of your word and would not try to escape, I cannot trust your own people, and we fear that they would try to kidnap you.' It added to my grief that I was not able to bury my mother, which was my responsibility as her eldest child and only son.

Over the next few months I thought about her a great deal. Her life had been far from easy. I had been able to support her when I was practising as an attorney but, once I went to prison, I was unable to help her. I had never been as attentive as I should have been.

A mother's death causes a man to look back on

and evaluate his own life. Her difficulties, her poverty, made me question once again whether I had taken the right path. That was always the conundrum: Had I made the right choice in putting the people's welfare even before that of my own family? For a long time, my mother had not understood my commitment to the struggle. My family had not asked for or even wanted to be involved in the struggle, but my involvement penalized them.

But I came back to the same answer. In South Africa it is hard for a man to ignore the needs of the people, even at the expense of his own family. I had made my choice and, in the end, she had supported it. But that did not lessen the sadness I felt at not being able to make her life more comfortable, or the pain of not being able to lay her to rest.

* * *

In the early hours of the morning of 12 May 1969 the security police woke Winnie at our home in Orlando and detained her without charge under the 1967 Terrorism Act, which gave the government unprecedented powers of arrest and detention without trial. The raid, I later learned, was part of a nationwide crackdown in which dozens of others were detained, including Winnie's sister. The police dragged Winnie away while Zeni and Zindzi clung to her skirts. She was placed in solitary confinement in Pretoria, where she was denied bail and visitors; over the next weeks and months she was relentlessly and brutally interrogated.

When Winnie was finally charged—six months later—I managed to send instructions for her to be represented by Joel Carlson, a long-time anti-apartheid lawyer. Winnie and twenty-two others were charged under the Suppression of Communism Act for attempting to revive the ANC. Later, George Bizos and Arthur Chaskalson, both members of the Rivonia team, joined the defence. In October, seventeen months after her arrest, the state withdrew its case without explanation, and Winnie was released. Within two weeks, she was again banned, and placed under house arrest. She immediately applied for permission to visit me but was rebuffed.

There was nothing I found so agonizing in prison as the thought that Winnie was in prison too. I put a brave face on the situation, but inwardly I was deeply disturbed and worried. Nothing tested my inner equilibrium as much as the time that Winnie was in solitary confinement. Although I often urged others not to worry about what they could not control, I was unable to take my own advice. I had many sleepless nights. What were the authorities doing to my wife? How would she bear up? Who was looking after our daughters? Who would pay the bills? It is a form of mental torture to be constantly plagued by such questions and not have the means to answer them.

Brigadier Aucamp allowed me to send letters to Winnie, and relayed one or two from her. Normally, prisoners awaiting trial are not permitted mail, but Aucamp permitted it as a favour to me. I was grateful, but knew the authorities had not granted permission out of altruism: they were reading our letters, hoping to glean some information that would assist their case against Winnie.

*   *   *

During this time I experienced another grievous loss. One cold morning in July 1969, three months after I learned of Winnie's incarceration, I was called to the main office on Robben Island and handed a telegram. It was from my youngest son, Makgatho, and only a sentence long. He informed me that his elder brother, my first and oldest son, Madiba Thembekile, whom we called Thembi, had been killed in a motor accident in the Transkei. Thembi was then twenty-five, and the father of two small children.

What can one say about such a tragedy? I was already overwrought about my wife, I was still grieving for my mother, and then to hear such news . . . I do not have words to express the sorrow, or the loss I felt. It left a hole in my heart that can never be filled.

I returned to my cell and lay on my bed. I do not know how long I stayed there, but I did not emerge for dinner. Some of the men looked in, but I said nothing. Finally, Walter came to me and knelt beside my bed, and I handed him the telegram. He said nothing, but only held my hand. I do not know how long he remained with me. There is nothing that one man can say to another at such a time.

I asked the authorities for permission to attend my son's funeral. As a father, it was my responsibility to make sure that my son's spirit would rest peacefully. I told them they could send a security cordon with me, and that I would give my word that I would return. Permission was denied. All I was permitted to do was write a letter to Thembi's mother, Evelyn, in which I did my best to comfort her and tell her that I shared her suffering.

I thought back to one afternoon when Thembi was a boy and he came to visit me at a safe house in Cyrildene that I used for secret ANC work. Between my underground political work and legal cases, I had not been able to see him for some time. I surprised him at home and found him wearing an old jacket of mine that came to his knees. He must have taken some comfort and pride in wearing his father's clothing, just as I once did with my own father's. When I had to say good-bye again, he stood up tall, as if he were already grown, and said, 'I shall look after the family while you are gone.'

PART NINE

Robben Island:
Beginning to Hope

71

The graph of improvement in prison was never steady. Progress was halting, and typically accompanied by setbacks. An advancement might take years to win, and then be rescinded in a day. We would push the rock up the hill, only to have it tumble down again. But conditions did improve. We had won a host of small battles that added up to a change in the atmosphere of the island. While we did not run it, the authorities could not run it without us, and in the aftermath of van Rensburg's departure, our life became more tolerable.

Within our first three years on the island we were all given long trousers. By 1969, we received our own individual prison uniforms instead of being issued a different set each week. These uniforms actually fitted us and we were allowed to wash them ourselves. We were permitted out in the courtyard at all hours during the weekend. Although our food was not yet equalized, African prisoners would occasionally receive bread in the morning. We were allowed to pool our food anyway, so that the differences did not matter. We had been given board games and cards, which we often played on Saturdays and Sundays. At the quarry, our talk was rarely interrupted. If the commanding officer was coming, the warders on duty would blow a whistle to warn us to pick up our tools. We had neutralized the worst warders and befriended the more reasonable ones, though the authorities realized this and rotated warders every few months.

We were able to meet among ourselves virtually whenever we wanted. Meetings of the High Organ, general members' meetings and meetings of Ulundi were generally not broken up unless they were too conspicuous. The inmates, not the authorities, seemed to be running the prison.

*　　*　　*

Stern and God-fearing, the Afrikaner takes his religion seriously. The one inflexible event in our weekly schedule was Sunday morning religious services. This was an observance the authorities considered mandatory. It was as though they believed their own mortal souls would be in peril if they did not give us the benefit of worship on Sunday.

Every Sunday morning a minister from a different denomination would preach to us. One Sunday it would be an Anglican priest, the next a Dutch Reformed predicant, the next a Methodist minister. The clerics were recruited by the prison service, whose one edict was that they must preach exclusively on religious matters. Warders were present at all services, and if the minister strayed from religion he was not invited back.

During the first two years on the island, we were not allowed to leave our cells even for Sunday services. The minister would preach from the head of our corridor. By our third year, services were held in the courtyard, which we preferred. In those years, this was the only time we were permitted in the courtyard on Sunday, except for our half hour of exercise. Few of our men were religious, but no one minded long sermons; we enjoyed being outside.

Once services were held outside, we were given the option of attending. Some men attended services only in their own denomination. Though I am a Methodist, I would attend each different religious service.

*　　　*　　　*

One of our first ministers was an Anglican priest by the name of Father Hughes, a gruff, burly Welshman who had served as a chaplain in the submarine corps during the Second World War. When he first arrived, he was perturbed by having to preach in the corridor, which he found inimical to the contemplation of God. On his first visit, instead of preaching to us, he recited passages of Winston Churchill's wartime radio addresses in his beautiful baritone: 'We shall fight on the beaches, we shall fight on the landing grounds, we shall fight in the fields and in the streets, we shall fight in the hills; we shall never surrender.'

Father Hughes soon preached to us in the courtyard and we found his sermons splendid. He made a point of discreetly inserting bits and pieces of news into his sermons, something we appreciated. He might say, for example, that like the pharaoh of ancient Egypt, the prime minister of South Africa was raising an army.

We always sang hymns at the end of services, and I think Father Hughes visited us so frequently just to hear us sing. He brought along a portable organ, and he would play for us. He praised our singing, saying that it was the only singing that matched the choirs in his native Wales.

The Methodist minister was a Reverend Jones, a nervous and gloomy fellow who had been based in the Congo during its revolution. His experience there seemed to be the source of his melancholy. Over and over, he preached the importance of reconciliation—implying that it was we who needed to reconcile ourselves to the whites.

One Sunday, during the Methodist's one-sided message, I noticed Eddie Daniels shifting uneasily. Finally, Eddie could take it no longer. 'You're preaching reconciliation to the wrong people,' he called out. 'We've been seeking reconciliation for the last seventy-five years.' This was enough for Reverend Jones, and we never saw him again.

Reverend Jones was not the only minister Eddie scared away. We were visited by a Coloured minister known as Brother September. One Sunday, a prisoner named Hennie Ferris, who was an eloquent speaker, volunteered to lead a prayer. Brother September was pleased to recognize such devotion. Hennie began speaking in lofty language and, at one point, asked the congregation to close its eyes and pray. Everyone, including Brother September, obliged. Eddie then tiptoed to the front, opened Brother September's briefcase, and removed the *Sunday Times* of that day. No one suspected anything at the time, but Brother September never brought newspapers again.

The Reverend André Scheffer was a minister of the Dutch Reformed Mission Church in Africa, a sister church of the Dutch Reformed Church, the faith of nearly all the Afrikaner people. The Mission Church catered only to Africans. Reverend Scheffer was a crusty, conservative fellow who usually preached to the general prisoners. One

Sunday, he wandered over to our section and we asked him why he didn't preach to us. 'You men think you are freedom fighters,' he said contemptuously. 'You must have been drunk on liquor or high on *dagga* [marijuana] when you were arrested. Freedom fighters, my foot!' But we challenged him to come to preach to us and, eventually, in the late 1960s, he responded.

Reverend Scheffer was unorthodox in one respect: he took a scientific approach to religion. I found this very appealing. Many people use science to debunk religion, but he enlisted science to bolster his beliefs. I recall one sermon in which he talked about the Three Wise Men from the East who followed a star until it led them to Bethlehem. 'This is not just a superstition or a myth,' he said, and then cited evidence from astronomers that at that time in history there was a comet that followed the path outlined in the Bible.

As Reverend Scheffer became familiar with us, he became more sympathetic. He had a dry sense of humour and liked to poke fun at us. 'You know,' he would say, 'the white man has a more difficult task than the black man in this country. Whenever there is a problem, we have to find a solution. But whenever you blacks have a problem, you have an excuse. You can simply say, "*Ingabilungu*".' We burst into laughter not only because his pronunciation was unintentionally comical, but also because we were amused by the idea. *Ngabelungu* is a Xhosa expression that means 'It is the whites.' He was saying that we could always blame all our troubles on the white man. His message was that we must also look within ourselves and become responsible for our actions—sentiments with which

I wholeheartedly agreed.

*　　　*　　　*

What Sundays were to the rest of the week, Christmas was to the rest of the year. It was the one day on which the authorities showed any goodwill towards men. We did not have to go to the quarry on Christmas Day, and we were permitted to purchase a small quantity of sweets. We did not have a traditional Christmas meal, but we were given an extra mug of coffee for supper.

The authorities permitted us to organize a concert, hold competitions and put on a play. The concert was the centrepiece. Our choirmaster was Selby Ngendane of the PAC. Selby had been a member of the ANC Youth League before switching allegiance to the Pan-Africanist Congress. He was a natural entertainer with a lovely voice and a fine ear.

Selby chose the songs, arranged the harmonies, selected the soloists and conducted the performance. The concert took place on Christmas morning in the courtyard. We would mix traditional English Christmas songs with African ones, and include a few protest songs—the authorities did not seem to mind or know the difference. The warders were our audience, and they enjoyed our singing as much as we did.

Before coming to prison, Selby was perceived as something of a political lightweight. But in prison, he showed his mettle. In prison, one likes to be around men who have a sunny disposition, and Selby had one.

Prison was a kind of crucible that tested a man's

character. Some men, under the pressure of incarceration, showed true mettle, while others revealed themselves as less than what they had appeared to be.

*   *   *

In addition to the concerts, we held a chess and draughts tournament, and also played Scrabble and bridge. Every year I competed in the draughts competition, and some years I won the grand prize, which was usually a candy bar. My style of play was slow and deliberate; my strategy conservative. I carefully considered the ramifications of every option and took a long time between moves. I resist such analogies, but it is my preferred mode of operating not only in draughts but in politics.

Most of my opponents played more swiftly, and often lost patience with my manner of play. One of my most frequent opponents was Don Davis. A member of the Non-European Unity Movement, Don had grown up in the diamond-mining area of Kimberley and was a rugged, fearless fellow who was also highly strung. Don was an excellent draughts player, but his style contrasted with mine. When he played, perspiration would flow down his face. He became tense and agitated as he played, and made his moves rapidly as though points were awarded for speed. Several times he and I found ourselves in the finals of the annual tournament.

Don called me Qhipu because of a habit I had when playing draughts. I would ponder each possibility, and then when I was about to move I would call out, 'Qhipu!'—which means 'I strike!'—and then move the piece. Don found this frustrating and he called me Qhipu more in irritation than in amiability.

Don and I played in many tournaments and, even if he won, he would come back within a few minutes, challenging me to another match. Don always wanted to play draughts, and did not seem satisfied until I responded. Soon I was spending so much time playing with Don that my other pursuits languished. When I once failed to pass an exam in my studies, a few colleagues asked me why, and I responded, to much laughter, 'Don Davis!'

*   *   *

Our amateur drama society made its yearly offering at Christmas. My thespian career, which had lain dormant since I played John Wilkes Booth while at Fort Hare, had a modest revival on Robben Island. Our productions were what might now be called minimalist: no stage, no scenery, no costumes. All we had was the text of the play.

I performed in only a few dramas, but I had one memorable role: that of Creon, the king of Thebes, in Sophocles' *Antigone*. I had read some of the classic Greek plays in prison, and found them enormously elevating. What I took out of them was that character was measured by facing up to difficult situations and that a hero was a man who would not break down even under the most trying circumstances.

When *Antigone* was chosen as the play I volunteered my services, and was asked to play Creon, an elderly king fighting a civil war over the throne of his beloved city-state. At the outset, Creon is sincere and patriotic, and there is wisdom

184

in his early speeches when he suggests that experience is the foundation of leadership and that obligations to the people take precedence over loyalty to an individual.

> Of course you cannot know a man completely, his character, his principles, sense of judgment, not till he's shown his colours, ruling the people, making laws. Experience, there's the test.

But Creon deals with his enemies mercilessly. He has decreed that the body of Polynices, Antigone's brother, who had rebelled against the city, does not deserve a proper burial. Antigone rebels, on the grounds that there is a higher law than that of the state. Creon will not listen to Antigone, neither does he listen to anyone but his own inner demons. His inflexibility and blindness ill become a leader, for a leader must temper justice with mercy. It was Antigone who symbolized our struggle; she was, in her own way, a freedom fighter, for she defied the law on the ground that it was unjust.

72

Some of the warders began to engage us in conversation. I never initiated conversations with warders, but if they addressed a question to me, I tried to answer. It is easier to educate a man when he wants to learn. Usually, these questions were posed with a kind of exasperation: 'All right, Mandela, what is it you really want?' Or, 'Look,

185

you have a roof over your head and enough food, why are you causing so much trouble?' I would then calmly explain our policies to the warders. I wanted to demystify the ANC for them, to peel away their prejudices.

In 1969 a young warder arrived who seemed particularly eager to get to know me. I had heard rumours that our people on the outside were organizing an escape for me, and had infiltrated a warder on to the island who would assist me. Gradually, this fellow communicated to me that he was planning my escape.

In bits and pieces he explained the plan: one night, he would drug the warders on duty at the lighthouse to allow for the landing of a boat on the beach. He would furnish me with a key to get out of our section so that I could meet the boat. On the boat I was to be equipped with underwater diving gear, which I would use to swim into the harbour at Cape Town. From Cape Town I would be taken to a local airport and flown out of the country.

I listened to the plan in its entirety and did not reveal to him how far-fetched and unreliable it sounded. I consulted Walter, and we agreed that this fellow was not to be trusted. I never told him that I would not do it, but I never took any of the actions required to implement the plan. He must have got the message, for he was soon transferred off the island.

As it turned out, my mistrust was justified, for we later learned that the warder was an agent of the Bureau of State Security (BOSS), South Africa's secret intelligence agency. The plot was that I was to be successfully taken off the island, but killed in a dramatic shoot-out with security forces at the airport as I tried to leave the country. The entire plan had been dreamed up by BOSS, even the rumours that reached me about the ANC's planning an escape. It was not the last time they would try to eliminate me.

*   *   *

The term of a commanding officer was usually no more than three years, and we had been through several by 1970. That year, Robben Island's CO was Colonel van Aarde, a rather amiable, harmless fellow who allowed us a free rein. But at the end of the year, the authorities concluded that they wanted a different atmosphere on the island, and Colonel Piet Badenhorst was named the new CO.

This was an ominous development. Badenhorst was reputed to be one of the most brutal and authoritarian officers in the entire prison service. His appointment indicated one thing: the government believed that discipline on the island was too lax, and that a strong hand was needed to keep us in line. Badenhorst would supposedly make us yearn for the days of Suitcase.

Whenever a new commanding officer was appointed, I requested a meeting with him. I did this in order to impress upon him the seriousness of our cause and also to evaluate his character. I requested a meeting with Colonel Badenhorst and was turned down. He was the first CO to spurn such a meeting.

We felt the effects of his regime before we ever saw him. A number of the newer regulations regarding study and free time were immediately rescinded. It was obvious that he intended to roll

187

back every privilege we had won over the years. Our old warders were transferred off the island and replaced by Badenhorst's handpicked guards. They were younger, coarser men who enforced every niggling regulation, whose job was to harass and demoralize us. Within days of Badenhorst's appointment, our cells were raided and searched, books and papers were confiscated, meals were suspended without warning and men were jostled on the way to the quarry.

Badenhorst attempted to turn back the clock to the way the island was in the early 1960s. The answer to every question was always no. Prisoners who requested to see their lawyers were given solitary confinement instead. Complaints were completely ignored. Visits were cancelled without explanation. The food deteriorated. Censorship increased.

About a week after Badenhorst arrived, we were working at the quarry one morning when, without introduction or fanfare, he and his driver pulled up in the commander's car. He got out and surveyed us from a distance. We paused to look at our new commander. Badenhorst returned my glance and called out, 'Mandela, *Jy moet jou vinger uit jou gat trek*' ('You must pull your finger out of your arse'). I did not care for this expression at all, and without thinking, I started advancing towards Badenhorst. He was still some distance away, and before I got close he had returned to his car and driven off.

From his car, Badenhorst radioed a command to his staff, and within minutes a truck had arrived to transport us back to section B. We were commanded to be silent in the truck, and when we arrived at the courtyard we were ordered to stand at attention. Badenhorst appeared in front of us, pacing back and forth. He seemed incapable of uttering a sentence without including an oath or swear-word. '*Jou ma se moer*', was his favourite expression. 'Your mother is a *moer*'—*moer* being a vulgar term for an intimate part of a woman's anatomy.

In his guttural voice, he told us he was disgusted to have observed our laziness at the quarry. As a result, he said, he was arbitrarily dropping all our classifications by one notch. Though we despised the classification system, most of the men had by that time risen to at least C level, where they were permitted to study. D level prisoners were not allowed to study. The authorities rued the fact that they had allowed us study privileges, and Badenhorst was determined to rectify that mistake.

Later, after my anger abated, I realized that Badenhorst's crude remark to me at the quarry was a calculated one. He had been brought to Robben Island to restore order, and he had singled out the individual he assumed was the source of the disorder. Like a teacher who takes over a rowdy class, he sought to discipline the student he regarded as the principal troublemaker.

73

In late May 1971 a number of men from SWAPO (the South West African People's Organization), an ally of the ANC fighting for independence in Namibia, were brought to the isolation section. They were led by Andimba Toivo ja Toivo, a founder of SWAPO and a formidable freedom fighter. We learned that they had embarked on a hunger strike to protest against their isolation, and we immediately decided to join in. This angered Badenhorst and the authorities, who regarded this as unacceptable insubordination.

Late on the night of 28 May we were woken by shouts and fierce knocking on our cell doors. 'Get up! Get up!' the warders yelled. We were ordered to strip and then line up against the wall of the courtyard. The warders were obviously drunk and were yelling and taunting us. They were led by a sadistic fellow named Fourie, whom we privately called Gangster.

It was a bitterly cold night, and for the next hour, while we stood to attention naked and shivering, our cells were searched one by one. Warders kept up their abuse for the entire time. Towards the end of the hour, Govan experienced severe chest pains and collapsed. This seemed to scare Fourie, and he ordered us to return to our cells.

The warders searched high and low, and found nothing. But the search seemed only an excuse for Fourie's sadistic impulses. Only later did we learn that he was reputed to have molested prisoners in the general section. The following day we discovered that the warders had brutally beaten some general prisoners before they came to us, and afterwards assaulted Toivo ja Toivo, who hit back and knocked down the warder who was beating him. Toivo was severely punished for this.

We filed a formal complaint about our treatment, but it was ignored. The incident stands out in my memory, but it was by no means unique: incidents like it were the rule rather than the exception under Badenhorst's command.

* * *

We were determined not to let conditions deteriorate entirely under Badenhorst. We smuggled messages to our people on the outside to agitate for his dismissal. At the same time, we resolved to create a delegation among ourselves to see Badenhorst. We discussed this for months and gradually decided on its composition; Walter and I represented the ANC, and each of the other parties had two representatives as well.

Badenhorst agreed to meet us, and at our parley we threatened work stoppages, go-slows, hunger strikes—every weapon at our disposal—unless he reformed his ways and restored many of the privileges that he had rescinded. He merely said he would take what we said into consideration. We regarded this confrontation as a victory, for he was wary of us and knew that we had alerted people on the outside to our complaints. These efforts soon produced a response.

A few weeks later, we knew an important visit must be imminent because when it rained that day at the quarry we were allowed to take shelter instead of continuing working. The following day we were informed that a troika of judges was coming to the island. The authorities asked us to nominate a spokesman to express our grievances, and I was chosen.

As I was preparing for my meeting with the judges, I was informed by a reliable source that a prisoner in the general section had recently been severely beaten by a guard. The three judges were

Justices Jan Steyn, M.E. Theron and Michael Corbett of the Cape provincial division of the Supreme Court. They were escorted by the commissioner of prisons, General Steyn, and accompanied by Colonel Badenhorst. I met them that day outside, where we were working.

General Steyn introduced me to the judges and explained that I had been selected to represent the other prisoners. The judges then indicated that as a matter of course they would talk with me privately. I replied that I had nothing to hide and that in fact I welcomed the presence of General Steyn and the colonel. I could see that they were taken aback by my statement, and I added that it would be only proper for them to have the opportunity to reply to my charges. The judges reluctantly acquiesced.

I began by recounting the recent assault in the general section. I told them the details that had been reported to me, the viciousness of the beating and the cover-up of the crime. I had barely begun to speak when I noticed Badenhorst shifting uncomfortably. When I had finished describing the incident, he interjected in a gruff, aggressive manner: 'Did you actually witness this assault?' I replied calmly that I had not but that I trusted the people who had told me of it. He snorted and wagged his finger in my face. 'Be careful, Mandela,' he said. 'If you talk about things you haven't seen, you will get yourself into trouble. You know what I mean.'

I ignored Badenhorst's remarks and turned to the judges and said, 'Gentlemen, you can see for yourselves the type of man we are dealing with as commanding officer. If he can threaten me here, in your presence, you can imagine what he does when you are not here.' Judge Corbett then turned to the others and said, 'The prisoner is quite right.'

I spent the remainder of the meeting enumerating complaints about our diet, work and studying. Inwardly Badenhorst must have been fuming, but outwardly he seemed chastened. At the end of the session, the judges thanked me, and I bade them good-bye.

I have no idea what the judges said or did after the meeting, but over the next few months Badenhorst seemed to have his hands tied. The harshness abated, and within three months of the judges' visit, we received word that he was to be transferred.

*   *   *

A few days before Badenhorst's departure, I was called to the main office. General Steyn was visiting the island and wanted to know if we had any complaints. Badenhorst was there as I went through a list of demands. When I had finished, Badenhorst spoke to me directly. He told me that he would be leaving the island, and added, 'I just want to wish you people good luck.' I do not know if I looked dumbfounded, but I was amazed. He spoke these words like a human being, and showed a side of himself we had never seen before. I thanked him for his good wishes, and wished him luck in his endeavours.

I thought about this moment for a long time afterwards. Badenhorst had perhaps been the most callous and barbaric commanding officer we had had on Robben Island. But that day in the office, he had revealed that there was another side to his nature, a side that had been obscured but that still existed. It was a useful reminder that all men, even the most seemingly cold-blooded, have a core of decency, and that if their hearts are touched, they are capable of changing. Ultimately, Badenhorst was not evil; his inhumanity had been foisted upon him by an inhuman system. He behaved like a brute because he was rewarded for brutish behaviour.

74

It was announced that Colonel Willemse would succeed Colonel Badenhorst as commanding officer. I requested a meeting with the colonel after his appointment and visited him shortly after his arrival. While he was obviously not a progressive man, he was courteous and reasonable, in marked contrast to his predecessor. Badenhorst's tenure, we hoped, would simply be a dip on the graph of the steady improvement of our conditions.

The aggressive young warders departed with Badenhorst as well, and we quickly resumed our customary behaviour at the quarry and in our section. Willemse might have been a reasonable man, but when he saw that we spent more time at the quarry talking than working, he was shocked.

He had been on the island for only a few weeks when I was summoned to his office. 'Mandela,' he said frankly, 'you must help me.' I asked him how. 'Your men are not working. They don't listen to orders. They only do what they want to do. This is a prison. There must be some discipline. It is not only good for us but good for you. We must have some order or they will bring back someone like the previous head of prison.'

What the colonel said made sense. I listened and told him that his request was a legitimate one, but before I could respond to him, I would need to have a meeting with all my men. At that time, a meeting of all prisoners in the single cells was something that was expressly forbidden. By asking him to permit this, I was asking him for a significant extension of the rules. He knew this as well as I did, and he wanted some time to consider it.

Within days, I received a communication from Willemse saying he would allow it. All of us met one afternoon in the courtyard, without guards watching over us. I told the men what Willemse had said, and noted that by compromising a bit now, we would be making our conditions better in the long run. We decided that we would at least appear to be working, but what work we did would be at a pace that suited us. From then on, that is what we did, and we heard no more complaints from the commanding officer.

*   *   *

During the early part of Willemse's tenure, in 1971–2, there was a steady influx of captured MK soldiers. These men had seen combat, and were well informed about the state of the movement in exile. While I was never happy to see ANC men imprisoned, I was keen to debrief them after they arrived. I was extremely eager to know about Oliver, about the training camps, about MK's

195

successes and failures.

The men were extremely militant, and they did not take to prison life easily. One of the first of them was Jimmy April, an MK officer who had trained under Joe Slovo, and had fought against the enemy in Rhodesia. MK had been slowly infiltrating men back into the country with forged identity documents. Jimmy had been one of them and he was arrested in South Africa.

Jimmy regaled us with war stories, but I also took him aside and asked him about MK's problems. As I was founder of MK and its first commander-in-chief, Jimmy and the others were more candid with me than with the others. He told me stories of discontent in the camps, and of abuses by MK officers. I asked him to keep the matter to himself, and managed to smuggle a letter out to Oliver suggesting that some reforms must be made in the camps.

One day I was at head office, meeting Colonel Willemse, when I saw Jimmy outside the office of another official. He turned to me and said in some agitation, 'They are refusing to give me my letter.'

'On what ground?' I replied.

'They claim it contains matter which I am not allowed to see,' he said. I entered the official's room to discuss the point, but before I could even open my mouth, Jimmy had barged in and loudly said to him, 'Give me my letter!' Jimmy began to push me aside to get to the officer's desk and take the letter himself. At this point, the officer took the letter and moved behind me as if for protection from Jimmy. It might have been a comical scene in a film, but at the time it was nerve-racking. I turned to Jimmy and said quietly but sternly, 'Please don't do this. Calm down. I'll sort out this matter and see that you get your letter. Now, please leave.'

My speech had the intended effect, and Jimmy left the room. I then turned to the officer, who was extremely rattled. It was, for me, an odd position. I was not opposing the authorities but mediating between my own people and the men I had so long fought against. The militancy of those who were coming to the island put me in this position more and more frequently. While we were encouraged by their radicalism, these men sometimes made our day-to-day life more burdensome.

Within a week, the officer handed me Jimmy's letter.

75

One morning, instead of walking to the quarry, we were ordered into the back of a truck. It rumbled off in a new direction, and fifteen minutes later we were ordered to jump out. There in front of us, glinting in the morning light, we saw the ocean, the rocky shore, and in the distance, winking in the sunshine, the glass towers of Cape Town. Although it was surely an illusion, the city, with Table Mountain looming behind it, looked agonizingly close, as though one could almost reach out and grasp it.

The senior officer explained that we had been brought to the shore to collect seaweed. We were instructed to pick up the large pieces that had washed up on the beach, and wade out to collect weed attached to rocks or coral. The seaweed itself was long and slimy and brownish-green in colour. Sometimes the pieces were six to eight feet in length and thirty pounds in weight. After fishing out the seaweed from the shallows, we lined it up in rows on the beach. When it was dry, we loaded it into the back of the truck. We were told it was then shipped to Japan, where it was used as a fertilizer.

The work did not seem too taxing to us that day, but in the coming weeks and months we found it could be quite strenuous. But that hardly mattered because we had the pleasures and distractions of such a panoramic tableau: we watched ships trawling, stately oil tankers moving slowly across the horizon; we saw gulls spearing fish from the sea and seals cavorting on the waves; we laughed at the colony of penguins, which resembled a brigade of clumsy, flat-footed soldiers; and we marvelled at the daily drama of the weather over Table Mountain, with its shifting canopy of clouds and sun.

In the summer the water felt wonderful, but in winter the icy Benguela Current made wading out into the waves a torture. The rocks on and around the shore were jagged, and we often cut and scraped our legs as we worked. But we preferred the sea to the quarry, although we never spent more than a few days there at a time.

*   *   *

The ocean proved to be a treasure chest. I found beautiful pieces of coral and elaborate shells, which I sometimes brought back to my cell. Once someone discovered a bottle of wine stuck in the sand that was still corked. I am told it tasted like

198

vinegar. Jeff Masemola of the PAC was an extremely talented artist and sculptor and the authorities allowed him to harvest pieces of driftwood, which he carved into fantastic figures, some of which the warders offered to buy. He constructed a bookcase for me, which I used for many years. The authorities told visitors that they had provided me with it.

The atmosphere at the shore was more relaxed than at the quarry. We also relished the seaside because we ate extremely well there. Each morning when we went to the shore, we would take a large drum of fresh water. Later we would bring along a second drum, which we would use to make a kind of Robben Island seafood stew. For our stew we would pick up clams and mussels. We also caught crayfish, which hid in the crevices of rocks. Capturing a crayfish was tricky; one had to grab it firmly between its head and tail or it would wriggle free.

Abalone, or what we call *perlemoen*, were my favourite. Abalone are molluscs that cling tenaciously to rocks, and one had to prise them loose. They were stubborn creatures, difficult to open, and if they were the slightest bit overcooked, they were too tough to eat.

We would take our catch and pile it into the second drum. Wilton Mkwayi, the chef among us, would concoct the stew. When it was ready, the warders would join us and we would all sit down on the beach and have a kind of picnic lunch. In 1973, in a smuggled newspaper, we read about the wedding of Princess Anne and Mark Phillips, and the story detailed the bridal luncheon of rare and delicate dishes. The menu included mussels,

199

crayfish and abalone, which made us laugh; we were dining on such delicacies every day.

One afternoon, we were sitting on the beach eating our stew when Lieutenant Terblanche, who was then head of prison, made a surprise visit. We quickly pretended to be working, but we had not fooled him. He soon discovered the second drum containing a mussel stew bubbling over the fire. The lieutenant opened the pot and looked inside. He then speared a mussel, ate it, and pronounced it '*smaaklik*', Afrikaans for 'tasty'.

76

In the struggle, Robben Island was known as 'the University'. This was not only because of what we learned from books, or because prisoners studied English, Afrikaans, art, geography and mathematics, or because so many of our men like Billy Nair, Ahmed Kathrada, Mike Dingake and Eddie Daniels earned multiple degrees. Robben Island was known as 'the University' because of what we learned from each other. We became our own faculty, with our own professors, our own curriculum, our own courses. We made a distinction between academic studies, which were official, and political studies, which were not.

Our university grew up partly out of necessity. As young men came to the island, we realized that they knew very little about the history of the ANC. Walter, perhaps the greatest living historian of the ANC, began to tell them about the genesis of the organization and its early days. His teaching was wise and full of understanding. Gradually this informal history grew into a course of study, constructed by the High Organ, which became known as Syllabus A, involving two years of lectures on the ANC and the liberation struggle. Syllabus A also included a course taught by Kathy, 'A History of the Indian Struggle'. Another comrade added a history of the Coloured people. Mac, who had studied in the German Democratic Republic, taught a course on Marxism.

Teaching conditions were not ideal. Study groups would work together at the quarry and station themselves in a circle around the leader of the seminar. The style of teaching was Socratic in nature; ideas and theories were elucidated through the leaders asking and answering questions.

It was Walter's course that was at the heart of all our education. Many of the young ANC members who came to the island had no idea that the organization had even been in existence in the 1920s and 1930s. Walter guided them from the founding of the ANC in 1912, through to the present day. For many of these young men, it was the only political education they had ever received.

As these courses became known in the general section, we began to get queries from our men on the other side. This started what became a kind of correspondence course with the prisoners in the general section. The teachers would smuggle lectures over to them and they would respond with questions and comments.

This was beneficial for us as well as for them. These men had little formal education, but a great knowledge of the hardships of the world. Their concerns tended to be practical rather than philosophical. If one of the lectures stated that a tenet of socialism is 'From each according to his ability, to each according to his need', we might receive a question back that said, 'Yes, but what does that mean in practice? If I have land and no money, and my friend has money but no land, which of us has a greater need?' Such questions were immensely valuable and forced us to think hard about our views.

For a number of years, I taught a course in political economy. In it, I attempted to trace the evolution of economic man from the earliest times up to the present, sketching out the path from ancient communal societies to feudalism to capitalism and socialism. I am by no means a scholar and not much of a teacher, and I would generally prefer to be asked questions than to lecture. My approach was not ideological, but it was biased in favour of socialism, which I saw as the most advanced stage of economic life then evolved by man.

*   *   *

In addition to my informal studies, my legal work continued. I sometimes considered hanging a name-plate outside my cell, because I was spending so many hours a week preparing judicial appeals for other prisoners, though this was forbidden under prison service regulations. Prisoners with very different political ideas sought my help.

South African law does not guarantee a defendant the right to legal representation, and thousands upon thousands of indigent men and women went to prison every year for lack of such representation. Few Africans could afford a lawyer, and most had no choice but to accept whatever verdict the court handed down. Many men in the general section had been sentenced without benefit of counsel, and a number of them sought me out to make an appeal. For most of these men, it was the first time they had ever dealt with an attorney.

I would receive a smuggled note from a prisoner in F or G asking for help. I would then request the particulars of the case, the charge, the evidence and the testimony. Because of the clandestine nature of these exchanges, information would come slowly in bits and pieces. A consultation that would last no more than half an hour in my old Mandela and Tambo office might take a year or more on the island.

I advised my 'clients' to write a letter to the registrar of the Supreme Court asking for a record of the case. I told the prisoner to inform the registrar that he had limited funds and would like the record at no charge. Sometimes the registrars were kind enough to supply that material gratis.

Once I had the record of the case, I could put together an appeal, usually based on some judicial irregularity such as bias, incorrect procedure or insufficient evidence. I drafted a letter to the judge or magistrate in my own handwriting, and then sent it to the other side. Because it was a violation of regulations for me to prepare a man's case, I would instruct the prisoner to copy the document in his own hand. If he could not write, and many prisoners could not, I told him to find someone who could.

I enjoyed keeping my legal skills sharp, and in a

few cases verdicts were overturned and sentences reduced. These were gratifying victories; prison is contrived to make one feel powerless, and this was one of the few ways to move the system. Often I never met the men I worked for, and sometimes, out of the blue, a man who was serving us pap for lunch would whisper a thank you to me for the work I had done on his behalf.

77

The oppression of my wife did not let up. In 1972, security policemen kicked down the door of No. 8115 Orlando West. Bricks were hurled through the window. Gunshots were fired at the front door. In 1974 Winnie was charged with violating her banning orders, which restricted her from having any visitors apart from her children and her doctor. She was then working at a lawyer's office, and a friend brought Zeni and Zindzi to see her during her lunch hour. For this, Winnie was charged and then sentenced to six months' imprisonment. She was put in Kroonstad Prison in the Orange Free State, but her experience there was not as horrendous as her previous stay in Pretoria. Winnie wrote to me that she felt liberated in prison this time, and it served to reaffirm her commitment to the struggle. The authorities permitted Zindzi and Zeni to visit her on Sundays.

When Winnie was released in 1975, we managed, through letters and communications with our lawyers, to work out a plan for me to see Zindzi. Prison regulations stated that no child between the ages of two and sixteen might visit a prisoner. When I went to Robben Island, all my children were in this legal limbo of age restrictions. The reasoning behind the rule was not pernicious: the lawmakers presumed that a prison visit would negatively affect the sensitive psyches of children. But the effect on prisoners was perhaps equally damaging; it is a source of deep sorrow not to be able to see one's children.

In 1975, Zindzi turned fifteen. The plan was for her mother to alter her birth documents to show that she was turning sixteen, not fifteen, and therefore able to see me. Birth records are not kept in a very uniform or organized way for Africans, and Winnie found that it was not hard to modify her documents to show that Zindzi was born a year earlier. She applied for a permit, and it was approved.

*   *   *

A few weeks before Zindzi's scheduled visit in December, I had a previously arranged visit from Winnie's mother. When I was seated across from her in the visiting area, I said to her, 'Well, Ma, I'm very excited because I'm going to see Zindzi.' My mother-in-law, who was a former teacher, regarded me with some surprise and then said in a rather peevish way, 'No, Zindzi cannot come and see you because she is not yet sixteen.'

I realized immediately that no one had told her about our gambit. There was a warder behind each of us, and I decided I would simply gloss over what she had said, and mumbled, 'Ah, well, Ma, it is nothing.'

But my mother-in-law is a stubborn woman and she did not let it pass. 'Well, Mkonyanisi'—an affectionate term for 'son-in-law' in Xhosa, which is what she called me—'you have made a serious error because Zindzi is only fifteen.'

I widened my eyes in a gesture of alarm and she must have got the message, because she did not mention Zindzi again.

* * *

I had not seen Zindzi since she was three years old. She was a daughter who knew her father from old photographs rather than memory. I put on a fresh shirt that morning, and took more trouble than usual with my appearance: it is my own vanity, but I did not want to look like an old man for my youngest daughter.

I had not seen Winnie for over a year, and I was pleased to find that she looked well. But I was delighted to behold what a beautiful woman my youngest daughter had become and how closely she resembled her equally beautiful mother.

Zindzi was shy and hesitant at first. I am sure it was not easy for her finally to see a father she had never really known, a father who could love her only from a distance, who seemed to belong not to her but to the people. Somewhere deep inside she must have harboured resentment and anger for a father who was absent during her childhood and adolescence. I could see right away that she was a strong and fiery young woman like her own mother had been when she was Zindzi's age.

I knew she would be feeling uncomfortable, and I did my best to lighten the atmosphere. When she arrived I said to her, 'Have you met my guard of honour?', gesturing to the warders who followed me everywhere. I asked her questions about her life, her schooling and her friends, and then tried to take her back to the old days that she hardly remembered. I told her how I often recalled Sunday mornings at home when I dandled her on my knee while Mum was in the kitchen preparing a roast. I recollected small incidents and adventures in Orlando when she was a baby, and how she had rarely cried even when she was small. Through the glass, I could see her holding back her tears as I talked.

*   *   *

The one tragic note of the visit was when I learned from Winnie that Bram Fischer had died of cancer shortly after being let out of prison. Bram's death affected me deeply. Although the government left no fingerprints on Bram's body, it was the state's relentless harassment of him that brought on the final illness that took him too soon. They hounded him even after death—the state confiscated his ashes after his cremation.

Bram was a purist, and after the Rivonia Trial he decided he could best serve the struggle by going underground and living the life of an outlaw. It burdened him that the men whom he was representing in court were going to prison while he lived freely. During the trial, I advised Bram not to take this route, stressing that he served the struggle best in the courtroom, where people could see this Afrikaner son of a judge president fighting for the rights of the powerless. But he could not let others suffer while he remained free. Like the general who fights side by side with his troops at the front, Bram did not want to ask others to make a sacrifice that he was unwilling to make himself.

Bram went underground while out on bail and was captured in 1965, and sentenced to life imprisonment for conspiracy to commit sabotage. I had tried to write to him in prison, but regulations forbade prisoners to correspond with each other. After he had been diagnosed with cancer, a newspaper campaign calling for his release on humanitarian grounds had influenced the government. Just a few weeks after the authorities released him to his brother's house in Bloemfontein, still under house arrest, he died.

In many ways, Bram Fischer, the grandson of the prime minister of the Orange River Colony, had made the greatest sacrifice of all. No matter what I suffered in my pursuit of freedom, I always took strength from the fact that I was fighting with and for my own people. Bram was a free man who fought against his own people to ensure the freedom of others.

*   *   *

A month after this visit I received word from Winnie that her most recent request for a visit had been turned down by the authorities on the absurd grounds that I did not wish to see her. I immediately made an appointment with Lieutenant Prins, who was then head of prison, to lodge a protest.

Prins was not what one would call a sophisticated man. When I went in to see him I explained the situation evenly and without animosity. But I said the situation as it stood was unacceptable and that my wife must be permitted to visit.

Prins did not appear to be listening, and when I had finished he said, 'Ag, Mandela, your wife is only seeking publicity.' I told him that I resented his remark, and before I had even finished, he uttered something so offensive and uncomplimentary about my wife that I immediately lost my temper.

I rose from my chair and started to move around the desk towards him. Prins began to retreat, but I soon checked myself. Instead of assaulting him with my fists, as I felt like doing, I pummelled him with words. I am not a man who approves of oaths or curses, but that day I violated my own principle. I finished by telling him that he was a contemptible man without honour, and that if he ever repeated those same words I would not hold myself back as I had that day.

When I had finished, I turned and stormed out of his office. As I was leaving, I saw Kathy and Eddie Daniels outside, but I did not even greet them as I walked back to my cell. Even though I had silenced Prins, he had caused me to violate my self-control and I considered that a defeat at the hands of my opponent.

*　　　*　　　*

After breakfast the following morning, two warders entered my cell and said I was wanted at head office. When I reached the office, I was surrounded by half a dozen armed warders. Off to one side was Lieutenant Prins and in the centre of this circle was a warrant officer who was the prison prosecutor. The atmosphere was tense.

'Well, Mandela,' the prosecutor said, 'I hear you had a nice time yesterday, but today will not be so pleasant. I am charging you for having insulted and threatened the head of prison. It is a grave charge.' He then handed me the summons.

'Do you have anything to say?' he asked.

'No,' I replied. 'You can speak to my attorney.' I then asked to be taken back to my cell. Prins did not say a word.

*   *   *

I knew immediately what I would do: prepare a counter suit charging everyone from the lieutenant all the way up to the minister of justice with misconduct. I would indict the prison system as a whole as a racist institution that sought to perpetuate white supremacy. I would make the case a *cause célèbre*, and make them regret they had ever charged me in the first place.

I asked George Bizos to represent me, and a meeting was soon arranged. Before George's visit I informed the authorities that I would be giving him written instructions. They asked me why, and I replied candidly that I assumed the consultation room was bugged. The authorities then refused permission for me to give a written statement; I must make an oral one. I told them that they had no right to withhold permission, and the fact that they did only confirmed my suspicions.

The truth was that the authorities were afraid George would leak a written statement to the press. This was indeed part of our strategy. They were also concerned that I was using George as a conduit to communicate with Oliver Tambo in Lusaka, and assumed that the written statement would contain sensitive information. I had previously used George for such purposes, but the document in question did not contain such material.

A date was set for the island's disciplinary court, and a magistrate from Cape Town was assigned. A day before the hearing, I was told that my attorney would be arriving the following day and I would be free to give him my written statement. I met George at head office in the morning and we briefly consulted before court was called into session. But the hearing had no sooner started than the prosecutor announced that the prison was withdrawing its case. The judge gavelled the session to a close and abruptly left the room. George and I looked at each other in surprise and we congratulated one another on an apparent victory. I was putting away my papers when another warrant officer came over and, pointing to my written statement, said, 'Hand me that file.'

I refused, saying it was a confidential matter between me and my attorney. I called over the prosecutor and said: 'Inform this man that these documents are protected by attorney–client privilege, and that I do not have to turn them over.' The prosecutor replied that they were, but that the case was over, court was no longer in session, and the only authority in the room was that of the warrant officer. The officer plucked the documents off the table. There was nothing I could do to stop him. I believe the authorities dropped the case simply to get hold of the documents—which, as they discovered, contained nothing they did not already know.

*　　*　　*

Unlikely a prospect as it might have seemed, I nevertheless thought about escape the entire time I was on the island. Mac Maharaj and Eddie Daniels, both brave and resourceful men, were always hatching plans and discussing possibilities. Most were far too risky, but that did not stop us from considering them.

We had made certain advances. Jeff Masemola, our master craftsman, had managed to make a passkey that unlocked most of the doors in and around our section. One day, a warder had left his key on the desk in the office at the end of our corridor. Jeff took a piece of soap and made an imprint of the key. Using that outline, he took a piece of metal and filed it into the shape of the key. This gave us access to some of the storerooms behind our cells as well as to the isolation section. But we never used it to leave our section. It was the sea, after all, that was the uncrossable moat around Robben Island.

In 1974 Mac had an idea how to cross that barrier. He had recently been taken to the dentist in Cape Town and discovered that the dentist himself was related by marriage to a well-known political prisoner. The dentist was sympathetic; he had refused to treat Mac unless Mac's leg irons were first removed. Mac had also noticed that the window in the dentist's second-floor waiting room was just a short drop to a small side-street where we might make a run for it.

When Mac returned, he met a few of us and urged us to make appointments at the dentist. We did so, and learned that a day had been arranged for Mac, Wilton Mkwayi, me, and one other prisoner to go to Cape Town. The three of us were willing to make the attempt, but when Mac contacted the fourth man, he refused to come with us. We had doubts about this man's loyalty, and it concerned me that he knew what we were planning.

The three of us were taken by boat to Cape Town and then to the dentist's office under heavy guard. All three of us had trained as soldiers and we probably had the best chance of actually executing an escape. Mac was also carrying a knife, and was prepared to use it. At the dentist's office, the guards first cleared away all the other patients. We demanded to have our leg irons removed, and with the support of the dentist, our guards took them off.

Mac led us over to the window and pointed out the street that was our escape route. But something about the street bothered him as soon as he saw it: we were in the centre of Cape Town in the middle of the day, and yet the street was empty. When he had been here before, the street had been filled with traffic. 'It's a trap,' Mac whispered. I, too, had the sense that something was not right. Wilton, whose adrenaline was flowing, said Mac was talking nonsense. 'Madiba, you're losing your nerve,' he said. But I agreed with Mac, and the three of us simply ended up having our teeth examined. The dentist was curious as to why I had come, because my teeth were fine.

While Mac considered the most practical escape plans, Eddie Daniels hatched the most imaginative ones. During the early years, aeroplanes were not permitted to fly over the island. But by the mid-1970s, we noticed that not only were planes flying over our heads, but helicopters on their way to and from the tankers that sailed off the coast. Eddie came to me with a plan that would involve the organization using a helicopter, painted with the South African military colours, to pick me up on the island and then deposit me on the roof of a friendly foreign embassy in Cape Town where I would seek asylum. It was not an ill-conceived plan, and I told Eddie he should smuggle out the suggestion to Oliver in Lusaka. Eddie did manage to get his idea to Lusaka, but we never received a response.

78

Birthday celebrations were bare-bone affairs on Robben Island. In lieu of cake and gifts, we would pool our food and present an extra slice of bread or cup of coffee to the birthday honouree. Fikile Bam and I were born on the same date, 18 July, and I would save a few sweets that I had purchased at Christmas for the two of us to share on our common anniversary. My fiftieth birthday had passed without much notice in 1968, but in 1975, when I turned fifty-seven, Walter and Kathy approached me with a long-term plan that would make my sixtieth birthday rather more memorable.

One of the issues that always concerned us was how to keep the idea of the struggle before the people. During the previous decade, the

214

government had silenced most of the radical press, and there remained a proscription on publishing the words or pictures of any banned or imprisoned individuals. An editor could go to jail and his newspaper be closed down for publishing so much as a snapshot of me or my colleagues.

One day, Kathy, Walter and I were talking in the courtyard when they suggested that I ought to write my memoirs. Kathy noted that the perfect time for such a book to be published would be on my sixtieth birthday. Walter said that such a story, if told truly and fairly, would serve to remind people of what we had fought and were still fighting for. He added that it could become a source of inspiration for young freedom fighters. The idea appealed to me, and during a subsequent discussion, I agreed to go ahead.

When I decide to do something, I like to start immediately, and I threw myself into this new project. I adopted a rather unorthodox work schedule: I would write most of the night and sleep during the day. During the first week or two I would take a nap after dinner, wake at 10 p.m. and then write until it was time for breakfast. After working at the quarry, I would then sleep until dinner, and the process would begin again. After a few weeks of this, I notified the authorities that I was not feeling well and would not be going to the quarry. They did not seem to care, and from then on I was able to sleep most of the day.

We created an assembly line to process the manuscript. Each day I passed what I wrote to Kathy, who reviewed it and then read it to Walter. Kathy then wrote their comments in the margins. Walter and Kathy have never hesitated to criticize me, and I took their suggestions to heart, often incorporating their changes. This marked-up manuscript was then given to Laloo Chiba, who spent the next night transferring my writing to his own almost microscopic shorthand, reducing ten pages of foolscap to a single small piece of paper. It would be Mac's job to smuggle the manuscript to the outside world.

The warders grew suspicious. They went to Mac and said, 'What is Mandela up to? Why is he sitting up late at night?' But Mac merely shrugged his shoulders and said he had no idea. I wrote rapidly, completing a draft in four months. I did not hesitate over choosing a word or phrase. I covered the period from my birth through to the Rivonia Trial, and ended with some notes about Robben Island.

I relived my experiences as I wrote about them. Those nights, as I wrote in silence, I could once again experience the sights and sounds of my youth in Qunu and Mqhekezweni; the excitement and fear of coming to Johannesburg; the tempests of the Youth League; the endless delays of the Treason Trial; the drama of Rivonia. It was like a waking dream and I attempted to transfer it to paper as simply and truthfully as I could.

Mac ingeniously hid the transcribed version of the manuscript inside the binding of a number of notebooks he used for his studies. In this way, he was able to conceal the entire text from the authorities and smuggle it out when he was released in 1976. The arrangement was that Mac would secretly communicate when the manuscript was safely out of the country; only then would we destroy the original. In the meantime, we still had to dispose of a five-hundred-page manuscript. We did the only thing we thought we could do: we buried it in the garden in the courtyard. Surveillance in the courtyard had become careless and sporadic. The warders usually sat talking in an office at the northern end. From that office, they could not see the southern end next to the isolation area where there was a small garden. I had casually inspected this area on my early morning walks, and it was there that I decided to bury the manuscript.

In order not to have to dig a great hole, we decided to bury the manuscript in three separate places. We divided it into two smaller segments and one larger one, each wrapped in plastic, and placed them inside empty cocoa containers. The work would have to be done quickly, and I asked Jeff Masemola to fashion some digging tools. Within a few days I was equipped with several sharp iron stakes.

One morning after breakfast, Kathy, Walter, Eddie Daniels and I drifted over to the garden at the southern end of the courtyard where we appeared to be having a political discussion. We were each hiding portions of the manuscript in our shirts. At a signal from me, we bent down and began digging. I dug in the centre, near a manhole cover that led to a drainpipe. When I reached the pipe, I carved out a space beneath it, and it was there that I placed the largest of the three containers. The others dug two shallower holes for their portions.

We finished just in time to line up for our march to the quarry. As I walked that morning, I felt a sense of relief that the manuscript was safely hidden. I then thought no more about it.

*   *   *

A few weeks later, just after our wake-up call, I heard a sound in the courtyard that made me uneasy: it was the thud of picks and shovels on the ground. When we were allowed out of our cells to wash, I walked to the end of the corridor and managed to peer out of the door and around the corner. There, at the south end of the courtyard was a work crew from the general section. To my alarm, they were digging in the area where the manuscript was buried.

The authorities had decided to build a wall in front of the isolation section because they had discovered that the prisoners in isolation were able to communicate with us in the courtyard. The work crew was digging a shallow trench for the concrete foundation of the wall.

While washing, I managed to inform Walter and Kathy about the digging outside. Kathy thought that the main part of the manuscript, which was buried under the pipe, would probably be safe, but that the other two were vulnerable. When the drums of breakfast porridge were wheeled into the courtyard, the warders in charge of the work crew ordered the men out of the yard. This was done to prevent any fraternization with the political prisoners.

With our bowls of porridge in hand, I led Walter and Kathy over to the south end of the courtyard as though I wanted to confer with them privately. The beginnings of the trench were already perilously close to the two smaller containers. At the same time we were joined by Eddie Daniels, who

218

immediately recognized the problem.

There was only one thing to do: as inconspicuously as possible, the four of us began digging in the area where the two smaller pieces of manuscript would be. We managed to unearth the two containers fairly quickly, and covered the area again with soil. To rescue the chunk of manuscript under the pipe would require more time, but we were confident that they would not find it because they would not have to dislodge the pipe in order to build the wall.

We hid the manuscript in our shirts as we walked back to our cells. Eddie was not going to the quarry that day, and we gave the containers to him, instructing him to destroy them as soon as possible. At great personal risk, Eddie agreed to do so. I breathed more easily knowing that we had salvaged the two containers, and tried not to dwell on the remaining piece of manuscript as I worked that day.

*   *   *

When we returned from the quarry that afternoon, instead of washing, which I normally did, I strolled over to the far end of the courtyard. I attempted to appear as casual as possible, but I was alarmed by what I saw. The prisoners had dug a trench that ran parallel to the wall of the isolation section and had actually removed the pipe altogether. They could not help but to have uncovered the manuscript.

I must have flinched or reacted in some way that was noticeable. Unknown to me, I was being watched by a number of warders, who later said that my reaction confirmed that I knew something

219

had been hidden there. I returned to the corridor to wash, and told Walter and Kathy that I suspected the manuscript had been discovered. Eddie had meanwhile successfully disposed of the other two pieces.

Early the next morning, I was summoned to the office to see the commanding officer. Next to him stood a high prison official who had just arrived from Pretoria. Without any greeting whatsoever, the commanding officer announced: 'Mandela, we have found your manuscript.'

I did not reply. The commanding officer then reached behind his desk and produced a sheaf of papers.

'This is your handwriting, is it not?' he demanded. Again, I remained silent. 'Mandela,' the commander said in some exasperation. 'We know this is your work.'

'Well,' I replied, 'you must produce some proof of that.'

They scoffed at this, and said they knew the notations in the margin had been made by Walter Sisulu and Ahmed Kathrada. Again, I said that they must furnish evidence if they were going to impose any penalties.

'We do not need evidence,' the commander said. 'We have the evidence.'

Although he did not impose a penalty that day, a short while later Walter, Kathy and I were called before General Rue, the deputy commissioner of prisons, who told us that we had abused our study privileges in order to write the manuscript illegally. For that offence, our study privileges were being suspended indefinitely. As it turned out, we lost study privileges for four years.

After Mac was released in December, he sent the notebooks overseas to England. He spent the next six months under house arrest in South Africa before slipping out of the country and going first to Lusaka to see Oliver Tambo, and then to London. He stayed there for six months; with a typist, he reconstructed the manuscript and put together a typescript. He then returned to Lusaka and presented Oliver with a copy.

From there, the trail grows cold. I heard nothing from Lusaka about the manuscript and still don't know precisely what Oliver did with it. Although it was not published while I was in prison, it forms the basis of this memoir.

79

In 1976 I received an extraordinary visit: Jimmy Kruger, the minister of prisons, a prominent member of the prime minister's cabinet, came to see me. Kruger was not only influential about prisons policy but was critical of the government's handling of the liberation struggle.

I had an inkling as to why he had come. The government was then engaged in a massive effort to make a success of its separate development policy, and the 'quasi-independent' homelands. The showpiece of separate development was the Transkei, led by my nephew and one-time benefactor, K.D. Matanzima, who had successfully repressed almost all legitimate opposition to his rule. I recalled that the commanding officer had recently said to me in a bantering way, 'Mandela, you ought to retire to the Transkei and take a good long rest.'

As it turned out, that was precisely what Jimmy Kruger was proposing as well. He was a stout, blunt man, not nearly as polished as I would have expected from a cabinet minister. I approached the meeting as another opportunity to present our grievances, and at first he seemed content to listen. I began by reminding him of the letter we had sent him in 1969, which had gone unanswered. He merely shrugged. I then detailed the poor conditions on the island, reiterating once more that we were political prisoners, not criminals, and expected to be treated as such. But Kruger scoffed at this, saying, 'Nah, you are all violent communists!'

I then began to tell him a bit about the history of our organization and why we had turned to violence. It was clear that he knew almost nothing about the ANC, and what he did know was gleaned from the propaganda of the right-wing press. When I told him the organization was far older than the National Party, he was dumbfounded. I said that if he considered us to be communists, he should reread the Freedom Charter. He looked at me blankly. He had never heard of the Freedom Charter. I found it extraordinary that a cabinet minister should be so uninformed. Yet I should not have been surprised; Nationalist politicians routinely condemned what they didn't understand.

I raised the question of our release and reminded him of the case of the 1914 Afrikaner

222

rebels, who had resorted to violence although they were represented in Parliament, could hold meetings and could even vote. Even though General de Wet and Major Kemp had led a force of twelve thousand and occupied towns and caused many deaths, they were both released soon after their convictions for high treason. I mentioned the case of Robey Leibbrandt, who set up an underground organization during the Second World War to oppose South Africa's support for the Allies, who was sentenced to life imprisonment but soon pardoned. Kruger seemed as ignorant of these episodes in the history of his own people as he was of the Freedom Charter. It is difficult to negotiate with those who do not share the same frame of reference.

Kruger waved all of this aside. 'That is ancient history,' he said. He came armed with a specific offer. Despite his reputation for brusqueness, he made his proposal in a deferential manner. He stated the matter simply: if I recognized the legitimacy of the Transkei government and was willing to move there, my sentence would be dramatically reduced.

I listened respectfully until he had finished. First, I said, I wholly rejected the Bantustan policy and would do nothing to support it, and second, I was from Johannesburg, and it was to Johannesburg that I would return. Kruger remonstrated with me, but to no avail. A month later he returned with the same proposal, and again I turned him down. It was an offer only a turncoat could accept.

80

Diligent as we were in gathering news and information, our knowledge of current events was always sketchy. Happenings in the outside world were muffled by the fact that we heard of them first through rumour; only later might they be confirmed by a newspaper account or an outside visitor.

In June 1976 we began to hear vague reports of a great uprising in the country. The whispers were fanciful and improbable: the youth of Soweto had overthrown the military and the soldiers had dropped their guns and fled. It was only when the first young prisoners who had been involved in the 16 June uprising began to arrive on Robben Island in August that we learned what had truly happened.

On 16 June 1976 fifteen thousand school-children gathered in Soweto to protest at the government's ruling that half of all classes in secondary schools must be taught in Afrikaans. Students did not want to learn and teachers did not want to teach in the language of the oppressor. Pleadings and petitions by parents and teachers had fallen on deaf ears. A detachment of police confronted this army of earnest schoolchildren and without warning opened fire, killing thirteen-year-old Hector Pieterson and many others. The children fought with sticks and stones, and mass chaos ensued, with hundreds of children wounded and killed and two white men stoned to death.

The events of that day reverberated in every

town and township of South Africa. The uprising triggered riots and violence across the country. Mass funerals for the victims of state violence became national rallying points. Suddenly the young people of South Africa were fired with the spirit of protest and rebellion. Students boycotted schools all across the country. ANC organizers joined with students to actively support the protest. Bantu Education had come back to haunt its creators, for these angry and audacious young people were its progeny.

*   *   *

In September, the isolation section was filled with young men who had been arrested in the aftermath of the uprising. Through whispered conversations in an adjacent corridor we learned first-hand what had taken place. My comrades and I were enormously cheered; the spirit of mass protest that had seemed dormant during the 1960s was erupting in the 1970s. Many of these young people had left the country to join our own military movement, and then smuggled themselves back. Thousands of them were trained in our camps in Tanzania, Angola and Mozambique. There is nothing so encouraging in prison as learning that the people outside are supporting the cause for which you are inside.

These young men were a different breed of prisoner from those we had seen before. They were brave, hostile and aggressive; they would not take orders, and shouted 'Amandla!' at every opportunity. Their instinct was to confront rather than cooperate. The authorities did not know how to handle them, and they turned the island upside down. During the Rivonia Trial, I remarked to a security policeman that if the government did not reform itself, the freedom fighters who would take our place would someday make the authorities yearn for us. That day had indeed come on Robben Island.

In these young men we saw the angry revolutionary spirit of the times. I had had some warning. On a visit with Winnie a few months before, she had managed to tell me through our coded conversation that there was a rising class of discontented youths who were militant and Africanist in orientation. She said they were changing the nature of the struggle and that I should be aware of them.

The new prisoners were appalled by what they considered the barbaric conditions of the island, and said they could not understand how we could live in such a way. We told them that they should have seen the island in 1964. But they were almost as sceptical of us as they were of the authorities. They chose to ignore our calls for discipline and thought our advice feeble and unassertive.

It was obvious that they regarded us, the Rivonia Trialists, as moderates. After so many years of being branded a radical revolutionary, to be perceived as a moderate was a novel and not altogether pleasant feeling. I knew that I could react in one of two ways: I could scold them for their impertinence or I could listen to what they were saying. I chose the latter.

When some of these men, such as Strini Moodley of the South African Students' Organization and Saths Cooper of the Black

People's Convention, came into our section, I asked them to give us papers on their movement and philosophy. I wanted to know what had brought them to the struggle, what motivated them, what their ideas were for the future.

Shortly after their arrival on the island, the commanding officer came to me and asked me as a favour to address the young men. He wanted me to tell them to restrain themselves, to recognize the fact that they were in prison and to accept the discipline of prison life. I told him that I was not prepared to do that. Under the circumstances, they would have regarded me as a collaborator of the oppressor.

*   *   *

These fellows refused to conform to even basic prison regulations. One day I was at head office conferring with the commanding officer. As I was walking out with the major, we came upon a young prisoner being interviewed by a prison official. The young man, who was no more than eighteen, was wearing his prison cap in the presence of senior officers, a violation of regulations. Nor did he stand up when the major entered the room, another violation.

The major looked at him and said, 'Please take off your cap.' The prisoner ignored him. Then in an irritated tone, the major said, 'Take off your cap.' The prisoner turned and looked at the major and said, 'What for?'

I could hardly believe what I had just heard. It was a revolutionary question: What for? The major also seemed taken aback, but managed a reply. 'It

227

is against regulations,' he said. The young prisoner responded, 'Why do you have this regulation? What is the purpose of it?' This questioning on the part of the prisoner was too much for the major, and he stomped out of the room, saying, 'Mandela, you talk to him.' But I would not intervene on his behalf, and simply bowed in the direction of the prisoner to let him know that I was on his side.

*   *   *

This was our first exposure to the Black Consciousness Movement. With the banning of the ANC, PAC and Communist Party, the Black Consciousness Movement helped fill a vacuum among young people. Black Consciousness was less a movement than a philosophy and grew out of the idea that blacks must first liberate themselves from the sense of psychological inferiority bred by three centuries of white rule. Only then could the people rise in confidence and truly liberate themselves from repression. While the Black Consciousness Movement advocated a non-racial society, they excluded whites from playing a role in achieving that society.

These concepts were not unfamiliar to me: they closely mirrored ideas I myself had held at the time of the founding of the ANC Youth League a quarter of a century before. We, too, were Africanists; we, too, stressed ethnic pride and racial self-confidence; we, too, rejected white assistance in the struggle. In many ways, Black Consciousness represented the same response to the same problem that had never gone away.

But just as we had outgrown our Youth League

At work
sewing clothes
in prison in
Pretoria,
before being
sent to
Robben
Island.
*(Archive
Photos)*

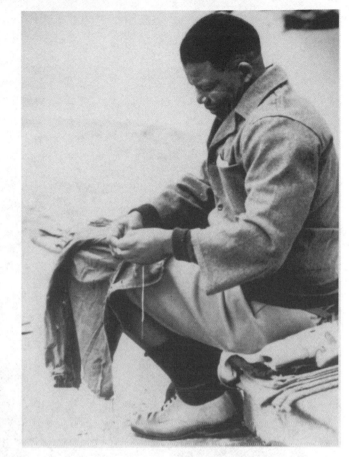

The books I
kept in my cell
during my
years on
Robben
Island.
*(Archive
Photos)*

With Walter in the prison yard, 1966.
(Archive Photos)

The prison yard at Robben Island.
(Archive Photos)

Freedom, February 1990.
(Gideon Mendel/Magnum)

At home in Orlando.
(Peter Magubane)

Walter and I had been imprisoned together on Robben Island for nearly two decades. In the Bishopscourt Gardens Residence of Archbishop Tutu in Cape Town, we gave the '*Afrika*' salute and prepared to take up the battle on the outside once again. *(Gideon Mendel/Magnum)*

A private exchange between old comrades.
(Peter Magubane)

In December of 1990 Oliver Tambo returned home to South Africa after more than thirty years in exile. *(Associated Press)*

Oliver's welcome home rally in Johannesburg
(Associated Press)

With Walter and Winnie in 1990. *(Gideon Mendel/ Magnum)*

Cyril Ramaphosa and Joe Slovo in Johannesburg, during preparatory talks for a new constitution. *(Associated Press)*

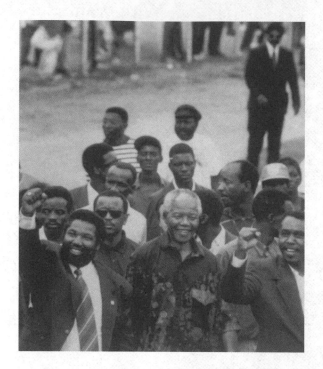

At the Chris Hani memorial at Orlando Stadium, Soweto, with Tokyo Sexwale (right) and Charles Ngekule (left). *(Magnum)*

Below: In 1994, I revisited Robben Island. *(Island Pictures/Karina Turok)*

The cell in which I lived for eighteen of my twenty-seven years in prison. *(Island Pictures/Karina Turok)*

The waters of Table Bay separate Robben Island from Cape Town. In the distance is Table Mountain. *(Island Pictures/Karina Turok)*

With Archbishop Tutu. *(Peter Magubane)*

With F. W. de Klerk. *(Peter Magubane)*

Casting my vote in South Africa's first general election. *(Peter Magubane)*

Singing the national anthem in my inauguration with Thabo Mbeki and my daughter Zenani. *(Ian Berry/Magnum)*

A warm embrace with Archbishop Tutu after the ceremony. *(Ian Berry/ Magnum)*

With my children Zindzi, Zenani, Makaziwe and Makgatho. *(Peter Magubane)*

With my great-granddaughter in September 1994. *(Peter Magubane)*

My family.
(Peter Magubane)

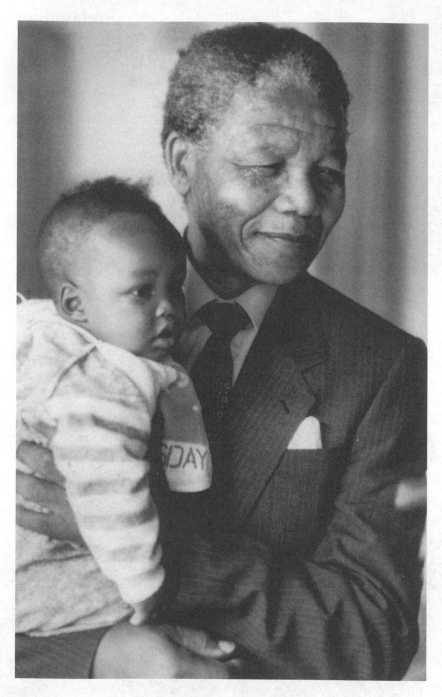

With my grandson Bambata. *(Peter Magubane)*

outlook, I was confident that these young men would transcend some of the strictures of Black Consciousness. While I was encouraged by their militancy, I thought that their philosophy, in its concentration on blackness, was sectarian, and represented an intermediate view that was not fully mature. I saw my role as an elder statesman who might help them move on to the more inclusive ideas of the Congress Movement. I knew also that these young men would eventually become frustrated because Black Consciousness offered no programme of action, no outlet for their protest.

Although we viewed the ranks of the BCM as a fertile ground for the ANC, we did not attempt to recruit these men. We knew that this would alienate both them and the other parties on the island. Our policy was to be friendly, to take an interest, to compliment them on their achievements, but not to proselytize. If they came to us and asked questions—'What is the ANC policy on the Bantustans?' 'What does the Freedom Charter say about nationalization?'—we would answer them, and a great many of them did come to us with questions.

I myself contacted some of these men through smuggled notes. I spoke with some who were from the Transkei and asked questions about my old home. Some of the men who arrived were already well known in the struggle. I had heard reports of the bravery of Patrick 'Terror' Lekota, a leader of the South African Students' Organization, and sent him a note of welcome to Robben Island.

Terror's nickname came from his prowess on the soccer field, but he was just as formidable in a debate. He disagreed with some of his colleagues

245

on the issue of racial exclusiveness and inched closer to the ideas of the ANC. Once on the island, Terror decided that he wanted to join us, but we discouraged him—not because we did not want him but because we thought such a manoeuvre would create tensions in the general section.

But Terror would not take no for an answer and publicly switched his allegiance to the ANC. One day, not long afterwards, he was assaulted with a garden fork by disgruntled BCM members. After he was treated, the authorities charged the attackers and planned to put them on trial. But in the interest of harmony, we advised Terror not to lodge a complaint. He agreed, and refused to testify against those who had hurt him. The case was dropped. Such a trial, I felt, would only play into the hands of the authorities. I wanted these young men to see that the ANC was a great tent that could accommodate many different views and affiliations.

After that incident, the floodgates seemed to open and dozens of BCM men decided to join the ANC, including some of those who had planned the attack on Terror. Terror rose to the top of the ANC hierarchy in the general section, and was soon teaching ANC policies to other prisoners. The courage and vision of men like him confirmed to us that our views remained potent, and still represented the best hope for unifying the liberation struggle as a whole.

*　　　*　　　*

Political feuding continued in sections F and G. We learned of a clash among the ANC, the PAC and the BCM in the general section. A number of ANC people had been beaten. A large number of ANC members were charged by the authorities, and a trial was set for the island's administrative court. The ANC men brought in an outside lawyer to handle the case. Although I had not witnessed the fight, I was asked to be a character witness. This was a troubling prospect. While I was more than willing to give testimonials for my comrades, I did not want to take any action that would heighten the bitterness between the ANC, the PAC and the BCM.

I regarded my role in prison as not just the leader of the ANC, but as a promoter of unity, an honest broker, a peacemaker, and I was reluctant to take a side in this dispute, even if it was the side of my own organization. If I testified on behalf of the ANC, I would jeopardize my chances of bringing about reconciliation among the different groups. If I preached unity, I must act like a unifier, even at the risk of perhaps alienating some of my own colleagues.

I decided not to testify. This disappointed some of my colleagues, but I thought the issue was serious enough to risk their displeasure. It was more important to show the young Black Consciousness men that the struggle was indivisible and that we all had the same enemy.

81

In their anxiousness to deal with these young lions, the authorities more or less let us fend for ourselves. We were in the second year of a go-slow strike at the quarry, demanding a complete end to all manual labour. Our requirement was for the right to do something useful with our days, such as studying or learning a trade. We no longer even went through the motions of working at the quarry; we simply talked among ourselves. In early 1977, the authorities announced the end of manual labour. Instead, we could spend our days in our section. They arranged some type of work for us to do in the courtyard, but it was merely a figleaf to hide their capitulation.

This victory was the combined result of our own unceasing protests and simple logistics. The authorities normally preferred to have a ratio of one warder for every three prisoners. Even before the arrival of the post-Soweto prisoners, there was a shortage of warders, and the rebellious young men required even greater supervision. They were so bold that each man seemed to require his own warder. If we remained in our section, we required less supervision.

The end of manual labour was liberating. I could now spend the day reading, writing letters, discussing issues with my comrades or formulating legal briefs. The free time allowed me to pursue what became two of my favourite hobbies on Robben Island: gardening and tennis.

To survive in prison, one must develop ways to take satisfaction in one's daily life. One can feel fulfilled by washing one's clothes so that they are particularly clean, by sweeping a corridor so that it is free of dust, by organizing one's cell to conserve as much space as possible. The same pride one takes in more consequential tasks outside prison one can find in doing small things inside prison.

Almost from the beginning of my sentence on Robben Island, I asked the authorities for permission to start a garden in the courtyard. For years, they refused without offering a reason. But eventually they relented, and we were able to cut out a small garden on a narrow patch of earth against the far wall.

The soil in the courtyard was dry and rocky. The courtyard had been constructed over a landfill, and in order to start my garden I had to excavate a great many rocks to allow the plants room to grow. At the time, some of my comrades jested that I was a miner at heart, for I spent my days at the quarry and my free time digging in the courtyard.

The authorities supplied me with seeds. I initially sowed tomatoes, chillies and onions— hardy plants that did not require rich earth or constant care. The early harvests were poor, but they soon improved. The authorities did not regret giving permission, for once the garden began to flourish, I often provided the warders with some of my best tomatoes and onions.

While I have always enjoyed gardening, it was not until I was behind bars that I was able to tend my own plot. My first experience in a garden was at Fort Hare where, as part of the university's manual labour requirement, I worked in the garden of one of my professors and enjoyed the contact with the soil as an antidote to my intellectual labours. Once I was in Johannesburg studying and then working, I had neither the time nor the space to cultivate a garden.

*   *   *

I began to order books on gardening and horticulture. I studied different gardening techniques and types of fertilizer. I did not have many of the materials that the books discussed, but I learned through trial and error. For a time I attempted to grow peanuts, and used different soils and fertilizers, but finally I gave up. It was one of my only failures.

A garden was one of the few things in prison that one could control. To plant a seed, watch it grow, to tend it and then harvest it offered a simple but enduring satisfaction. The sense of being the custodian of this small patch of earth offered a small taste of freedom.

In some ways, I saw the garden as a metaphor for certain aspects of my life. A leader must also tend his garden; he, too, sows seeds, and then watches, cultivates and harvests the result. Like the gardener, a leader must take responsibility for what he cultivates; he must mind his work, try to repel enemies, preserve what can be preserved and eliminate what cannot succeed.

I wrote Winnie two letters about a particularly beautiful tomato plant, how I coaxed it from a tender seedling to a robust plant that produced deep red fruit. But, then, either through some mistake or lack of care, the plant began to wither and decline, and nothing I did would bring it back to health. When it finally died, I removed the roots from the soil, washed them and buried them in a corner of the garden.

I narrated this small story at great length. I do not know what she read into that letter, but when I wrote it I had a mixture of feelings: I did not want

250

our relationship to go the way of that plant, and yet I felt that I had been unable to nourish many of the most important relationships in my life. Sometimes there is nothing one can do to save something that must die.

* * *

One unanticipated result of ending manual labour was that I began to gain weight. Though we were doing barely enough at the quarry to work up a sweat, the walk there and back was enough to keep me trim.

I have always believed that exercise is a key not only to physical health but to peace of mind. Many times in the old days I unleashed my anger and frustration on a punchbag rather than taking it out on a comrade or even a policeman. Exercise dissipates tension, and tension is the enemy of serenity. I found that I worked better and thought more clearly when I was in good physical condition, and so training became one of the inflexible disciplines of my life. In prison, having an outlet for my frustrations was absolutely essential.

Even on the island, I attempted to follow my old boxing routine of doing roadwork and muscle-building from Monday to Thursday and then resting for the next three days. On Mondays to Thursdays I would run on the spot in my cell in the morning for up to forty-five minutes. I would also perform a hundred fingertip push-ups, two hundred sit-ups, fifty deep knee-bends and various other callisthenics.

In my letters to my children, I regularly urged them to exercise, to play some fast-moving sport like basketball, soccer or tennis to take their mind off whatever might be bothering them. While I was not always successful with my children, I did manage to influence some of my more sedentary colleagues. Exercise was unusual for African men of my age and generation. After a while even Walter began to take a few turns around the courtyard in the morning. I know that some of my younger comrades looked at me and said to themselves, 'If that old man can do it, why can't I?' They, too, began to exercise.

*   *   *

From the very first meetings I had with outside visitors and the International Red Cross, I stressed the importance of having the time and facilities for proper exercise. Only in the mid-1970s, under the auspices of the International Red Cross, did we begin to receive things like volleyball equipment and a ping-pong table.

At roughly the same time as we stopped working at the quarry, one of the warders had the idea of converting our courtyard into a tennis court. Its dimensions were almost exact. Prisoners from the general section painted the cement surface green and then fashioned the traditional configuration of white lines. A few days later a net was put up and suddenly we had our own Wimbledon in our front yard.

I had played a bit of tennis when I was at Fort Hare, but I was by no means an expert. My forehand was relatively strong, my backhand regrettably weak. But I pursued the sport for exercise, not style; it was the best and only replacement for the walks to and from the quarry. I was one of the first in our section to play regularly. I was a back-court player, only rushing the net when I had a clean slam.

*   *   *

Once manual labour ended, I had much more time for reading, but the books I had been using were now out of bounds. When my studies were cancelled, I was still in the midst of pursuing my LLB at the University of London. I had started studying for the degree during the Rivonia Trial and the suspension of study privileges for four years would undoubtedly assure me the university record for taking the longest time in pursuit of that degree.

But the suspension of study privileges had an unintended benefit, and that was that I began to read many books that I would not otherwise have come across. Instead of poring over tomes about contract law, I was now absorbed by novels.

I did not have an unlimited library to choose from on Robben Island. We had access to many unmemorable mysteries and detective novels and all the works of Daphne du Maurier, but little more. Political books were off limits. Any book about socialism or communism was definitely out. A request for a book with the word *red* in the title, even if it was *Little Red Riding Hood*, would be rejected by the censors. *The War of the Worlds* by H. G. Wells, though it is a work of science fiction, would be turned down because the word *war* appeared in its title.

From the first, I tried to read books about South

253

Africa or by South African writers. I read all the unbanned novels of Nadine Gordimer and learned a great deal about the white liberal sensibility. I read many American novels, and recall especially John Steinbeck's *The Grapes of Wrath*, in which I found many similarities between the plight of the migrant workers in that novel and our own labourers and farmworkers.

One book that I returned to many times was Tolstoy's great work, *War and Peace*. (Although the word *war* was in the title, this book was permitted.) I was particularly taken with the portrait of General Kutuzov, whom everyone at the Russian court underestimated. Kutuzov defeated Napoleon precisely because he was not swayed by the ephemeral and superficial values of the court, and made his decisions on a visceral understanding of his men and his people. It reminded me once again that truly to lead one's people one must also truly know them.

82

In the wake of the Soweto student uprising, I learned that Winnie, along with my old friend and physician, Dr Nthato Motlana, had become involved with the Black Parents' Association, an organization of concerned local professionals and church leaders who acted as a guiding hand and intermediary for the students. The authorities seemed to be equally wary of the parents association and the young rebels. In August, less than two months after the student revolt, Winnie was detained under the Internal Security Act and imprisoned without charge in the Fort in Johannesburg, where she was held for five months. During that time I was able to write to her and my daughters, who were at boarding school in Swaziland, expressing support and solidarity. I was greatly distressed by her imprisonment, though she was apparently not mistreated this time and emerged from jail in December even firmer in her commitment to the struggle.

Though banned, Winnie picked up where she left off, and the authorities were dismayed about her popularity with the young radicals of Soweto. They were determined to lessen her influence and did it with a brazen and shameless act: they sent her into internal exile. On the night of 16 May 1977 police cars and a truck pulled up outside the house in Orlando West and began loading furniture and clothing into the back of the truck. This time Winnie was not being arrested, detained or interrogated; she was being banished to a remote township in the Free State called Brandfort. I discovered the details from Kathy, who had been given the information from a visiting Hindu priest.

Brandfort is about two hundred and fifty miles southwest of Johannesburg, just north of Bloemfontein, in the Free State. After a long and rough ride, Winnie, Zindzi and all their possessions were dumped in front of a three-room tin-roofed shack in Brandfort's bleak African township, a desperately poor and backward place where the people were under the thumb of the local white farmers. Winnie was regarded with wariness and trepidation. The local language was Sesotho, which Winnie did not speak.

Her new circumstances saddened and angered me. At least when she was home in Soweto, I could picture her cooking in the kitchen or reading in the lounge; I could imagine her waking up in the house I knew so well. That was a source of comfort to me. In Soweto, even if she was banned, there were friends and family near by. In Brandfort she and Zindzi would be alone.

I had passed through this township once on my way to Bloemfontein, and took no notice of it. There was nothing memorable in its all too typical poverty and desolation. I did not know at the time how familiar the address—house No. 802, Brandfort—would one day become to me. Once again, I felt as though Winnie and I were in prison at the same time.

*   *   *

Life in Brandfort was hard, as I learned from Winnie's letters. They had no heat, no toilet, no running water. The township had no shops and the stores in town were hostile to African customers. The whites for the most part were Afrikaans-speaking and deeply conservative.

Winnie and Zindzi were under constant police surveillance and intermittent harassment. Within a few months Zindzi—who was not banned—was upset by the security police's intimidation. In September, with the help of Winnie's lawyers, I brought an urgent application for an interdict against the local Brandfort security police to restrain them from harassing my daughter. Affidavits filed before the judge described policemen bursting into the house and threatening

Zindzi. The judge ruled that Zindzi could receive visitors in peace.

Winnie is a resilient person, and within a relatively short time she had won over the people of the township, including some sympathetic whites in the vicinity. She supplied food to the people in the township with the help of Operation Hunger, started a crèche for the township's children and raised funds to create a medical clinic in a place where few people had ever seen a doctor.

*   *   *

In 1978 Zeni, my second-youngest daughter and my first child with Winnie, married Prince Thumbumuzi, a son of King Sobhuza of Swaziland. They had met while Zeni was away at school. Being in prison, I was not able to fulfil the father's traditional duties. In our culture, the father of the bride must interview the prospective groom and assess his prospects. He must also determine *lobola*, the brideprice, which is paid by the groom to the bride's family. On the wedding day itself, the father gives away his daughter. Although I had no doubts about the young man, I asked my friend and legal adviser George Bizos to stand in for me. I instructed George to interview the prince about how he intended to look after my daughter.

George met the prince in his office and then arranged to have a consultation with me on Robben Island. Because Zeni was under twenty-one, it was necessary for me to give my legal consent for her to marry. I met George in the consulting room and he was surprised to find a warder in the room with us. I explained that it was

257

according to regulations because this was considered a family visit, not a legal one. I jestingly reassured George by saying that I had no secrets from my guards.

George reported how much the two children loved one another and the bright prospects of my future son-in-law. His father, King Sobhuza, was an enlightened traditional leader and also a member of the ANC. As George relayed to me some of the requirements made by the young man's family, he was at pains to point out that the boy was a Swazi prince. I told George to tell the young man that he was getting a Thembu princess.

*   *   *

There was a tremendous advantage in Zeni becoming a member of the Swazi royal family: she was immediately granted diplomatic privileges and could visit me virtually at will. That winter, after she and Thumbumuzi were married, they came to see me, along with their newborn baby daughter. Because of the prince's status, we were allowed to meet one another in the consulting room, not the normal visiting area where one is separated from one's family by thick walls and glass. I waited for them with some nervousness.

It was a truly wondrous moment when they came into the room. I stood up, and when Zeni saw me, she practically tossed her tiny daughter to her husband and ran across the room to embrace me. I had not held my now grown-up daughter since she was about her own daughter's age. It was a dizzying experience, as though time had sped forward in a science fiction novel, suddenly to hug one's fully grown child. I then embraced my new son and he handed me my tiny granddaughter, whom I did not let go of for the entire visit. To hold a newborn baby, so vulnerable and soft in my rough hands, hands that for too long had held only picks and shovels, was a profound joy. I don't think a man was ever happier to hold a baby than I was that day.

The visit had a more official purpose and that was for me to choose a name for the child. It is the custom for the grandfather to select a name, and the one I had chosen was Zaziwe—which means 'Hope'. The name had a special meaning for me, for during all my years in prison hope never left me—and now it never would. I was convinced that this child would be a part of a new generation of South Africans for whom apartheid would be a distant memory—that was my dream.

83

I do not know whether it was the upheaval inside the prison after the Soweto uprising or the upheaval in my family's life outside prison, but in the year or two following 1976 I was in a dreamy, nostalgic state of mind. In prison, one has time to review the past, and memory becomes both a friend and a foe. My memory transported me into moments of both great joy and sadness. My dream life became very rich, and I seemed to pass entire nights reliving the high and low times of the old days.

I had one recurring nightmare. In the dream, I had just been released from prison—only it was not

259

Robben Island, but a jail in Johannesburg. I walked outside the gates into the city and found no one to meet me. In fact there was no one there at all, no people, no cars, no taxis. I would then set out on foot towards Soweto. I walked for many hours before arriving in Orlando West, and then turned the corner towards No. 8115. Finally I would see my home, but it turned out to be empty, a ghost house, with all the doors and windows open but no one there at all.

But not all my dreams of release were so dark. In 1976 I wrote to Winnie of a happier vision:

> The night of 24 February, I dreamt of arriving at No. 8115, finding the house full of youth dancing away a mixture of jive and *infiba*. I caught all of them by surprise as I walked in unexpectedly. Some greeted me warmly, whilst others simply melted away shyly. I found the bedroom equally full with members of the family and close friends. You were relaxing in bed, with Kgatho [my son Makgatho], looking young and sleeping against the opposite wall.
>
> Perhaps in that dream I was recalling the two weeks in December 1956 when he was six and when I left Makhulu [Evelyn's mother] alone in the house. He was living with his mother in OE [Orlando East] then, but a few days before I came back he joined Makhulu and slept in my bed. He was missing me very much and using the bed must have relieved the feeling of longing a bit.

While I took joy from dwelling on happy moments,

I rued the pain I had often caused my family through my absence. Here is another letter from 1976:

As I woke up on the morning of 25 February I was missing you and the children a great deal as always. These days I spend quite some time thinking of you both as Dadewethu [Sister], Mum, pal and mentor. What you perhaps don't know is how I often think and actually picture in my mind all that makes you up physically and spiritually—the loving remarks which came daily and the blind eye you've always turned against those numerous irritations that would have frustrated another woman . . . I even remember a day when you were bulging with Zindzi, struggling to cut your nails. I now recall those incidents with a sense of shame. I could have done it for you. Whether or not I was conscious of it, my attitude was: I've done my duty, a second brat is on the way, the difficulties you are now facing as a result of your physical condition are all yours. My only consolation is the knowledge that I then led a life where I'd hardly enough time even to think. Only I wonder what it'll be like when I return . . .

Your beautiful photo still stands about two feet above my left shoulder as I write this note. I dust it carefully every morning, for to do so gives me the pleasant feeling that I'm caressing you as in the old days. I even touch your nose with mine to recapture the electric current that used to flush through my blood whenever I did so. Nolitha stands on the table

261

directly opposite me. How can my spirits ever be down when I enjoy the fond attentions of such wonderful ladies.

Nolitha was the one person who was not a member of the family whose photo I kept. I revealed the secret of her identity to my daughter Zindzi in another letter from 1976:

> By the way, has Mum ever told you about Nolitha, the other lady in my cell from the Andaman Islands? She keeps you, Zeni, Ndindi and Nandi, Mandla [these last three are grandchildren], Maki and Mum company. It's one matter over which Mum's comments are surprisingly economic. She regards the pygmy beauty as some sort of rival and hardly suspects that I took her picture out of the *National Geographic*.

I thought continually of the day when I would walk free. Over and over, I fantasized about what I would like to do. This was one of the pleasantest ways to pass the time. I put my daydreams on paper, again in 1976.

> I wish I could drive you on a long, long journey just as I did on 12/6/58, with the one difference that this time I'd prefer us to be alone. I've been away from you for so long that the very first thing I would like to do on my return would be to take you away from that suffocating atmosphere, drive you along carefully, so that you could have the opportunity of breathing fresh and clean air,

seeing the beauty spots of South Africa, its green grass and trees, colourful wild flowers, sparkling streams, animals grazing in the veld and be able to talk to the simple people we meet along the road. Our first stop would be to the place where Ma Radebe and CK [Winnie's mother and father] sleep. I hope they lie next to each other. Then I would be able to pay my respects to those who have made it possible for me to be as happy and free as I am now. Perhaps the stories I've so much wanted to tell you all these years would begin there. The atmosphere should probably sharpen your ears and restrain me to concentrate on those aspects which are tasty, edifying and constructive. Thereafter, we would adjourn and resume next to Mphakanyiswa and Nosekeni [my parents] where the environment would be similar. I believe we would then be fresh and solid as we drive back to No. 8115.

When the authorities began to allow us to receive photographs of immediate family members in the early 1970s, Winnie sent me an album. Whenever I received a photograph of Winnie, the children or the grandchildren, I would carefully paste it in. I cherished this album; it was the one way that I could see those I loved whenever I wanted.

But in prison no privilege comes without some accompanying pain. Though I was permitted to receive pictures and to keep the album, warders would often search my cell and confiscate pictures of Winnie. Eventually, however, the practice of seizing pictures ceased, and I built up my album so that it was thick with pictures of my entire family.

I do not remember who first asked to borrow my photo album, but it was undoubtedly someone in my section. I happily lent it, and someone else asked, and then someone else. Soon it became so widely known that I possessed a photo album that I was receiving requests from men in F and G.

The men of F and G rarely received visitors or even letters, and it would have been ungenerous to deny them this window on the world. But before long I found that my precious photo album was in tatters, and that many of my irreplaceable photographs had been removed. These men were desperate to have something personal in their cells and could not help themselves. Each time this happened, I resolved to build up my album once more.

Sometimes men would just ask me for a photograph rather than the album. I recall one day when a young BCM fellow from the general section who was bringing us food took me aside and said, 'Madiba, I would like a photograph.' I said fine, I would send him one. 'When?' he said rather brusquely. I replied that I would try to send it that weekend. This seemed to satisfy him, and he began to walk away, but suddenly he turned round and said, 'Look, don't send me a photograph of the old lady. Send me one of the young girls, Zindzi or Zeni—remember, not the old lady!'

84

In 1978, after we had spent almost fifteen years agitating for the right to receive news, the authorities offered us a compromise. Instead of permitting us to receive newspapers or listen to radio, they started their own radio news service, which consisted of a daily canned summary of the news read over the prison's intercom system.

The broadcasts were far from objective or comprehensive. Several of the island's censors would compile a brief news digest from other daily radio bulletins. The broadcasts consisted of good news for the government and bad news for all its opponents.

The first broadcast opened with a report about the death of Robert Sobukwe. Other early reports concerned the victories of Ian Smith's troops in Rhodesia and detentions of government opponents in South Africa. Despite the slanted nature of the news, we were glad to have it, and prided ourselves on reading between the lines and making educated guesses based on the obvious omissions.

That year, we learned via the intercom that P. W. Botha had succeeded John Vorster as prime minister. What the warders did not tell us was that Vorster resigned as a result of press revelations about the Department of Information's misuse of government funds. I knew little about Botha apart from the fact that he had been an aggressive defence minister and had supported a military strike into Angola in 1975. We had no sense that he would be a reformer in any way.

I had recently read an authorized biography of Vorster (this was one of the books the prison library did have) and found that he was a man willing to pay for his beliefs; he went to prison for his support of Germany during the Second World War. We were not sorry to see Vorster go. He had escalated the battle against freedom to new heights of repression.

But even without our expurgated radio broadcasts, we had learned what the authorities did not want us to know. We learned of the successful liberation struggles in Mozambique and Angola in 1975 and their emergence as independent states with revolutionary governments. The tide was turning our way.

*　　*　　*

In keeping with the increased openness on the island, we now had our own cinema. Almost every week we watched films on a sheet in a large room adjacent to our corridor. Later, we had a proper screen. The films were a wonderful diversion, a vivid escape from the bleakness of prison life.

The first films we saw were silent, black-and-white Hollywood action movies and Westerns that were made before even my time. I recall one of the first ones was *The Mark of Zorro*, with the swashbuckling Douglas Fairbanks, a movie that was made in 1920. The authorities seemed to have a weakness for historical films, particularly ones with a stern moral message. Among the early films we saw—now in colour, with dialogue—were *The Ten Commandments* with Charlton Heston as Moses, *The King and I* with Yul Brynner and *Cleopatra* with Richard Burton and Elizabeth Taylor.

We were intrigued by *The King and I*, for to us it depicted the clash between the values of East and West, and seemed to suggest that the West had much to learn from the East. *Cleopatra* proved controversial; many of my comrades took exception to the fact that the queen of Egypt was depicted by a raven-haired, violet-eyed American actress, however beautiful. The detractors asserted that the movie was an example of Western propaganda that sought to erase the fact that Cleopatra was an African woman. I related how on my trip to Egypt I had seen a splendid sculpture of a young ebony-skinned Cleopatra.

Later, we also saw local South African films with black stars whom we all knew from the old days. On those nights, our little makeshift theatre echoed with the shouts, whistles and cheers that greeted the appearance of an old friend on screen. Later, we were permitted to select documentaries—a form that I preferred—and I began to skip the conventional films. (Although I would never miss a movie with Sophia Loren in it.) The documentaries were ordered from the state library and usually selected by Ahmed Kathrada, who was our section's librarian. I was particularly affected by a documentary we saw about the great naval battles of the Second World War, which showed newsreel footage of the sinking of HMS *Prince of Wales* by the Japanese. What moved me most was a brief image of Winston Churchill weeping after he heard the news of the loss of the British vessel. The image stayed in my memory a long time, and demonstrated to me that there are times when a leader can show sorrow in public, and that it will not diminish him in the eyes of his people.

*   *   *

One of the documentaries we watched concerned a controversial American motorcycle group, the Hell's Angels. The film depicted them as reckless, violent and antisocial, and the police as decent, upstanding and trustworthy. When the film ended, we immediately began to discuss its meaning. Almost without exception the men criticized the Hell's Angels for their lawless ways. But then Strini Moodley, a bright young Black Consciousness member, stood up and accused the assembled group of being out of touch with the times, for the bikers represented the equivalent of the Soweto students of 1976 who rebelled against the authorities. He reproached us for being elderly middle-class intellectuals who identified with the movie's right-wing authorities instead of the bikers.

Strini's accusations caused a furore, and a number of men rose to speak against him, saying the Hell's Angels were indefensible and it was an insult to compare our struggle with this band of amoral sociopaths. But I considered what Strini said, and while I did not agree with him, I came to his defence. Even though the Hell's Angels were unsympathetic, they were rebels against the authorities, unsavoury rebels though they were.

*   *   *

I was not interested in the Hell's Angels, but the larger question that concerned me was whether we had, as Strini suggested, become stuck in a mind-set that was no longer revolutionary. We had been jailed for more than fifteen years; I had been in prison for nearly eighteen. The world that we left was long gone. The danger was that our ideas had become frozen in time. Prison is a still point in a turning world, and it is very easy to remain in the same place in jail while the world moves on.

I had always attempted to remain open to new ideas, not to reject a position because it was new or different. During our years on the island we kept up a continuing dialogue about our beliefs and ideas; we debated them, questioned them and thereby refined them. I did not think we had stayed in one place; I believed we had evolved.

Although Robben Island was becoming more open, there was as yet no sign that the state was reforming its views. Even so, I did not doubt that I would some day be a free man. We might have been stuck in one place, but I was confident that the world was moving towards our position, not away from it. The movie reminded me once again that on the day I did walk out of prison, I did not want to appear to be a political fossil from an age long past.

*　　　*　　　*

It took fifteen years, but in 1979 the authorities announced over the intercom system that the diet for African, Coloured and Indian prisoners would henceforth be the same. But just as justice delayed is justice denied, a reform so long postponed and so grudgingly enacted was hardly worth celebrating.

All prisoners were to receive the same amount of sugar in the morning: a spoonful and a half. But instead of simply increasing the African quota, the authorities reduced the amount of sugar that Coloured and Indian prisoners received by half a spoonful, while adding that amount for African prisoners. A while before, African prisoners had begun to receive bread in the morning, but that made little difference. We had been pooling bread for years.

Our food had already improved in the previous two years, but not because of the authorities. In the wake of the Soweto uprising, the authorities had decided that the island would become the exclusive home of South Africa's 'security prisoners'. The number of general prisoners had been drastically reduced. As a result, political prisoners were recruited to work in the kitchen for the first time. Once political prisoners were in the kitchen, our diet improved dramatically. This was not because they were better chefs, but because the smuggling of food immediately stopped. Instead of siphoning off food for themselves or to bribe the warders, the new cooks used all the food allotted to us. Vegetables became more abundant, and chunks of meat began to appear in our soups and stews. Only then did we realize we should have been eating such food for years.

85

In the summer of 1979, I was playing tennis in the courtyard when my opponent hit a cross-court shot that I strained to reach. As I ran across the court, I felt a pain in my right heel so intense that I had to stop playing. For the next few days I walked with a severe limp.

I was examined by a doctor on the island who decided I should go to Cape Town to see a specialist. The authorities had become more solicitous of our health, afraid that if we died in prison they would be condemned by the international community.

Although under normal circumstances I and the other men would relish a visit to Cape Town, going as a prisoner was altogether different. I was handcuffed and kept in a remote corner of the boat surrounded by five armed warders. The sea was rough that day, and the boat shuddered at every wave. About midway between the island and Cape Town, I thought we were in danger of capsizing. I spied a lifejacket behind two warders young enough to be my grandsons. I said to myself, 'If this boat goes under, I will commit my last sin on earth and run over those two boys to get that lifejacket.' But in the end, it was unnecessary.

On the docks, we were met by more armed guards and a small crowd. It is a humiliating experience to watch the fear and disgust on ordinary citizens' faces when they watch a convict go by. My inclination was to duck down and hide, but one could not do that.

I was examined by a young surgeon, who asked if I had ever before injured my heel. In fact, I had when I was at Fort Hare. One afternoon, I was playing soccer when I attempted to steal the ball and felt a searing pain in my heel. I was taken to the local hospital, the first time in my life I had ever been to a hospital or seen a doctor. Where I grew up, there was no such thing as an African doctor, and going to see a white doctor was unheard of.

The Fort Hare doctor had examined my heel and said he would need to operate. The diagnosis alarmed me, and I abruptly told him that I did not want him to touch me. At that stage in my life I regarded seeing a doctor as unmanly, and having any medical procedure seemed even worse. 'Suit yourself,' he said, 'but when you are old this thing will worry you.'

The Cape Town surgeon X-rayed my heel and discovered bone fragments that had probably been there since Fort Hare. He said he could remove them in his surgery with a local anaesthetic. I immediately agreed.

The surgery went well, and when it was over, the doctor was explaining how to care for my heel. He was abruptly interrupted by the head warder, who said that I had to return immediately to Robben Island. The surgeon was incensed by this and in his most authoritative manner said that it was necessary for Mr Mandela to remain in hospital overnight and that he would not release me under any circumstances. The warder was intimidated and acquiesced.

My first night in a proper hospital turned out to be quite pleasant. The nurses fussed over me a good deal. I slept very well, and in the morning a group of nurses came in and said that I should keep the pyjamas and dressing gown I had been given. I thanked them and told them that I would be the envy of all my comrades.

I found the trip instructive in another way because in that hospital I sensed a thawing in the relationship between black and white. The doctor and nurses had treated me in a natural way as though they had been dealing with blacks on a basis of equality all their lives. This was something new and different to me, and an encouraging sign. It reaffirmed my long-held belief that education was the enemy of prejudice. These were men and women of science, and science had no room for racism.

My only regret was that I did not have the opportunity to contact Winnie before I went into hospital. Rumours had appeared in newspapers that I was at death's door, and she had become quite concerned. But when I returned, I wrote to her to dispel her fears.

*   *   *

In 1980 we were granted the right to buy newspapers. This was a victory but, as always, each new privilege contained within it a catch. The new regulation stated that A group prisoners were granted the right to buy one English-language newspaper and one Afrikaans newspaper a day. But the annoying caveat was that any A group prisoner found sharing his newspaper with a non-A group prisoner would lose his newspaper privileges. We protested against this restriction, but to no avail.

We received two daily newspapers: *Cape Times* and *Die Burger*. Both were conservative papers, especially the latter. Yet the prison censors went through each of those newspapers every day with scissors, clipping out articles that they deemed unsafe for us to see. By the time we received them,

273

they were filled with holes. We were soon able to supplement these papers with copies of the *Star*, the *Rand Daily Mail* and the *Sunday Times*, but these papers were even more heavily censored.

*   *   *

One story I was certainly not able to read was in the *Johannesburg Sunday Post* in March 1980. The headline was 'FREE MANDELA!' Inside was a petition that people could sign to ask for my release and that of my fellow political prisoners. While newspapers were still barred from printing my picture or any words I had ever said or written, the *Post*'s campaign ignited a public discussion of our release.

The idea had been conceived in Lusaka by Oliver Tambo and the ANC, and the campaign was the cornerstone of a new strategy that would put our cause in the forefront of people's minds. The ANC had decided to personalize the quest for our release by centring the campaign on a single figure. There is no doubt that the millions of people who subsequently became supporters of this campaign had no idea of precisely who Nelson Mandela was. (I am told that when 'Free Mandela' posters went up in London, most young people thought my Christian name was 'Free'.) There was a handful of dissenting voices on the island who felt that personalizing the campaign was a betrayal of the collectivity of the organization, but most people realized that it was a technique to rouse the people.

The previous year I had been awarded the Jawaharlal Nehru Human Rights Award in India, another piece of evidence of the resurgence of the struggle. I was of course refused permission to attend the ceremony, as was Winnie, but Oliver accepted the award in my absence. We had a sense of a reviving ANC. Umkhonto we Sizwe was stepping up its sabotage campaign, which had become far more sophisticated. In June, MK men set off bombs at the vast Sasolburg refinery just south of Johannesburg. MK was orchestrating an explosion a week at some strategic site or another. Bombs exploded at power stations in the eastern Transvaal, at police stations in Germiston, Daveyton, New Brighton and elsewhere, and at the Voortrekkerhoogte military base outside Pretoria. These were all strategically significant locations, places that would attract attention and worry the state. The defence minister, General Magnus Malan, backed by P. W. Botha, introduced a policy known as 'total onslaught', which was a militarization of the country to combat the liberation struggle.

The Free Mandela campaign had its lighter side as well. In 1981 I learned that the students at the University of London had nominated me as a candidate for the honorific post of university chancellor. This was a wonderful honour, to be sure, and my rivals were none other than Princess Anne and the trade union leader Jack Jones. In the end, I polled 7,199 votes and lost to the daughter of the Queen. I wrote to Winnie in Brandfort that I hoped the voting might have for a moment turned her humble shack into a castle, making its tiny rooms as grand as the ballroom at Windsor.

The campaign for our release rekindled our hopes. During the harsh days of the early 1970s, when the ANC seemed to sink into the shadows, we had to force ourselves not to give in to despair.

In many ways we had miscalculated; we had thought that by the 1970s we would be living in a democratic, non-racial South Africa. Yet as we entered the new decade my hopes for that South Africa rose once again. Some mornings I walked out into the courtyard and every living thing there, the seagulls and wagtails, the small trees, and even the stray blades of grass seemed to smile and shine in the sun. It was at such times, when I perceived the beauty of even this small, closed-in corner of the world, that I knew that some day my people and I would be free.

86

Like my father before me, I had been groomed to be a counsellor to the king of the Thembu. Although I had chosen a different path, I tried in my own fashion to live up to the responsibilities of the role for which I had been schooled. From prison, I did my best to remain in contact with the king and advise him as best I could. As I grew older, my thoughts turned more and more often to the green hills of the Transkei. Although I would never move there under the government's auspices, I dreamed of one day returning to a free Transkei. Thus it was with great dismay that I learned in 1980 that the king, Sabata Dalindyebo, the paramount chief of the Thembu, had been deposed by my nephew, K.D. Matanzima, the prime minister of the Transkei.

A group of Thembu chiefs requested an urgent visit with me, which was approved by the authorities, who were usually willing to countenance visits by traditional leaders—believing that the more involved I was in tribal and Transkei matters, the less committed I would be to the struggle.

The government promoted the power of traditional leaders as a counterpoint to the ANC. While many of my comrades thought we should disclaim those leaders, my inclination was to reach out to them. There is no contradiction between being a traditional leader and a member of the ANC. This spurred one of the longest and most delicate debates we had on the island: whether or not the ANC should participate in government-sponsored institutions. Many of the men considered this collaborationist. Once again, I thought it necessary to draw a distinction between principle and tactics. To me, the critical question was a tactical one: Will our organization emerge stronger through participating in these organizations or by boycotting them? In this case, I thought we would emerge stronger by participating.

*　　　*　　　*

I met the chiefs in a large room in the visiting area, and they explained their dilemma. Although their hearts were with Sabata, they feared Matanzima. After listening to their presentation, I advised them to support Sabata against Matanzima, who was illegally and shamefully usurping power from the king. I sympathized with their situation, but I could not condone Matanzima's actions. I asked them to convey my support to Sabata and my disapproval to Matanzima.

Matanzima had also proposed a visit to discuss Sabata and family matters. As my nephew, he had actually been requesting such a visit for a number of years. Although Matanzima claimed to want to discuss family matters, such a visit would have political consequences. From the moment of Matanzima's first request, I referred the matter to the High Organ and the ANC men in our section. Some simply shrugged their shoulders and said, 'He's your nephew; he has a right to visit.' Raymond, Govan and Kathy, however, insisted that although such a visit could be explained away as a family matter, it would be interpreted by many people inside and outside as a sign of my endorsement of the man and his policies. That was the reason why Matanzima wanted to see me, and the reason such a visit was unacceptable.

I understood and in large part agreed with their arguments, but I wanted to meet my nephew. I have always had perhaps too high a regard for the importance of face-to-face meetings and of my own ability in such a meeting to persuade men to change their views. I was hoping I could convince Matanzima to modify his policies.

Eventually the ANC men in our section decided not to object to a visit. In the interests of democracy, we then consulted with our men in F and G on the matter, and they were adamantly opposed. Steve Tshwete, who was one of the leading ANC figures in the general section, said such a visit would help Matanzima politically and was therefore out of the question. Many of them noted that Matanzima had already tried to coopt my approval by appointing Winnie's father, Columbus Madikizela, the minister of agriculture in his government. This was bad enough, they said, without Madiba agreeing to see him. I bowed to the views of the membership in the general section and regretfully informed the authorities that I would not accept a visit from my nephew.

*   *   *

In March 1982, I was told by the prison authorities that my wife had been in a car accident, and that she was in hospital. They had very little information, and I had no idea of her condition or what her circumstances were. I accused the authorities of holding back information, and made an urgent application for my attorney to visit me. The authorities used information as a weapon, and it was a successful one. I was preoccupied with my wife's health until I was visited on 31 March by Winnie's attorney and my friend Dullah Omar.

Dullah quickly eased my mind about Winnie. She had been in a car that had overturned, but she was all right. Our visit was brief, and as I was led back to section B my mind was still dwelling on Winnie, and I was plagued by the feeling of powerlessness and my inability to help her.

I had not been in my cell long when I was visited by the commanding officer and a number of other prison officials. This was highly unusual; the CO did not generally pay calls on prisoners in their cells. I stood up when they arrived, and the commander actually entered my cell. There was barely room for the two of us.

'Mandela,' he said, 'I want you to pack up your things.'

I asked him why.

'We are transferring you,' he said simply.

Where?

'I cannot say,' he replied.

I demanded to know why. He told me only that he had received instructions from Pretoria that I was to be transferred off the island immediately. The commanding officer left and went in turn to the cells of Walter, Raymond Mhlaba and Andrew Mlangeni and gave them the same order.

*　　　*　　　*

I was disturbed and unsettled. What did it mean? Where were we going? In prison, one can only question and resist an order to a certain point, then one must succumb. We had no warning, no preparation. I had been on the island for over eighteen years, and to leave so abruptly?

We were each given several large cardboard boxes in which to pack our things. Everything that I had accumulated in nearly two decades could fit into these few boxes. We packed in little more than half an hour.

There was a commotion in the corridor when the other men learned we were leaving, but we had no time to say a proper good-bye to our comrades of many years. This is another one of the indignities of prison. The bonds of friendship and loyalty with other prisoners count for nothing with the authorities.

Within minutes we were on board the ferry headed for Cape Town. I looked back at the island as the light was fading, not knowing whether I would ever see it again. A man can get used to anything, and I had grown used to Robben Island. I had lived there for almost two decades and while it was never a home—my home was in Johannesburg—it had become a place where I felt comfortable. I have always found change difficult, and leaving Robben Island, however grim it had been at times, was no exception. I had no idea what to look forward to.

At the docks, surrounded by armed guards, we were hustled into a windowless truck. The four of us stood in the dark while the truck drove for what seemed considerably more than an hour. We passed through various checkpoints, and finally came to a stop. The back doors swung open, and in the dark we were marched up some concrete steps and through metal doors into another security facility. I managed to ask a guard where we were.

'Pollsmoor Prison,' he said.

PART TEN

Talking with the Enemy

87

Pollsmoor maximum security prison is located on the edge of a prosperous white suburb of green lawns and tidy houses called Tokai, a few miles southeast of Cape Town. The prison itself is set amid the strikingly beautiful scenery of the Cape, between the mountains of Constantiaberg to the north and hundreds of acres of vineyards to the south. But this natural beauty was invisible to us behind Pollsmoor's high concrete walls. At Pollsmoor I first understood the truth of Oscar Wilde's haunting line about the tent of blue that prisoners call the sky.

Pollsmoor had a modern face but a primitive heart. The buildings, particularly the ones for the prison staff, were clean and contemporary; but the housing for the prisoners was archaic and dirty. With the exception of ourselves, all men at Pollsmoor were common-law prisoners and their treatment was oppressive. We were kept separately from them and treated differently.

It was not until the next morning that we got a proper sense of our surroundings. The four of us had been given what was in effect the prison's penthouse: a spacious room on the third and topmost floor. We were the only prisoners on the entire floor. The main room was clean, modern and rectangular, about fifty by thirty feet and had a separate section with a toilet, urinal, two basins and two showers. There were four proper beds, with sheets, and towels, a great luxury for men who had spent much of the last eighteen years sleeping on thin mats on a stone floor. Compared with Robben Island, we were in a five-star hotel.

We also had our own L-shaped terrace, an open, outdoor section that was as long as half a soccer field, where we were allowed out during the day. It had white concrete walls about twelve feet high, so that we could see only the sky, except in one corner where we could make out the ridges of the Constantiaberg mountains, in particular a section known as the Elephant's Eye. I sometimes thought of this bit of mountain as the tip of the iceberg of the rest of the world.

It was greatly disorienting to be uprooted so suddenly and without explanation. One must be prepared for precipitate movements in prison, but one does not ever get used to them. Though we were now on the mainland, we felt more isolated. For us, the island had become the locus of the struggle. We took solace in each other's company, and spent those early weeks speculating on why we had been transferred. We knew the authorities had long resented and feared the influence we had on younger prisoners. But the reason seemed to be more strategic: we believed the authorities were attempting to cut off the head of the ANC on the island by removing its leadership. Robben Island itself was becoming a sustaining myth in the struggle, and they wanted to rob it of some of its symbolic import by removing us. Walter, Raymond and I were members of the High Organ, but the one piece that did not fit was the presence of Mlangeni. Andrew was not a member of the High Organ and had not been in the forefront of the island leadership, although we considered the possibility that the authorities did not know this.

Their intelligence about the organization was often inexact.

One of our hypotheses seemed to be confirmed a few months later when we were joined by Kathy, who had indeed been a member of the High Organ. More important, Kathy had been our chief of communications, and it was because of his work that we were able to communicate with new young prisoners.

A few weeks after Kathy arrived, we were also joined by a man we did not know who had not even come from Robben Island. Patrick Maqubela was a young lawyer and ANC member from the eastern Cape. He had been articled to Griffiths Mxenge, a highly respected attorney who had appeared for many detained ANC men and who had been assassinated near Durban the year before. Maqubela was serving a twenty-year sentence for treason and had been transferred to Pollsmoor from Diepkloof in Johannesburg, where he had made waves by organizing prisoners.

At first, we were sceptical about this new arrival, and wondered if he could perhaps be a security plant by the authorities. But we soon saw that this was not the case. Patrick was a bright, amiable, undaunted fellow with whom we got along very well. It could not have been easy for him bunking in with a group of old men set in their ways who had been together for the previous two decades.

*   *   *

We were now in a world of concrete. I missed the natural splendour of Robben Island. But our new home had many consolations. For one thing, the

287

food at Pollsmoor was far superior; after years of eating pap three meals a day, Pollsmoor's dinners of proper meat and vegetables were like a feast. We were permitted a fairly wide range of newspapers and magazines, and could receive such previously contraband publications as *Time* magazine and the *Guardian Weekly* from London. This gave us a window on the wider world. We also had a radio, but one that received only local stations and not what we really wanted: the BBC World Service. We were allowed out on our terrace all day long, except between twelve and two when the warders had their lunch. There was not even a pretence that we had to work. I had a small cell near our large one that functioned as a study, with a chair, desk and bookshelves, where I could read and write during the day.

On Robben Island I would do my exercises in my own cramped cell, but now I had room to stretch out. At Pollsmoor I would wake up at five and do an hour and a half of exercise in our communal cell. I followed my usual regimen of stationary running, skipping, sit-ups, fingertip press-ups. My comrades were not early risers and my programme soon made me a very unpopular fellow in our cell.

I was visited by Winnie shortly after arriving at Pollsmoor and was pleased to find that the visiting area was far better and more modern than the one on Robben Island. We had a large glass barrier through which one could see the visitor from the waist up and far more sophisticated microphones so that we did not have to strain to hear. The window gave at least the illusion of greater intimacy, and in prison, illusions can offer comfort.

It was far easier for my wife and family to get to

Pollsmoor than to Robben Island, and this made a tremendous difference. The supervision of visits also became more humane. Often, Winnie's visits were overseen by Warrant Officer James Gregory, who had been a censor on Robben Island. I had not known him terribly well, but he knew us, because he had been responsible for reviewing our incoming and outgoing mail.

At Pollsmoor I got to know Gregory better and found him a welcome contrast to the typical warder. He was polished and soft-spoken, and treated Winnie with courtesy and deference. Instead of barking, 'Time up!' he would say, 'Mrs Mandela, you have five more minutes.'

* * *

The Bible tells us that gardens preceded gardeners, but that was not the case at Pollsmoor, where I cultivated a garden that became one of my happiest diversions. It was my way of escaping from the monolithic concrete world that surrounded us. Within a few weeks of surveying all the empty space we had on the building's roof and how it was bathed in sun the whole day, I decided to start a garden and received permission to do so from the commanding officer. I requested that the prison service supply me with sixteen forty-four-gallon oil drums that they sliced in half for me. The authorities then filled each half with rich, moist soil, creating in effect thirty-two giant flowerpots.

I grew onions, aubergines, cabbage, cauliflower, beans, spinach, carrots, cucumbers, broccoli, beetroot, lettuce, tomatoes, peppers, strawberries, and much more. At its height, I had a small farm

289

with nearly nine hundred plants; a garden far grander than the one I had on Robben Island.

Some of the seeds I purchased and some—for example, broccoli and carrots—were given to me by the commanding officer, Brigadier Munro, who was particularly fond of these vegetables. Warders also gave me seeds of vegetables they liked, and I was supplied with excellent manure to use as fertilizer.

Each morning, I put on a straw hat and rough gloves and worked in the garden for two hours. Every Sunday I would supply vegetables to the kitchen so that they could cook a special meal for the common-law prisoners. I also gave quite a lot of my harvest to the warders, who used to bring satchels to take away their fresh vegetables.

*   *   *

At Pollsmoor, our problems tended to be less consequential than those we experienced on Robben Island. Brigadier Munro was a decent, helpful man, who took extra pains to make sure we had what we wanted. Nevertheless, small problems sometimes got blown up out of proportion. In 1983, during a visit from Winnie and Zindzi, I mentioned to my wife that I had been given shoes that were a size too small and were pinching my toe. Winnie was concerned, and I soon learned that there were press reports that I was having a toe amputated. Because of the difficulty of communication, information from prison often becomes exaggerated in the outside world. If I had simply been able to telephone my wife and tell her that my foot was fine, such confusion would not have happened. A short while later, Helen Suzman was permitted to visit, and she inquired about my toe. I thought the best answer was a demonstration: I took off my socks, held my bare foot up to the glass, and wiggled my toes.

We complained about the dampness in our cell, which was causing us to catch colds. Later, I heard reports that South African newspapers were writing that our cell was flooded. We asked for contact with other prisoners, and in general made the same basic complaint that we always had: to be treated as political prisoners.

In May 1984, I found some consolation that seemed to make up for all the discomforts. On a scheduled visit from Winnie, Zeni and her youngest daughter, I was escorted by Warrant Officer Gregory who, instead of taking me to the normal visiting area, ushered me into a separate room where there was only a small table, and no dividers of any kind. He very softly said to me that the authorities had made a change. That day was the beginning of what were known as 'contact' visits.

He then went outside to see my wife and daughter and asked to speak to Winnie privately. Winnie actually got a fright when Gregory took her aside, thinking that I was perhaps ill. But Gregory escorted her around the door and before either of us knew it, we were in the same room and in each other's arms. I kissed and held my wife for the first time in all these many years. It was a moment I had dreamed about a thousand times. It was as if I were still dreaming. I held her to me for what seemed like an eternity. We were still and silent except for the sound of our hearts. I did not want to let go of her at all, but I broke free and embraced my daughter and then took her child onto my lap. It had been twenty-one years since I had even touched my wife's hand.

88

At Pollsmoor, we were more connected to outside events. We were aware that the struggle was intensifying, and that the efforts of the enemy were similarly increasing. In 1981, the South African Defence Force launched a raid on ANC offices in Maputo, Mozambique, killing thirteen of our people, including women and children. In December 1982, MK set off explosions at the unfinished Koeberg nuclear power plant outside Cape Town and placed bombs at many other military and apartheid targets around the country. That same month, the South African military again attacked an ANC outpost in Maseru, Lesotho, killing forty-two people, including a dozen women and children.

In August 1982 the activist Ruth First was opening her post in Maputo, where she was living in exile, when she was murdered by a letter bomb. Ruth, the wife of Joe Slovo, was a brave anti-apartheid activist who had spent a number of months in prison. She was a forceful, engaging woman whom I first met when I was studying at Wits, and her death revealed the extent of the state's cruelty in combating our struggle.

MK's first car bomb attack took place in May 1983, and was aimed at an air force and military intelligence office in the heart of Pretoria. This was an effort to retaliate for the unprovoked attacks the military had launched on the ANC in Maseru and elsewhere and was a clear escalation of the armed struggle. Nineteen people were killed and more than two hundred injured.

The killing of civilians was a tragic accident, and I felt a profound horror at the death toll. But disturbed as I was by these casualties, I knew that such accidents were the inevitable consequence of the decision to embark on a military struggle. Human fallibility is always a part of war, and the price of it is always high. It was precisely because we knew that such incidents would occur that our decision to take up arms had been so grave and reluctant. But as Oliver said at the time of the bombing, the armed struggle was imposed upon us by the violence of the apartheid regime.

Both the government and the ANC were working on two tracks: military and political. On the political front, the government was pursuing its standard divide-and-rule strategy in attempting to separate Africans from Coloureds and Indians. In a referendum in November 1983, the white electorate endorsed P.W. Botha's plan to create a so-called tricameral Parliament, with Indian and Coloured chambers in addition to the white Parliament. This was an effort to lure Indians and Coloureds into the system, and divide them from Africans. But the offer was merely a 'toy telephone', as all parliamentary action by Indians and Coloureds was subject to a white veto. It was also a way of fooling the outside world into thinking that the government was reforming apartheid. Botha's ruse did not deceive the people, as more than 80 per cent of eligible Indian and Coloured voters boycotted the election to the new houses of Parliament in 1984.

Powerful grassroots political movements were being formed inside the country that had firm links to the ANC, the principal one being the United Democratic Front, of which I was named a patron. The UDF had been created to coordinate protest against the new apartheid constitution in 1983, and the first elections to the segregated tricameral Parliament in 1984. The UDF soon blossomed into a powerful organization that united over six hundred anti-apartheid organizations—trade unions, community groups, church groups, student associations.

The ANC was experiencing a new birth of popularity. Opinion polls showed that the Congress was far and away the most popular political organization among Africans even though it had been banned for a quarter of a century. The anti-apartheid struggle as a whole had captured the attention of the world; in 1984 Bishop Desmond Tutu was awarded the Nobel Peace Prize. (The authorities refused to send Bishop Tutu my letter of congratulations.) The South African government was under growing international pressure, as nations all across the globe began to impose economic sanctions on Pretoria.

*　　　*　　　*

The government had sent 'feelers' to me over the years, beginning with Minister Kruger's efforts to persuade me to move to the Transkei. These were not efforts to negotiate, but attempts to isolate me from my organization. On several other occasions, Kruger said to me: 'Mandela, we can work with you, but not your colleagues. Be reasonable.' Although I did not respond to these overtures, the mere fact that they were talking rather than attacking could be seen as a prelude to genuine negotiations.

The government was testing the waters. In late 1984 and early 1985 I had visits from two prominent Western statesmen, Lord Nicholas Bethell, a member of the British House of Lords and the European Parliament, and Samuel Dash, a professor of law at Georgetown University and a former counsel to the US Senate Watergate Committee. Both visits were authorized by the new minister of justice, Kobie Coetsee, who appeared to be a new sort of Afrikaner leader.

I met Lord Bethell in the prison commander's office, which was dominated by a large photograph of a glowering President Botha. Bethell was a jovial, rotund man and when I first met him, I teased him about his stoutness. 'You look as though you are related to Winston Churchill,' I said as we shook hands, and he laughed.

Lord Bethell wanted to know about our conditions at Pollsmoor and I told him. We discussed the armed struggle and I explained to him it was not up to us to renounce violence, but the government. I reaffirmed that we aimed for hard military targets, not people. 'I would not want our men to assassinate, for instance, the major here,' I said, pointing to Major Fritz van Sittert, who was monitoring the talks. Van Sittert was a good-natured fellow who did not say much, but he started at my remark.

In my visit from Professor Dash, which quickly followed that of Lord Bethell, I laid out what I saw as the minimum for a future non-racial South Africa: a unitary state without homelands, non-racial elections for the central Parliament and one-person one-vote. Professor Dash asked me whether I took any encouragement from the government's stated intention of repealing the mixed-marriage laws and certain other apartheid statutes. 'This is a pinprick,' I said. 'It is not my ambition to marry a white woman or swim in a white pool. It is political equality that we want.' I told Dash quite candidly that at the moment we could not defeat the government on the battlefield, but could make governing difficult for them.

I had one not-so-pleasant visit from two Americans, editors of the conservative newspaper the *Washington Times*. They seemed less intent on finding out my views than on proving that I was a communist and a terrorist. All their questions were slanted in that direction, and when I reiterated that I was neither a communist nor a terrorist, they attempted to show that I was not a Christian either by asserting that the Reverend Martin Luther King never resorted to violence. I told them that the conditions in which Martin Luther King struggled were totally different from my own: the United States was a democracy with constitutional guarantees of equal rights that protected non-violent protest (though there was still prejudice against blacks); South Africa was a police state with a constitution that enshrined inequality and an army that responded to non-violence with force. I told them that I was a Christian and had always been a Christian. Even Christ, I said, when he was left with no alternative, used force to expel the moneylenders from the temple. He was not a man of violence, but had no choice but to use force against evil. I do not think I persuaded them.

*   *   *

Faced with trouble at home and pressure from abroad, P. W. Botha offered a tepid, halfway measure. On 31 January 1985, in a debate in Parliament, the state president publicly offered me my freedom if I 'unconditionally rejected violence as a political instrument'. This offer was extended to all political prisoners. Then, as though he were staking me to a public challenge, he added, 'It is therefore not the South African government which now stands in the way of Mr Mandela's freedom. It is he himself.'

I had been warned by the authorities that the government was going to make a proposal involving my freedom, but I had not been prepared for the fact that it would be made in Parliament by the state president. By my reckoning, it was the sixth conditional offer the government had made for my release in the past ten years. After I listened to the speech on the radio, I made a request to the commander of the prison for an urgent visit by my wife and my lawyer, Ismail Ayob, so that I could dictate my response to the state president's offer.

Winnie and Ismail were not given permission to visit for a week, and in the meantime I wrote a letter to the foreign minister, Pik Botha, rejecting the conditions for my release, while also preparing a public response. I was keen to do a number of things in this response, because Botha's offer was an attempt to drive a wedge between me and my colleagues by tempting me to accept a policy the ANC rejected. I wanted to reassure the ANC in general and Oliver Tambo in particular that my loyalty to the organization was beyond question. I also wished to send a message to the government that while I rejected its offer because of the conditions attached to it, I nevertheless thought negotiation, not war, was the path to a solution.

Botha wanted the onus of violence to rest on my shoulders and I wanted to reaffirm to the world that we were only responding to the violence done to us. I intended to make it clear that if I emerged from prison into the same circumstances under which I was arrested, I would be forced to resume the same activities for which I was arrested.

I met Winnie and Ismail on a Friday; on Sunday, a UDF rally was to be held in Soweto's Jabulani Stadium, where my response would be made public. Some guards with whom I was not familiar supervised the visit, and as we began discussing my response to the state president, one of the warders, a relatively young fellow, interrupted to say that only family matters were permitted to be discussed. I ignored him, and he returned minutes later with a senior warder whom I barely knew. This warder said that I must cease discussing politics, and I told him that I was dealing with a matter of national importance involving an offer from the state president. I warned him that if he wanted to halt the discussion he must get direct orders from the state president himself. 'If you are not willing to telephone the state president to get those orders,' I said coldly, 'then kindly do not interrupt us again.' He did not.

I gave Ismail and Winnie the speech I had prepared. In addition to responding to the government, I wanted to thank publicly the UDF for its fine work and to congratulate Archbishop Tutu on his prize, adding that his award belonged to all the people. On Sunday 10 February 1985, my daughter Zindzi read my response to a cheering crowd of people who had not been able to hear my words legally anywhere in South Africa for more than twenty years.

Zindzi was a dynamic speaker like her mother, and said that her father should be at the stadium to speak the words himself. I was proud to know that it was she who spoke my words.

I am a member of the African National Congress. I have always been a member of the African National Congress and I will remain a member of the African National Congress until the day I die. Oliver Tambo is more than a brother to me. He is my greatest friend and comrade for nearly fifty years. If there is any one amongst you who cherishes my freedom, Oliver Tambo cherishes it more, and I know that he would give his life to see me free . . .

I am surprised at the conditions that the government wants to impose on me. I am not a violent man . . . It was only then, when all other forms of resistance were no longer open to us, that we turned to armed struggle. Let Botha show that he is different to Malan, Strijdom and Verwoerd. Let him renounce violence. Let him say that he will dismantle apartheid. Let him unban the people's organization, the African National Congress.

299

Let him free all who have been imprisoned, banished or exiled for their opposition to apartheid. Let him guarantee free political activity so that people may decide who will govern them.

I cherish my own freedom dearly, but I care even more for your freedom. Too many have died since I went to prison. Too many have suffered for the love of freedom. I owe it to their widows, to their orphans, to their mothers and to their fathers who have grieved and wept for them. Not only I have suffered during these long, lonely, wasted years. I am not less life-loving than you are. But I cannot sell my birthright, nor am I prepared to sell the birthright of the people to be free . . .

What freedom am I being offered while the organization of the people remains banned? What freedom am I being offered when I may be arrested on a pass offence? What freedom am I being offered to live my life as a family with my dear wife who remains in banishment in Brandfort? What freedom am I being offered when I must ask for permission to live in an urban area? . . . What freedom am I being offered when my very South African citizenship is not respected?

Only free men can negotiate. Prisoners cannot enter into contracts . . . I cannot and will not give any undertaking at a time when I and you, the people, are not free. Your freedom and mine cannot be separated. I will return.

89

In 1985 after a routine medical examination from the prison doctor, I was referred to a urologist, who diagnosed an enlarged prostate gland and recommended surgery. He said the procedure was routine. I consulted with my family and decided to go ahead with the operation.

I was taken to Volks Hospital in Cape Town under heavy security. Winnie flew down and was able to see me prior to the surgery. But I had another visitor, a surprising and unexpected one: Kobie Coetsee, the minister of justice. Not long before, I had written to Coetsee pressing him for a meeting to discuss talks between the ANC and the government. He did not respond. But that morning, he dropped by the hospital unannounced as if he were visiting an old friend who was laid up for a few days. He was altogether gracious and cordial, and for the most part we simply made pleasantries. Though I acted as though this was the most normal thing in the world, I was amazed. The government, in its slow and tentative way, was reckoning that they had to come to some accommodation with the ANC. Coetsee's visit was an olive branch.

Although we did not discuss politics, I did bring up one sensitive issue, and that was the status of my wife. In August, shortly before I entered hospital, Winnie had gone to Johannesburg to receive medical treatment. The only trips she was permitted from Brandfort were to visit either me or her doctor. While in Johannesburg, her house in

Brandfort and the clinic behind it were firebombed and destroyed. Winnie had no place in which to reside, and she decided to remain in Johannesburg despite the fact that the city was off-limits to her. Nothing happened for a few weeks, and then the security police wrote to inform her that the house in Brandfort had been repaired and she must return. But she refused to do so. I asked Coetsee to allow Winnie to remain in Johannesburg and not force her to return to Brandfort. He said he could promise nothing, but he would indeed look into it. I thanked him.

*　　　*　　　*

I spent several days in hospital recuperating from the surgery. When I was discharged, I was collected from the hospital by Brigadier Munro. Commanding officers do not usually pick up prisoners from hospitals, so my suspicions were immediately aroused.

On the ride back, Brigadier Munro said to me in a casual way, as though he were simply making conversation, 'Mandela, we are not taking you back to your friends now.' I asked him what he meant. 'From now on, you are going to be alone.' I asked him why. He shook his head. 'I don't know. I've just been given these instructions from headquarters.' Once again, there was no warning and no explanation.

Upon my return to Pollsmoor I was taken to a new cell on the ground floor of the prison, three floors below and in an entirely different wing. I was given three rooms and a separate toilet, with one room to be used for sleeping, one across the hall

302

for studying, and another for exercise. By prison standards, this was palatial, but the rooms were damp and musty and received very little natural light. I said nothing to the brigadier, for I knew the decision had not been his. I wanted time to consider the implications of the move. Why had the state taken this step?

It would be too strong to call it a revelation, but over the next few days and weeks I came to a realization about my new circumstances. The change, I decided, was not a liability but an opportunity. I was not happy to be separated from my colleagues and I missed my garden and the sunny terrace on the third floor. But my solitude gave me a certain liberty, and I resolved to use it to do something I had been pondering for a long while: begin discussions with the government. I had concluded that the time had come when the struggle could best be pushed forward through negotiations. If we did not start a dialogue soon, both sides would soon be plunged into a dark night of oppression, violence and war. My solitude would give me an opportunity to take the first steps in that direction, without the kind of scrutiny that might destroy such efforts.

We had been fighting against white minority rule for three-quarters of a century. We had been engaged in the armed struggle for more than two decades. Many people on both sides had already died. The enemy was strong and resolute. Yet even with all their bombers and tanks, they must have sensed they were on the wrong side of history. We had right on our side, but not yet might. It was clear to me that a military victory was a distant if not impossible dream. It simply did not make sense for both sides to lose thousands if not millions of lives in a conflict that was unnecessary. They must have known this as well. It was time to talk.

This would be extremely sensitive. Both sides regarded discussions as a sign of weakness and betrayal. Neither would come to the table until the other made significant concessions. The government asserted over and over that we were a terrorist organization of communists, and that they would never talk to terrorists or communists. This was National Party dogma. The ANC asserted over and over that the government were fascistic and racist and that there was nothing to talk about until they unbanned the ANC, unconditionally released all political prisoners and removed the troops from the townships.

A decision to talk to the government was of such importance that it should only have been made in Lusaka. But I felt that the process needed to begin, and I had neither the time nor the means to communicate fully with Oliver. Someone from our side needed to take the first step, and my new isolation gave me both the freedom to do so and the assurance, at least for a while, of the confidentiality of my efforts.

*　　　*　　　*

I was now in a kind of splendid isolation. Though my colleagues were only three floors above me, they might as well have been in Johannesburg. In order to see them, I had to put in a formal request for a visit, which had to be approved by the head office in Pretoria. It often took weeks to receive a response. If it was approved, I would then meet

304

them in the visiting area. This was a novel experience: my comrades and fellow prisoners were now official visitors. For years we had been able to talk for hours a day, now we had to make official requests and appointments, and our conversations were monitored.

After I had been in my new cell for a few days, I asked the commanding officer to arrange such a meeting. He did so, and the four of us discussed the issue of my transfer. Walter, Kathy and Ray were angry that we had been separated. They wanted to lodge a strong protest, and demand that we be reunited. My response was not what they expected. 'Look, chaps,' I said, 'I don't think we should oppose this thing.' I mentioned that my new accommodation was superior, and maybe this would set a precedent for all political prisoners. I then added somewhat ambiguously, 'Perhaps something good will come of this. I'm now in a position where the government can make an approach to us.' They did not care too much for this latter explanation, as I knew they would not.

I chose to tell no one what I was about to do. Not my colleagues upstairs nor those in Lusaka. The ANC is a collective, but the government had made collectivity in this case impossible. I did not have the security or the time to discuss these issues with my organization. I knew that my colleagues upstairs would condemn my proposal, and that would kill my initiative even before it was born. There are times when a leader must move out ahead of the flock, go off in a new direction, confident that he is leading his people the right way. Finally, my isolation furnished my organization with an excuse in case matters went awry: the old man was alone and completely cut off, and his actions were taken by him as an individual, not a representative of the ANC.

90

Within a few weeks of my move, I wrote to Kobie Coetsee to propose talks about talks. As before, I received no response. I wrote once more, and again there was no response. I found this peculiar and demoralizing, and I realized I had to look for another opportunity to be heard. That came in early 1986.

At a meeting of the British Commonwealth in Nassau in October 1985, the leaders could not reach agreement on whether to participate in international sanctions against South Africa. This was mainly because British Prime Minister Margaret Thatcher was adamantly opposed. To resolve the deadlock, the assembled nations agreed that a delegation of 'eminent persons' would visit South Africa and report back on whether sanctions were the appropriate tool to help bring about the end of apartheid. In early 1986 the seven-member Eminent Persons Group, led by General Olusegun Obasanjo, the former military leader of Nigeria, and the former Australian Prime Minister Malcolm Fraser, arrived in South Africa on their fact-finding mission.

In February, I was visited by General Obasanjo to discuss the nature of the delegation's brief. He was eager to facilitate a meeting between me and the full group. With the government's permission, such a meeting was scheduled for May. The group would be talking with the cabinet after they had seen me, and I viewed this as a chance to raise the subject of negotiations.

The government regarded my session with the group as something extraordinary. Two days before the meeting I was visited by Brigadier Munro, who had brought along a tailor. 'Mandela,' the commander said, 'we want you to see these people on an equal footing. We don't want you to wear those old prison clothes, so this tailor will take your measurements and outfit you with a proper suit.' The tailor must have been some kind of wizard, for the very next day I tried on a pinstriped suit that fitted me like a glove. I was also given a shirt, tie, shoes, socks and underwear. The commander admired my new attire. 'Mandela, you look like a prime minister now, not a prisoner,' he said and smiled.

*　　　*　　　*

At the meeting between me and the Eminent Persons Group, we were joined by two significant observers: Kobie Coetsee, and Lieutenant General W. H. Willemse, the commissioner of prisons. Like the tailor, these two men were there to take my measure. But, curiously, they left shortly after the session started. I pressed them to remain, saying I had nothing to hide, but they left anyway. Before they took their leave, I told them the time had come for negotiations, not fighting, and that the government and the ANC should sit down and talk.

The Eminent Persons Group had come with many questions involving the issues of violence, negotiations and international sanctions. At the outset, I set the ground rules for our discussions. 'I am not the head of the movement,' I told them. 'The head of the movement is Oliver Tambo in Lusaka. You must go and see him. You can tell him what my views are, but they are my personal views alone. They don't even represent the views of my colleagues here in prison. All that being said, I favour the ANC beginning discussions with the government.'

Various members of the group had concerns about my political ideology and what a South Africa under ANC leadership might look like. I told them I was a South African nationalist, not a communist, that nationalists came in every hue and colour, and that I was firmly committed to a non-racial society. I told them I believed in the Freedom Charter, that the charter embodied principles of democracy and human rights, and that it was not a blueprint for socialism. I spoke of my concern that the white minority should feel a sense of security in any new South Africa. I told them I thought many of our problems were a result of lack of communication between the government and the ANC, and that some of these could be resolved through actual talks.

They questioned me extensively on the issue of violence, and while I was not yet willing to renounce violence, I affirmed in the strongest possible terms that violence could never be the ultimate solution to the situation in South Africa and that men and women by their very nature required some kind of negotiated understanding. While I once again reiterated that these were my views and not those of the ANC, I suggested that if the government withdrew the army and the police from the townships, the ANC might agree to a suspension of the armed struggle as a prelude to talks. I told them that my release alone would not stem the violence in the country or stimulate negotiations.

After the group had finished with me, they planned to see both Oliver in Lusaka and government officials in Pretoria. In my remarks, I had sent messages to both places. I wanted the government to see that under the right circumstances we would talk, and I wanted Oliver to know that my position and his were the same.

In May, the Eminent Persons Group was scheduled to see me one last time. I was optimistic, as they had been to both Lusaka and Pretoria, and I hoped that the seed of negotiations had been sown. But the day before we were to meet, the South African government took a step that sabotaged whatever goodwill had been engendered by the Commonwealth visitors. On the day the Eminent Persons Group was scheduled to meet cabinet ministers, the South African Defence Force, under the orders of President Botha, launched air raid and commando attacks on ANC bases in Botswana, Zambia and Zimbabwe. This utterly poisoned the talks, and the Eminent Persons Group immediately left South Africa. Once again, I felt my efforts to move negotiations forward had stalled.

*   *   *

Oliver Tambo and the ANC had called for the people of South Africa to render the country ungovernable, and the people were obliging. The state of unrest and political violence was reaching new heights. The anger of the masses was unrestrained; the townships were in upheaval. International pressure was growing stronger every day. On 12 June 1986 the government imposed a State of Emergency in an attempt to keep a lid on protest. In every outward way, the time seemed inauspicious for negotiations. But often, the most discouraging moments are precisely the time to launch an initiative. At such times people are searching for a way out of their dilemma. That month I wrote a very simple letter to General Willemse, the commissioner of prisons, saying merely, 'I wish to see you on a matter of national importance.' I handed the letter to Brigadier Munro on a Wednesday.

That weekend, I was told by the commanding officer to be prepared to see General Willemse, who was coming down from Pretoria. This meeting was not treated in the usual fashion. Instead of conferring with the general in the visiting area, I was taken to his residence in the grounds of Pollsmoor itself.

Willemse is a direct fellow and we got down to business immediately. I told him I wanted to see Kobie Coetsee, the minister of justice. He asked me why. I hesitated for a moment, reluctant to discuss political matters with a prison official. But I responded with frankness: 'I want to see the minister in order to raise the question of talks between the government and the ANC.'

He pondered this for a moment, and then said, 'Mandela, as you know, I am not a politician. I cannot discuss such issues myself, for they are beyond my authority.' He then paused, as if something had just occurred to him. 'It just so happens,' he said, 'that the minister of justice is in Cape Town. Perhaps you can see him. I will find out.'

The general then telephoned the minister and the two spoke for a few moments. After putting down the phone, the general turned to me and said, 'The minister said, "Bring him round."' Minutes later, we left the general's residence in his car bound for the minister's house in Cape Town. Security was light; only one other car accompanied the general's vehicle. The ease and rapidity with which this meeting was set up made me suspect that the government might have planned this rendezvous in advance. Whether they had or not was immaterial; it was an opportunity to take the first step towards negotiations.

At his official residence in the city, Coetsee greeted me warmly and we settled down on comfortable chairs in his lounge. He apologized that I had not had a chance to change out of my prison clothes. I spent three hours in conversation with him and was struck by his sophistication and willingness to listen. He asked knowledgeable and relevant questions—questions that reflected a familiarity with the issues that divided the government and the ANC. He asked me under what circumstances we would suspend the armed struggle; whether or not I spoke for the ANC as a whole; whether I envisioned any constitutional guarantees for minorities in a new South Africa. His questions went to the heart of the issues dividing the government and the ANC.

After responding in much the same way as I did

to the Eminent Persons Group, I sensed that Coetsee wanted some resolution. 'What is the next step?' he asked. I told him I wanted to see the state president and the foreign minister, Pik Botha. Coetsee noted this on a small pad he had kept beside him, and said he would send my request through the proper channels. We then shook hands, and I was driven back to my solitary cell on the ground floor of Pollsmoor prison.

I was greatly encouraged. I sensed the government was anxious to overcome the impasse in the country, that they were now convinced they had to depart from their old positions. In ghostly outline, I saw the beginnings of a compromise.

I told no one of my encounter. I wanted the process to be under way before I informed anyone. Sometimes it is necessary to present one's colleagues with a policy that is already a *fait accompli*. I knew that once they examined the situation carefully, my colleagues at Pollsmoor and in Lusaka would support me. But again, after this promising start, nothing happened. Weeks and then months passed without a word from Coetsee. In some frustration, I wrote him another letter.

91

Although I did not get a direct response from Kobie Coetsee, there were other signs that the government was preparing me for a different kind of existence. On the day before Christmas, Lieutenant Colonel Gawie Marx, the deputy commander of Pollsmoor, wandered by my cell after breakfast and said quite casually, 'Mandela, would you like to see the city?' I was not exactly certain what he had in mind, but I thought there was no harm in saying yes. Good, he said, come along. I walked with the colonel through the fifteen locked metal doors between my cell and the entrance, and when we emerged, I found his car waiting for us.

We drove into Cape Town along the lovely road that runs parallel to the coast. He had no destination in mind and we simply meandered around the city in a leisurely fashion. It was absolutely riveting to watch the simple activities of people out in the world: old men sitting in the sun, women doing their shopping, people walking their dogs. It is precisely those mundane activities of daily life that one misses most in prison. I felt like a curious tourist in a strange and remarkable land.

After an hour or so, Colonel Marx stopped the car in front of a small shop in a quiet street. 'Would you like a cold drink?' he asked. I nodded, and he disappeared inside the shop. I sat there alone. For the first few moments, I did not think about my situation, but as the seconds ticked away, I became more and more agitated. For the first time in twenty-two years, I was out in the world and unguarded. I had a vision of opening the door, jumping out, and then running and running until I was out of sight. Something inside was urging me to do just that. I noticed a wooded area near the road where I could hide. I was extremely tense and began to perspire. Where was the colonel? But then I took control of myself; such an action would be unwise and irresponsible, not to mention dangerous. It was possible that the whole situation was contrived to try to get me to escape, though I do not think that was the case. I was greatly relieved a few moments later when I saw the colonel walking back to the car with two cans of Coca-Cola.

As it turned out, that day in Cape Town was the first of many excursions. Over the next few months, I went out again with the colonel not only to Cape Town but to some of the sights around the city, its beautiful beaches and lovely cool mountains. Soon, more junior officers were permitted to take me around. One of the places I regularly visited with these junior officers was known as the 'gardens', a series of smallholdings on the edge of the prison grounds where crops were grown for the prison kitchen. I enjoyed being out in nature, being able to see the horizon and feel the sun on my shoulders.

One day I went to the gardens with a captain, and after walking in the fields we strolled over to the stables. There were two young white men in overalls working with the horses. I walked over to them, praised one of the animals, and said to the fellow, 'Now, what is this horse's name?' The young man seemed quite nervous and did not look at me. He then mumbled the name of the horse, but to the captain, not to me. I then asked the other fellow in turn what the name of his horse was, and he had precisely the same reaction.

As I was walking back to the prison with the captain, I commented on what I thought was the curious behaviour of the two young men. The captain laughed. 'Mandela, don't you know what those two chaps were?' I said I did not. 'They were white prisoners. They had never been questioned

314

by a native prisoner in the presence of a white officer before.'

Some of the younger warders took me quite far afield, and we would walk on the beach and even stop at a café and have tea. At such places I often tried to see if people recognized me, but no one ever did; the last published picture of me had been taken in 1962.

These trips were instructive on a number of levels. I saw how life had changed in the time I had been away, and because we mainly went to white areas, I saw the extraordinary wealth and ease that whites enjoyed. Though the country was in upheaval and the townships were on the brink of open warfare, white life went on placidly and undisturbed. Their lives were unaffected. Once, one of the warders, a very pleasant young man named Warrant Officer Brand, actually took me to his family's flat and introduced me to his wife and children. From then on, I sent his children Christmas cards every year.

Much as I enjoyed these little adventures, I well knew that the authorities had a motive other than keeping me diverted. I sensed that they wanted to acclimatize me to life in South Africa and perhaps at the same time, get me so used to the pleasures of small freedoms that I might be willing to compromise in order to have complete freedom.

92

In 1987 I resumed contact with Kobie Coetsee. I had several private meetings with him at his residence, and later that year the government made its first concrete proposal. Coetsee said the government would like to appoint a committee of senior officials to conduct private discussions with me. This would be done with the full knowledge of the state president, Coetsee said. He himself would be head of the committee, and it would include General Willemse, the commissioner of prisons, Fanie van der Merwe, director general of the Prisons Department and Dr Niel Barnard, a former academic who was then head of the National Intelligence Service. The first three individuals were associated with the prison system, so if talks foundered or were leaked to the press, both sides would be able to cover up and say we were discussing prison conditions and nothing more.

The presence of Dr Barnard, however, disturbed me. He was the head of South Africa's equivalent of the CIA, and was also involved with military intelligence. I could justify to my organization discussions with the other officials, but not Barnard. His presence made the talks more problematic and suggested a larger agenda. I told Coetsee that I would like to think about the proposal overnight.

That night I considered all the ramifications. I knew that P. W. Botha had created something called the State Security Council, a shadowy secretariat of security experts and intelligence officials. He had done this, according to the press, to circumvent the authority of the cabinet and increase his own power. Dr Barnard was a key player in this inner council and was said to be a protégé of the president. I thought that my refusing Barnard would alienate Botha, and decided that such a tack was too risky. If the state president was not brought on board, nothing would happen. In the morning, I sent word to Coetsee that I accepted his offer.

I knew that I had three crucial matters that I needed to address: first, I wanted to sound out my colleagues on the third floor before I proceeded any further, second, it was essential to communicate with Oliver in Lusaka about what was taking place and, finally, I intended to draft a memorandum to P. W. Botha laying out my views and those of the ANC on the vital issues before the country. This memorandum would create talking points for any future discussion.

I requested a meeting with my colleagues, and to my surprise, the authorities summarily refused. This was remarkable, and I assumed it reflected a great deal of nervousness about the prospect of secret talks between myself and the government. I took my complaints to more senior officials. Finally the request was approved, with the proviso that I could see my colleagues one by one, not together.

I met them in the visiting area. I had resolved to leave out a few details; I would seek their counsel about the idea of having talks with the government without mentioning that an actual committee had been formed. Walter was first. I told him about my letter to the commissioner of prisons and my meeting with Coetsee. I said that I had discussed with Coetsee the idea of beginning talks with the government and that the government seemed interested. What were his views on the matter?

I have been through thick and thin with Walter. He was a man of reason and wisdom, and no man knew me better than he did. There was no one whose opinion I trusted or valued more. Walter considered what I told him. I could see he was uncomfortable and, at best, lukewarm. 'In principle,' he said, 'I am not against negotiations. But I would have wished that the government initiated talks with us rather than our initiating talks with them.'

I replied that if he was not against negotiations in principle, what did it matter who initiated them? What mattered was what they achieved, not how they started. I told Walter that I thought we should move forward with negotiations and not worry about who knocked on the door first. Walter saw that my mind was made up and he said he would not stop me, but that he hoped I knew what I was doing.

Next was Raymond Mhlaba. I explained the entire situation to him as I had to Walter. Ray was always a man of few words, and for several moments he digested what I had said. He then looked at me and said, 'Madiba, what have you been waiting for? We should have started this years ago.' Andrew Mlangeni's reaction was virtually the same as Ray's. The last man was Kathy. His response was negative; he was as resolutely against what I was suggesting as Raymond and Andrew were in favour. Even more strongly than Walter, he felt that by initiating talks it would appear that we were capitulating. Like Walter, he said he was not against negotiations in principle, and I responded exactly as I had with Walter. But Kathy was adamant; he felt I was going down the wrong path. But, despite his misgivings, he said he would not stand in my way.

Not long after this I received a note from Oliver Tambo that was smuggled to me by one of my lawyers. He had heard reports that I was having secret discussions with the government and he was concerned. He said he knew I had been alone for some time and separated from my colleagues. He must have been wondering: what is going on with Mandela? Oliver's note was brief and to the point: what, he wanted to know, was I discussing with the government? Oliver could not have believed that I was selling out, but he might have thought I was making an error in judgment. In fact, the tenor of his note suggested that.

I replied to Oliver in a very terse letter saying that I was talking to the government about one thing and one thing only: a meeting between the National Executive of the ANC and the South African government. I would not spell out the details, for I could not trust the confidentiality of the communication. I simply said the time had come for such talks and that I would not compromise the organization in any way.

Although the ANC had called for talks with the government for decades, we had never been confronted with the actual prospect of such talks. It is one thing to consider them in theory, and quite another to engage in them. As I was writing my response to Oliver, I was also beginning to draft my memorandum to P. W. Botha. I would make sure that Oliver saw this as well. I knew that when Oliver and the National Executive read my memo, their fears that I had gone off the road would be allayed.

The first formal meeting of the secret working group took place in May 1988, at a posh officers' club within the precincts of Pollsmoor. While I knew both Coetsee and Willemse, I had never before met van der Merwe and Dr Barnard. Van der Merwe was a quiet, even-handed man who spoke only when he had something important to say. Dr Barnard was in his mid-thirties and was exceedingly bright, a man of controlled intelligence and self-discipline.

The initial meeting was quite stiff, but in subsequent sessions we were able to talk more freely and directly. I met them almost every week for a few months, and then the meetings occurred at irregular intervals, sometimes not for a month, and then suddenly every week. The meetings were usually scheduled by the government, but sometimes I would request a session.

During our early meetings, I discovered that my new colleagues, with the exception of Dr Barnard, knew little about the ANC. They were all sophisticated Afrikaners, and far more open-minded than nearly all of their brethren. But they were the victims of so much propaganda that it was necessary to straighten them out about certain facts. Even Dr Barnard, who had made a study of the ANC, had received most of his information from police and intelligence files, which were in the main inaccurate and sullied by the prejudices of the men who had gathered them. He could not help but be infected by the same biases.

I spent some time in the beginning sketching out the history of the ANC and then explaining our positions on the primary issues that divided the organization from the government. After these preliminaries, we focused on the critical issues: the armed struggle, the ANC's alliance with the Communist Party, the goal of majority rule and the idea of racial reconciliation.

The first issue to arise was in many ways the most crucial, and that was the armed struggle. We spent a number of months discussing it. They insisted that the ANC must renounce violence and give up the armed struggle before the government would agree to negotiations—and before I could meet President Botha. Their contention was that violence was nothing more than criminal behaviour that could not be tolerated by the state.

I responded that the state was responsible for the violence and that it is always the oppressor, not the oppressed, who dictates the form of the struggle. If the oppressor uses violence, the oppressed have no alternative but to respond violently. In our case it was simply a legitimate form of self-defence. I ventured that if the state decided to use peaceful methods, the ANC would also use peaceful means. 'It is up to you,' I said, 'not us, to renounce violence.'

I think I advanced their understanding on this point, but the issue soon moved from a philosophical question to a practical one. As Minister Coetsee and Dr Barnard pointed out, the National Party had repeatedly stated that it would not negotiate with any organization that advocated violence: therefore, how could it suddenly announce talks with the ANC without losing its credibility? In order for us to begin talks, they said, the ANC must make some compromise so that the government would not lose face with its own people.

It was a fair point and one that I could well understand, but I would not offer them a way out. 'Gentlemen,' I said, 'it is not my job to resolve your dilemma for you.' I simply told them that they must tell their people that there could be no peace and no solution to the situation in South Africa without sitting down with the ANC. 'People will understand,' I said.

*   *   *

The ANC's alliance with the Communist Party seemed to trouble them almost as much as the armed struggle. The National Party accepted the most hide-bound of 1950s cold war ideology and regarded the Soviet Union as the evil empire and communism as the work of the devil. There was nothing that one could do to disabuse them of this notion. They maintained that the Communist Party dominated and controlled the ANC and that in order for negotiations to begin we must break from the party.

First of all, I said, no self-respecting freedom fighter would take orders from the government he is fighting against or jettison a longtime ally in the interest of pleasing an antagonist. I then explained at great length that the party and the ANC were separate and distinct organizations that shared the same short-term objectives, the overthrow of racial oppression and the birth of a non-racial South Africa, but that our long-term interests were not the same.

This discussion went on for months. Like most Afrikaners, they thought that because many of the communists in the ANC were white or Indian, they were controlling the blacks in the ANC. I cited many occasions when the ANC and the CP had differed on policy and the ANC had prevailed, but this did not seem to impress them. Finally, in exasperation, I said to them, 'You gentlemen consider yourselves intelligent, do you not? You consider yourselves forceful and persuasive, do you not? Well, there are four of you and only one of me, and you cannot control me or get me to change my mind. What makes you think the communists can succeed where you have failed?'

*   *   *

They were also concerned about the idea of nationalization, insisting that the ANC and the Freedom Charter supported the wholesale nationalization of the South African economy. I explained that we were for a more even distribution of the rewards of certain industries, industries that were already monopolies, and that nationalization might occur in some of those areas. But I referred them to an article I wrote in 1956 for *Liberation* in which I said that the Freedom Charter was not a blueprint for socialism but for African-style capitalism. I told them I had not changed my mind since then.

The other main area of discussion was the issue of majority rule. They felt that if there was majority rule, the rights of minorities would be trampled. How would the ANC protect the rights of the white minority? they wanted to know. I said that there was no organization in the history of South Africa to compare with the ANC in terms of trying to unite all the people and races of South Africa. I referred them to the preamble of the Freedom Charter: 'South Africa belongs to all who live in it, black and white.' I told them that whites were Africans as well, and that in any future dispensation the majority would need the minority. 'We do not want to drive you into the sea,' I said.

94

The meetings had a positive effect: I was told in the winter of 1988 that President Botha was planning to see me before the end of August. The country was still in turmoil. The government had reimposed a State of Emergency in both 1987 and 1988. International pressure mounted. More companies left South Africa. The American Congress had passed a sweeping sanctions bill.

In 1987, the ANC celebrated its seventy-fifth anniversary and held a conference at the end of the year in Tanzania attended by delegates from more than fifty nations. Oliver declared that the armed struggle would intensify until the government was prepared to negotiate the abolition of apartheid. Two years before, at the ANC's Kabwe conference in Zambia marking the thirtieth anniversary of the Freedom Charter, members of other races were elected to the National Executive Committee for the first time, and the NEC pledged that no discussions with the government could be held until all ANC leaders were released from prison.

Although violence was still pervasive, the National Party had never been stronger. In the white general election of May 1987, the Nationalists won an overwhelming majority. Worse still, the liberal Progressive Federal Party had been replaced as the official opposition by the Conservative Party, which was to the right of the Nationalists and campaigned on the theme that the government was too lenient with the black opposition.

Despite my optimism about the secret talks, it was a difficult time. I had recently had a visit from Winnie and I learned that No. 8115 Orlando West, the house in which we had been married and which I considered home, had been burned down by arsonists. We had lost invaluable family records, photographs and keepsakes—even the slice of wedding cake Winnie was saving for my release. I had always thought that some day when I left prison I would be able to recapture the past when looking over those pictures and letters, and now they were gone. Prison had robbed me of my freedom but not my memories, and now I felt some enemies of the struggle had tried to rob me of even those.

I was also suffering from a bad cough that I could not seem to shake off, and I often felt too weak to exercise. I had continued to complain about the dampness of my cell, but nothing had been done about it. One day, during a meeting in the visiting area with my attorney, Ismail Ayob, I felt ill and vomited. I was taken back to my cell, examined by a doctor, and soon recovered. A few days later, however, I was in my cell after dinner

325

when a number of warders and a doctor arrived. The physician gave me a cursory examination, and then one of the warders told me to get dressed. 'We are taking you to hospital in Cape Town,' I was told. Security was tight; I went in a convoy of cars and military vehicles accompanied by at least a dozen warders.

*   *   *

I was taken to Tygerberg Hospital, on the campus of the University of Stellenbosch in a rich and verdant area of the Cape. As I later discovered, they had nearly chosen a different facility because the authorities feared I might attract sympathetic attention at a university hospital. The warders went in first and cleared everyone out of the entrance area. I was then escorted up to a floor that had been entirely emptied; the hall was lined with more than a dozen armed guards.

While sitting on a table in the examining room, I was looked at by a young and amiable doctor who was also a professor at the university medical school. He inspected my throat, tapped my chest, took some cultures and in no time pronounced me fit. 'There is nothing wrong with you,' he said with a smile. 'We should be able to release you tomorrow.' I was anxious not to be diverted from my talks with the government, so I was pleased with his diagnosis.

After the examination, the doctor asked me if I would like some tea. I said I would, and a few minutes later a tall young Coloured nurse came in with a tray. The presence of all the armed guards and warders so frightened her that she dropped the

326

tray on my bed, spilling the tea, before rushing out.

*   *   *

I spent the night in the empty ward under heavy guard. The first thing next morning, even before I had breakfasted, I was visited by an older doctor who was head of internal medicine at the hospital. He was a no-nonsense fellow and had far less of a bedside manner than the cordial young physician of the night before. Without any preliminaries, he tapped me roughly on my chest and then said gruffly, 'There is water in your lung.' I told him that the previous doctor had done tests and said I was fine. With a hint of annoyance, he said, 'Mandela, take a look at your chest.' He pointed out that one side of my chest was actually larger than the other, and said that it was probably filled with water.

He asked a nurse to bring him a syringe, and without further ado he poked it into my chest and drew out some brownish liquid. 'Have you had breakfast?' he said. No, I replied. 'Good,' he said, 'we are taking you to the operating theatre immediately.' He told me I had a great deal of fluid on my lung and he wanted to draw it out right away.

In the operating room I was anaesthetized, and the next thing I recalled was waking up in a room with the doctor present. I was groggy, but I concentrated on what he said: he had removed two litres of fluid from my chest and when the liquid was analysed, tuberculosis had been discovered. He said it was in the very early stages of the illness, and that there was no damage to the lung. While full-blown tuberculosis normally took six months to

327

cure, he said, I should be better in two months. The doctor agreed that it was probably the damp cell that had helped to cause my illness.

*   *   *

I spent the next six weeks at Tygerberg recuperating and receiving treatment. In December, I was moved to the Constantiaberg Clinic, a luxurious facility near Pollsmoor that had never had a black patient before. My first morning there, I had an early visit from Kobie Coetsee, who was accompanied by Major Marais, a deputy commander responsible for looking after me. We had barely exchanged greetings when the orderly brought in my breakfast.

Because of my recent illness and my history of high blood pressure, I had been put on a strict low-cholesterol diet. That order had apparently not yet been conveyed to the clinic's kitchen, for the breakfast tray contained scrambled eggs, three rashers of bacon and several pieces of buttered toast. I could not remember the last time I had tasted bacon and eggs and I was ravenous. Just as I was about to take a delicious forkful of egg, Major Marais said, 'No, Mandela, that is against the orders of your physician,' and he reached over to take the tray. I held it tightly, and said, 'Major, I am sorry. If this breakfast will kill me, then today I am prepared to die.'

*   *   *

Once I was ensconced at Constantiaberg, I again began to meet Kobie Coetsee and the secret

328

committee. While I was still at the clinic Coetsee said he wanted to put me in a situation that was halfway between confinement and freedom. While he did not spell out what this meant, I had a notion of what he was talking about, and I merely nodded. I would not be so naive as to consider his proposal to be freedom, but I knew that it was a step in that direction.

In the meantime, the clinic was extremely comfortable and for the first time I actually enjoyed a hospital convalescence. The nurses— who were white or Coloured; no black nurses were permitted—spoiled me; they brought extra desserts and pillows and were constantly visiting, even during their time off.

One day, one of the nurses came and said, 'Mr Mandela, we are having a party tonight and we would like you to come.' I said I'd be honoured to attend, but that the authorities would undoubtedly have something to say about it. The prison authorities refused permission for me to go, which nettled the nurses, and as a result they decided to hold their party in my room, insisting they could not have it without me.

That night, a dozen or so of these young ladies in party frocks descended on my room with cake and punch and gifts. The guards seemed befuddled, but they could hardly consider these vivacious young girls a security risk. In fact, when one of the guards attempted to prevent some of the nurses from entering my room, I jestingly accused him of being jealous of an old man receiving so much attention from such beautiful young ladies.

95

In early December 1988, security on my ward was tightened and the officers on duty were more alert than usual. Some change was imminent. On the evening of 9 December, Major Marais came into my room and told me to prepare to leave. 'Where to?' I asked him. He could not say. I packed my things and looked around for some of my loyal nurses; I was disappointed at not being able to thank them and bid them farewell.

We left in a rush, and after about an hour on the road we entered a prison whose name I recognized: Victor Verster. Located in the lovely old Cape Dutch town of Paarl, Victor Verster is thirty-five miles northeast of Cape Town in the province's wine-growing region. The prison had the reputation of being a model facility. We drove through its entire length, and then along a winding dirt road through a rather wild, wooded area at the rear of the property. At the end of the road we came to an isolated whitewashed one-storey cottage set behind a concrete wall and shaded by tall fir trees.

I was ushered into the house by Major Marais and found a spacious lounge next to a large kitchen, with an even larger bedroom at the back. The place was sparsely but comfortably furnished. It had not been cleaned or swept before my arrival, and the bedroom and living room were teeming with all kinds of exotic insects, centipedes, monkey spiders and the like, some of which I had never seen before. That night, I swept the insects off my bed and windowsill and slept extremely well in what was to be my new home.

The next morning I surveyed my new abode and discovered a swimming pool in the back yard, and two smaller bedrooms. I walked outside and admired the trees that shaded the house and kept it cool. The entire place felt removed, isolated. The only thing spoiling the idyllic picture was that the walls were topped with razor wire, and there were guards at the entrance to the house. Even so, it was a lovely place and situation; a halfway house between prison and freedom.

That afternoon I was visited by Kobie Coetsee, who brought a case of Cape wine as a housewarming gift. The irony of a jailer bringing his prisoner such a gift was not lost on either of us. He was extremely solicitous and wanted to make sure that I liked my new home. He surveyed the house himself, and the only thing he recommended was that the walls outside the house be raised—for my privacy, he said. He told me that the cottage at Victor Verster would be my last home before becoming a free man. The reason behind this move, he said, was that I should have a place where I could hold discussions in privacy and comfort.

The cottage did in fact give me the illusion of freedom. I could go to sleep and wake up as I pleased, swim whenever I wanted, eat when I was hungry—all were delicious sensations. Simply to be able to go outside during the day and take a walk when I desired was a moment of private glory. There were no bars on the windows, no jangling keys, no doors to lock or unlock. It was altogether pleasant, but I never forgot that it was a gilded cage.

*   *   *

The prison service provided me with a cook, Warrant Officer Swart, a tall, quiet Afrikaner who had once been a warder on Robben Island. I did not remember him, but he said he sometimes drove us to the quarry and purposely steered the truck over bumps to give us a rocky ride. 'I did that to you,' he said sheepishly, and I laughed. He was a decent, sweet-tempered fellow without any prejudice and he became like a younger brother to me.

He arrived at seven in the morning and left at four, and would make my breakfast, lunch and dinner. I had a diet outlined by my physician and he would follow it in his preparations. He was a lovely cook, and when he went home, he would leave my supper to heat up in the microwave oven, a device that was new to me.

Warrant Officer Swart baked bread, made home-brewed ginger-beer and assorted other delicacies. When I had visitors, which was increasingly often, he would prepare gourmet meals. They always praised the food and I dare say my chef was the envy of all my visitors. When the authorities began to permit some of my ANC comrades and members of the United Democratic Front (UDF) and the Mass Democratic Movement (MDM) to visit, I accused them of coming only for the food.

One day, after a delicious meal prepared by Mr Swart, I went into the kitchen to wash the dishes. 'No,' he said, 'that is my duty. You must return to the sitting room.' I insisted that I had to do something, and that if he cooked, it was only fair

332

for me to do the dishes. Mr Swart protested, but finally gave in. He also objected to the fact that I would make my bed in the morning, saying it was his responsibility to do so. But I had been making my own bed for so long that it had become a reflex.

We also swapped favours in another respect. Like many Afrikaans-speaking warders, he was keen to improve his English. I was always looking for ways to improve my Afrikaans. We made an agreement: he would speak to me in English and I would answer in Afrikaans, and in that way we both practised the language at which we were weakest.

I would occasionally ask him to make certain dishes. I sometimes requested samp and beans, which I used to eat as a boy. One day, I asked, 'You know, I would like you to cook me some brown rice.' To my astonishment, he said, 'What is brown rice?' Swart was a young man, and I explained to him that brown rice was the unrefined rice kernel that we used to eat during the war when white rice was unavailable. I said it was far healthier than white rice. He was sceptical, but managed to find me some. He cooked it and I enjoyed it very much. But Mr Swart could not abide the taste and vowed that if I ever wanted it again, I would have to cook it myself.

*   *   *

Even though I was not a drinker, I wanted to be a proper host and serve wine to my guests. I would occasionally take a sip in order to make my guests feel comfortable, but the only wine I can stomach is a South African 'semi-sweet' wine, which is actually very sweet.

333

Before my guests came I would ask Mr Swart to get a certain type of Nederburg wine, which I had tasted before and knew was a semi-sweet. One day, I was expecting my friends and lawyers, Dullah Omar, George Bizos and Ismail Ayob, for lunch and asked Mr Swart to purchase some Nederburg wine should George Bizos, not a Muslim, want some with his meal. I noticed that he grimaced when I said this, and asked him what was wrong.

'Mr Mandela,' he said. 'I always buy that wine for you because you ask me to, but it is cheap stuff and not very nice.' I reminded him that I did not like dry wines and I was sure George could not tell the difference anyway. Mr Swart smiled at this and proposed a compromise: he would go out and buy two bottles, a dry wine and my Nederburg, and then he would ask my guest which he preferred. 'Fine,' I said, 'let us try your experiment.'

When all four of us were seated for lunch, Swart came out holding the two bottles and turned to the guests and said, 'Gentlemen, which wine would you like?' Without even looking at me, George pointed to the bottle of dry white. Warrant Officer Swart just smiled.

96

The meetings with the committee continued, but we stalled on the same issues that had always prevented us from moving forward: the armed struggle, the Communist Party, and majority rule. I was still pressing Coetsee for a meeting with P. W. Botha. By this time, the authorities permitted me to have rudimentary communications with my comrades at Pollsmoor and Robben Island and also the ANC in Lusaka. Although I knew I was going ahead of my colleagues, I did not want to go too far, and find that I was all alone.

In January 1989, I was visited by my four comrades from Pollsmoor and we discussed the memorandum I was planning to send to the state president. It reiterated most of the points I had made in our secret committee meetings, but I wanted to make sure the state president heard them directly from me. He would see that we were not wild-eyed terrorists, but reasonable men.

'I am disturbed,' I wrote to Mr Botha in the memorandum sent to him in March, 'as many other South Africans no doubt are, by the spectre of a South Africa split into two hostile camps—blacks on one side . . . and whites on the other, slaughtering one another.' To avert this and prepare the groundwork for negotiations, I proposed to deal with the three demands made of the ANC by the government as a precondition to negotiations: renouncing violence; breaking with the SACP; and abandoning the call for majority rule.

On the question of violence I wrote that the refusal of the ANC to renounce violence was not the problem: 'The truth is that the government is not yet ready . . . for the sharing of political power with blacks.' I explained our unwillingness to cast aside the SACP, and reiterated that we were not under its control. 'Which man of honour,' I wrote, 'will desert a life-long friend at the insistence of a common opponent and still retain a measure of credibility with his people?' I said the rejection of

335

majority rule by the government was a poorly disguised attempt to preserve power. I suggested he must face reality. 'Majority rule and internal peace are like the two sides of a single coin, and white South Africa simply has to accept that there will never be peace and stability in this country until the principle is fully applied.'

At the end of the letter, I offered a very rough framework for negotiations.

> Two political issues will have to be addressed; firstly, the demand for majority rule in a unitary state; secondly, the concern of white South Africa over this demand, as well as the insistence of whites on structural guarantees that majority rule will not mean domination of the white minority by blacks. The most crucial tasks which will face the government and the ANC will be to reconcile these two positions.

I proposed that this be done in two stages, the first being a discussion to create the proper conditions for negotiations, the second being the actual negotiations themselves. 'I must point out that the move I have taken provides you with the opportunity to overcome the current deadlock, and to normalize the country's political situation. I hope you will seize it without delay.'

*　　　*　　　*

But delay there was. In January, P. W. Botha suffered a stroke. While it did not incapacitate the president, it did weaken him and, according to his cabinet, made him even more irascible. In February

336

Botha unexpectedly resigned as head of the National Party, but kept his position as state president. This was an unparalleled situation in the country's history: in the South African parliamentary system, the leader of the majority party becomes the head of state. President Botha was now head of state but not of his own party. Some saw this as a positive development: that Botha wanted to be 'above party politics' in order to bring about true change in South Africa.

Political violence and international pressure both continued to intensify. Political detainees all across the country had held a successful hunger strike, persuading the minister of law and order to release over nine hundred detainees. In 1989 the UDF formed an alliance with the Congress of South African Trade Unions (COSATU) to form the Mass Democratic Movement (MDM), which then began organizing a countrywide 'defiance campaign' of civil disobedience to challenge apartheid institutions. On the international front, Oliver Tambo held talks with the governments of Great Britain and the Soviet Union, and in January 1987 met the US secretary of state, George Shultz, in Washington. The Americans recognized the ANC as an indispensable element of any solution in South Africa. Sanctions against South Africa remained in force and even increased.

Political violence also had its tragic side. As the violence in Soweto intensified, my wife permitted a group of young men to act as her bodyguards as she moved around the township. These young men were untrained and undisciplined and became involved in activities that were unbecoming to a liberation struggle. Winnie subsequently became legally entangled in the trial of one of her bodyguards who was convicted of murdering a young comrade. This situation was deeply disconcerting to me, for such a scandal only served to divide the movement at a time when unity was essential. I wholly supported my wife and maintained that while she had shown poor judgment, she was innocent of any serious charges.

That July, for my seventy-first birthday, I was visited at the cottage at Victor Verster by nearly my entire family. It was the first time I had ever had my wife and children and grandchildren all in one place, and it was a grand and happy occasion. Warrant Officer Swart outdid himself in preparing a feast, and he did not even get upset when I let some of the grandchildren eat their puddings before their main courses. After the meal, the grandchildren went into my bedroom to watch a video of a horror movie while the adults stayed outside gossiping in the lounge. It was a deep, deep pleasure to have my whole family around me, and the only pain was the knowledge that I had missed such occasions for so many years.

97

On 4 July I was visited by General Willemse who informed me that I was being taken to see President Botha the following day. He described the visit as a 'courtesy call', and I was told to be ready to leave at 5.30 a.m. I told the general that while I was looking forward to the meeting, I thought I ought to have a suit and tie in which to see Mr Botha. (The suit from the visit of the Eminent Persons Group had long since vanished.) The general agreed, and a short while later a tailor appeared to take my measurements. That afternoon I received a new suit, tie, shirt and shoes. Before leaving, the general also asked me my blood type, just in case anything untoward should happen the following day.

I prepared as best I could for the meeting. I reviewed my memo and the extensive notes I had made for it. I looked at as many newspapers and publications as I could to make sure I was up to date. After President Botha's resignation as head of the National Party, F. W. de Klerk had been elected in his place, and there was said to be considerable jockeying between the two men. Some might interpret Botha's willingness to meet me as his way of stealing the thunder from his rival, but that did not concern me. I rehearsed the arguments that the state president might make and the ones I would put in return. In every meeting with an adversary, you must make sure you have conveyed precisely the impression you intend to.

I was tense about seeing Mr Botha. He was known as *'die Groot Krokodil'*—'the Great Crocodile'—and I had heard many accounts of his ferocious temper. He seemed to me to be the very model of the old-fashioned, stiff-necked, stubborn Afrikaner who did not so much discuss matters with black leaders as dictate to them. His recent stroke had apparently only exacerbated this tendency. I resolved that if he acted in that finger-wagging fashion with me, I would have to inform him that I found such behaviour unacceptable, and I would then stand up and adjourn the meeting.

*   *   *

At precisely 5.30 in the morning Major Marais, the commander of Victor Verster, arrived at my cottage. He came into the lounge where I stood in front of him in my new suit for inspection. He walked around me, and then shook his head from side to side.

'No, Mandela, your tie,' he said. I did not have much use for ties in prison, and I realized that morning when I was putting it on that I had forgotten how to tie it properly. I made a knot as best I could and hoped no one would notice. Major Marais unbuttoned my collar, loosened and then removed my tie, and then, standing behind me, tied it in a double Windsor knot. He then stood back to admire his handiwork. 'Much better,' he said.

We drove from Victor Verster to Pollsmoor, to the home of General Willemse, where we were served breakfast by the general's wife. After breakfast, in a small convoy, we drove to Tuynhuys, the official presidential office, and parked in an underground garage where we would not be seen. Tuynhuys is a graceful, nineteenth-century Cape-Dutch-style building, but I did not get a proper look at it that day. I was essentially smuggled into the presidential suite.

We took a lift to the ground floor and emerged in a grand wood-panelled lobby in front of the president's office. There we were met by Kobie Coetsee, Niel Barnard and a retinue of prison officials. I had spoken extensively with both Coetsee and Dr Barnard about this meeting, and

340

they had always advised me to avoid controversial issues with the president. While we were waiting, Dr Barnard looked down and noticed that my shoelaces were not properly tied and he quickly knelt down to tie them for me. I realized just how nervous they were, and that did not make me any calmer. The door then opened and I walked in expecting the worst.

From the opposite side of his grand office, P.W. Botha walked towards me. He had planned his march perfectly, for we met exactly halfway. He had his hand out and was smiling broadly, and in fact, from that very first moment, he completely disarmed me. He was unfailingly courteous, deferential and friendly.

We very quickly posed for a photograph of the two of us shaking hands, and then were joined at a long table by Kobie Coetsee, General Willemse and Dr Barnard. Tea was served and we began to talk. From the first, it was not as though we were engaged in tense political arguments but a lively and interesting tutorial. We did not discuss substantive issues so much as history and South African culture. I mentioned that I had recently read an article in an Afrikaans magazine about the 1914 Afrikaner Rebellion, and mentioned how they had occupied towns in the Free State. I said I saw our struggle as a parallel to this famous rebellion, and we discussed this historical episode for quite a while. South African history, of course, looks very different to the black man and the white man. Their view was that the rebellion had been a quarrel between brothers, whereas my struggle was a revolutionary one. I said that it could also be seen as a struggle between brothers who happen to be different colours.

The meeting was not even half an hour long, and was friendly and breezy until the end. It was then that I raised a serious issue. I asked Mr Botha to release unconditionally all political prisoners, including myself. That was the only tense moment in the meeting, and Mr Botha said that he was afraid that he could not do that.

There was then a brief discussion as to what we should say if news of the meeting leaked out. We very quickly drafted a bland statement saying that we had met for tea in an effort to promote peace in the country. Once this was agreed upon, Mr Botha rose and shook my hand, saying what a pleasure it had been. Indeed, it had been. I thanked him, and left the way I had come.

While the meeting was not a breakthrough in terms of negotiations, it was one in another sense. Mr Botha had long talked about the need to cross the Rubicon, but he never did it himself until that morning at Tuynhuys. Now, I felt, there was no turning back.

*   *   *

A little more than a month later, in August 1989, P.W. Botha went on national television to announce his resignation as state president. In a curiously rambling farewell address, he accused cabinet members of a breach of trust, of ignoring him and of playing into the hands of the African National Congress. The following day, F.W. de Klerk was sworn in as acting president and affirmed his commitment to change and reform.

To us, Mr de Klerk was a cipher. When he

342

became head of the National Party, he seemed to be the quintessential party man, nothing more and nothing less. Nothing in his past seemed to hint at a spirit of reform. As education minister, he had attempted to keep black students out of white universities. But as soon as he took over the National Party, I began to follow him closely. I read all of his speeches, listened to what he said and began to see that he represented a genuine departure from his predecessor. He was not an ideologue but a pragmatist, a man who saw change as necessary and inevitable. On the day he was sworn in, I wrote him a letter requesting a meeting.

In his inaugural address, Mr de Klerk said his government was committed to peace and that it would negotiate with any other group committed to peace. But his commitment to a new order was demonstrated only after his inauguration when a march was planned in Cape Town to protest at police brutality. It was to be led by Bishop Tutu and the Reverend Allan Boesak. Under President Botha, the march would have been banned, marchers would have defied that ban and violence would have resulted. The new president lived up to his promise to ease restrictions on political gatherings and permitted the march to take place, only asking that the demonstrators remain peaceful. A new and different hand was on the tiller.

98

Even as de Klerk became president, I continued to meet the secret negotiating committee. We were joined by Gerrit Viljoen, the minister of constitutional development, a brilliant man with a doctorate in Classics, whose role was to bring our discussions into a constitutional framework. I pressed the government to display evidence of its good intentions, urging the state to show its bona fides by releasing my fellow political prisoners at Pollsmoor and Robben Island. While I told the committee that my colleagues had to be released unconditionally, I said the government could expect disciplined behaviour from them after their release. That was demonstrated by the conduct of Govan Mbeki, who had been unconditionally released at the end of 1987.

On 10 October 1989, President de Klerk announced that Walter Sisulu and seven of my former Robben Island comrades, Raymond Mhlaba, Ahmed Kathrada, Andrew Mlangeni, Elias Motsoaledi, Jeff Masemola, Wilton Mkwayi and Oscar Mpetha, were to be released. That morning, I had been visited by Walter, Kathy, Ray and Andrew, who were still at Pollsmoor, and I was able to say good-bye. It was an emotional moment, but I knew I would not be too far behind. The men were released five days later from Johannesburg Prison. It was an action that rightly evoked praise here and abroad, and I conveyed my appreciation to Mr de Klerk.

But my gratitude paled compared with my

unalloyed joy that Walter and the others were free. It was a day we had yearned for and fought for over so many years. De Klerk had lived up to his promise, and the men were released under no bans; they could speak in the name of the ANC. It was clear that the ban on the organization had effectively expired, a vindication of our long struggle and our resolute adherence to principle.

De Klerk began a systematic dismantling of many of the building blocks of apartheid. He opened South African beaches to people of all colours, and stated that the Reservation of Separate Amenities Act would soon be repealed. Since 1953 this act had enforced what was known as 'petty apartheid', segregating parks, theatres, restaurants, buses, libraries, toilets and other public facilities according to race. In November, he announced that the National Security Management System, a secret structure set up under P.W. Botha to combat anti-apartheid forces, would be dissolved.

In early December I was informed that a meeting with de Klerk was set for the twelfth of that month. By this time I was able to consult my colleagues new and old, and had meetings at the cottage with my old colleagues and the leaders of the Mass Democratic Movement and the UDF. I received ANC people from all of the regions, as well as delegates from the UDF and COSATU. One of these young men was Cyril Ramaphosa, the general secretary of the National Mine Workers' Union and one of the ablest of the new generation of leadership. I also had visits from colleagues of mine from Robben Island, including Terror Lekota and Tokyo Sexwale, who stayed for lunch. They are both men with large appetites, and the only complaint I heard about them was from Warrant Officer Swart, who said, 'Those fellows will eat us out of house and home!'

With guidance from a number of colleagues, I then drafted a letter to de Klerk not unlike the one I had sent to P. W. Botha. The subject was talks between the government and the ANC. I told the president that the current conflict was draining South Africa's lifeblood and that talks were the only solution. I said the ANC would accept no preconditions to talks, especially not the precondition that the government wanted: the suspension of the armed struggle. The government asked for an 'honest commitment to peace' and I pointed out that our readiness to negotiate was exactly that.

I told Mr de Klerk how impressed I was by his emphasis on reconciliation, enunciated in his inaugural address. His words had imbued millions of South Africans and people around the world with the hope that a new South Africa was about to be born. The very first step on the road to reconciliation, I said, would be the complete dismantling of apartheid and all the measures used to enforce it.

But I said that the spirit of that speech had not been much in evidence of late. The government's policies were perceived by many as a continuation of apartheid by other means. The government, I said, had spent too much time talking with black homeland leaders and others co-opted by the system; these men, I asserted, were the agents of an oppressive past that the mass of black South Africans rejected.

I reiterated my proposal that talks take place in two stages. I told him I fully supported the guidelines the ANC had adopted in the Harare Declaration of 1989, which put the onus on the government to eliminate the obstacles to negotiations that the state itself had created. Those demands included the release of all political prisoners, the lifting of all bans on restricted organizations and persons, the ending of the State of Emergency and the removal of all troops from the townships. I stressed that a mutually agreed-upon cease-fire to end hostilities ought to be the first order of business, for without that, no business could be conducted. The day before our meeting the letter was delivered to Mr de Klerk.

*   *   *

On the morning of 13 December I was again taken to Tuynhuys. I met de Klerk in the same room where I had had tea with his predecessor. He was accompanied by Kobie Coetsee, General Willemse, Dr Barnard and his colleague Mike Louw. I congratulated Mr de Klerk on becoming president and expressed the hope that we would be able to work together. He was extremely cordial and reciprocated these sentiments.

From the first I noticed that Mr de Klerk listened to what I had to say. This was a novel experience. National Party leaders generally heard what they wanted to hear in discussions with black leaders, but Mr de Klerk seemed to be making a real attempt to listen and understand.

One of the issues I emphasized that day was the National Party's recently introduced five-year plan,

347

which contained the concept of 'group rights'. The idea of 'group rights' was that no racial or ethnic group could take precedence over any other. Although they defined 'group rights' as a way of protecting the freedom of minorities in a new South Africa, in fact their proposal was a means of preserving white domination. I told Mr de Klerk that this was unacceptable to the ANC.

I added that it was not in his interest to retain this concept, for it gave the impression that he wanted to modernize apartheid without abandoning it; this was damaging his image and that of the National Party in the eyes of the progressive forces in this country and around the world. An oppressive system cannot be reformed, I said; it must be entirely cast aside. I mentioned an editorial that I had recently read in *Die Burger*, the mouthpiece of the National Party in the Cape, implying that the group rights concept was conceived as an attempt to bring back apartheid through the back door. I told Mr de Klerk that if that was how his party's paper perceived group rights, how did he think we regarded it? I added that the ANC had not struggled against apartheid for seventy-five years only to yield to a disguised form of it, and that if it was his true intention to preserve apartheid through the Trojan horse of group rights, then he did not truly believe in ending apartheid.

Mr de Klerk, I saw that day, does not react quickly to things. It was a mark of the man that he listened to what I had to say and did not argue with me. 'You know,' he said, 'my aim is no different than yours. Your memo to P. W. Botha said the ANC and the government should work together to deal with white fears of black domination, and the idea of "group rights" is how we propose to deal with it.' I was impressed with this response, but said that the idea of 'group rights' did more to increase black fears than allay white ones. De Klerk then said, 'We will have to change it, then.'

I then brought up the question of my freedom and said that if he expected me to go out to pasture upon my release he was greatly mistaken. I reaffirmed that if I was released into the same conditions under which I had been arrested I would go back to doing precisely those things for which I had been imprisoned. I made the case to him that the best way to move forward was to unban the ANC and all other political organizations, to lift the State of Emergency, to release political prisoners and to allow the exiles to return. If the government did not unban the ANC, as soon as I was out of prison I would be working for an illegal organization. 'Then,' I said, 'you must simply rearrest me after I walk through those gates.'

Again, he listened carefully to what I had to say. My suggestions certainly came as no surprise to him. He said he would take all I said into consideration, but that he would make no promises. The meeting was an exploratory one and I understood that nothing was going to be resolved that day. But it was extremely useful, for I had taken the measure of Mr de Klerk just as I had with new prison commanders when I was on Robben Island. I was able to write to our people in Lusaka that Mr de Klerk seemed to represent a true departure from the National Party politicians of the past. Mr de Klerk, I said, echoing Mrs Thatcher's famous description of Mr Gorbachev, was a man we could do business with.

99

On 2 February 1990 F.W. de Klerk stood before Parliament to make the traditional opening speech and did something no other South African head of state had ever done: he truly began to dismantle the apartheid system and lay the groundwork for a democratic South Africa. In dramatic fashion, he announced the lifting of the bans on the ANC, the PAC, the South African Communist Party and thirty-one other illegal organizations; the freeing of political prisoners incarcerated for non-violent activities; the suspension of capital punishment; and the lifting of various restrictions imposed by the State of Emergency. 'The time for negotiation has arrived,' he said.

It was a breathtaking moment, for in one sweeping action he had virtually normalized the situation in South Africa. Our world had changed overnight. After forty years of persecution and banishment, the ANC was now a legal organization. I and all my comrades could no longer be arrested for being a member of the ANC, for carrying its green, yellow and black banner, for speaking its name. For the first time in almost thirty years, my picture and my words, and those of all my banned comrades, could appear in South African newspapers. The international community applauded de Klerk's bold actions. Amid all the good news, however, the ANC objected to the fact that Mr de Klerk had not completely lifted the

State of Emergency or ordered the troops out of the townships.

On 9 February, seven days after Mr de Klerk's speech opening Parliament, I was informed that I was again going to Tuynhuys. I arrived at six o'clock in the evening. I met a smiling Mr de Klerk in his office and, as we shook hands, he informed me that he was going to release me from prison the following day. Although the press in South Africa and around the world had been speculating for weeks that my release was imminent, the announcement nevertheless came as a surprise to me. I had not been told that the reason de Klerk wanted to see me was to tell me that he was making me a free man.

I felt a conflict between my blood and my brain. I deeply wanted to leave prison as soon as I could, but to do so on such short notice would not be wise. I thanked Mr de Klerk, and then said that at the risk of appearing ungrateful I would prefer to have a week's notice in order that my family and my organization could be prepared for my release. Simply to walk out tomorrow, I said, would cause chaos. I asked de Klerk to release me a week from that day. After waiting twenty-seven years, I could certainly wait another seven days.

De Klerk was taken aback by my response. Instead of replying, he continued to relate the plan for my release. He said that the government would fly me to Johannesburg and officially release me there. Before he went any further, I told him that I strongly objected to that. I wanted to walk out of the gates of Victor Verster and be able to thank those who looked after me and greet the people of Cape Town. Though I was from Johannesburg,

Cape Town had been my home for nearly three decades. I would make my way back to Johannesburg, but when I chose to, not when the government wanted me to. 'Once I am free,' I said, 'I will look after myself.'

De Klerk was again nonplussed. But this time my objections caused a reaction. He excused himself and left his office to consult with others. After ten minutes he returned with a rather long face and said, 'Mr Mandela, it is too late to change the plan now.' I replied that the plan was unacceptable and that I wanted to be released a week hence and at Victor Verster, not Johannesburg. It was a tense moment and, at the time, neither of us saw any irony in a prisoner asking not be released and his jailer attempting to release him.

De Klerk again excused himself and left the room. After ten minutes he returned with a compromise: yes, I could be released at Victor Verster, but, no, the release could not be postponed. The government had already informed the foreign press that I was to be set free the next day and felt they could not renege on that statement. I felt I could not argue with that. In the end, we agreed on the compromise, and Mr de Klerk poured a tumbler of whisky for each of us to drink in celebration. I raised the glass in a toast, but only pretended to drink; such spirits are too strong for me.

I did not get back to my cottage until shortly before midnight, whereupon I immediately sent word to my colleagues in Cape Town that I was to be released the following day. I managed to get a message to Winnie, and telephoned Walter in

Johannesburg. They would all fly in on a chartered plane the next day. That evening, a number of ANC people on what was known as the National Reception Committee came to the cottage to draft a statement that I would make the following day. They left in the early hours of the morning and, despite my excitement, I had no trouble falling asleep.

PART ELEVEN

Freedom

100

I awoke on the day of my release after only a few hours' sleep at 4.30 a.m. 11 February was a cloudless, end-of-summer Cape Town day. I did a shortened version of my usual exercise regimen, washed and ate breakfast. I then telephoned a number of people from the ANC and the UDF in Cape Town to come to the cottage to prepare for my release and work on my speech. The prison doctor came by to give me a brief check-up. I did not dwell on the prospect of my release, but on all the many things I had to do before then. As so often happens in life, the momentousness of an occasion is lost in the welter of a thousand details.

There were numerous matters that had to be discussed and resolved with very little time to do so. A number of comrades from the Reception Committee, including Cyril Ramaphosa and Trevor Manuel, were at the house bright and early. I wanted initially to address the people of Paarl, who had been very kind to me during my incarceration, but the reception committee was adamant that that would not be a good idea: it would look curious if I gave my first speech to the prosperous white burghers of Paarl. Instead, as planned, I would speak first to the people of Cape Town at the Grand Parade in Cape Town.

One of the first questions to be resolved was where I would spend my first night of freedom. My inclination was to spend the night in the Cape Flats, the bustling black and Coloured townships of Cape Town, in order to show my solidarity with the people. But my colleagues and, later, my wife argued that for security reasons I should stay with Archbishop Desmond Tutu in Bishopscourt, a plush residence in a white suburb. It was not an area where I would have been permitted to live before I went to prison, and I thought it would send the wrong signal to spend my first night of freedom in a posh white area. But the committee explained that Bishopscourt had become multi-racial under Tutu's tenure, and symbolized an open, generous non-racialism.

The prison service supplied me with boxes and crates for packing. During my first twenty or so years in prison, I accumulated very few possessions, but in the last few years I had amassed enough property—mainly books and papers—to make up for previous decades. I filled over a dozen crates and boxes.

*   *   *

My actual release time was set for 3 p.m., but Winnie and Walter and the other passengers from the chartered flight from Johannesburg did not arrive until after two. There were already dozens of people at the house, and the entire scene took on the aspect of a celebration. Warrant Officer Swart prepared a final meal for all of us and I thanked him not only for the food he had provided for the last two years but also the companionship. Warrant Officer James Gregory was also there at the house, and I embraced him warmly. In the years that he had looked after me from Pollsmoor to Victor Verster, we had never discussed politics, but our bond was an unspoken one and I would miss his soothing presence. Men like Swart, Gregory and Warrant Officer Brand reinforced my belief in the essential humanity even of those who had kept me behind bars for the previous twenty-seven and a half years.

There was little time for lengthy farewells. The plan was that Winnie and I would be driven in a car to the front gate of the prison. I had told the authorities that I wanted to be able to say good-bye to the guards and warders who had looked after me and I asked that they and their families wait for me at the front gate, where I would be able to thank them individually.

At a few minutes after three, I was telephoned by a well-known SABC presenter who requested that I get out of the car a few hundred feet before the gate so that they could film me walking towards freedom. This seemed reasonable, and I agreed. This was my first inkling that things might not go as smoothly as I had imagined.

By 3.30, I began to get restless, as we were already behind schedule. I told the members of the Reception Committee that my people had been waiting for me for twenty-seven years and I did not want to keep them waiting any longer. Shortly before four, we left in a small motorcade from the cottage. About a quarter of a mile in front of the gate, the car slowed to a stop and Winnie and I got out and began to walk towards the prison gate.

At first I could not really make out what was going on in front of us, but when I was within 150 feet or so, I saw a tremendous commotion and a great crowd of people: hundreds of photographers and television cameras and newspeople as well as several thousand well-wishers. I was astounded and a little bit alarmed. I had truly not expected such a scene; at most, I had imagined that there would be several dozen people, mainly the warders and their families. But this proved to be only the beginning; I realized we had not thoroughly prepared for all that was about to happen.

Within twenty feet or so of the gate, the cameras started clicking, a noise that sounded like some great herd of metallic beasts. Reporters started shouting questions; television crews began crowding in; ANC supporters were yelling and cheering. It was a happy, if slightly disorienting, chaos. When a television crew thrust a long, dark and furry object at me, I recoiled slightly, wondering if it were some newfangled weapon developed while I was in prison. Winnie informed me that it was a microphone.

When I was among the crowd I raised my right fist, and there was a roar. I had not been able to do that for twenty-seven years and it gave me a surge of strength and joy. We stayed among the crowd for only a few minutes before jumping back into the car for the drive to Cape Town. Although I was pleased to have such a reception, I was greatly vexed by the fact that I did not have a chance to say good bye to the prison staff. As I finally walked through those gates to enter a car on the other side, I felt—even at the age of seventy-one—that my life was beginning anew. My ten thousand days of imprisonment were at last over.

*   *   *

Cape Town was thirty-five miles to the southwest, but because of the unexpected crowds at the gate, the driver elected to take a different path to the city. We drove round to the back of the prison, and our convoy took small roads and byways into town. We drove through beautiful green vineyards and manicured farms, and I relished the scenery around me.

The countryside was lush and well cared for, but what surprised me was how many white families were standing beside the road to get a glimpse of our motorcade. They had heard on the radio that we were taking an alternative route. Some, perhaps a dozen, even raised their clenched right fists in what had become the ANC power salute. This astonished me; I was tremendously encouraged by these few brave souls from a conservative farming area who expressed their solidarity. At one point I stopped and got out of the car to greet and thank one such white family and tell them how inspired I was by their support. It made me think that the South Africa I was returning to was far different from the one I had left.

As we entered the outskirts of the city, I could see people streaming towards the centre. The Reception Committee had organized a rally at the Grand Parade in Cape Town, a great open square that stretched out in front of the old City Hall. I would speak to the crowd from the balcony of that building, which overlooked the entire area. We had heard sketchy reports that a great sea of people had been waiting there since morning. The plan was for our motorcade to avoid the crowd and drive round to the back of City Hall, where I would quietly enter the building.

The drive to Cape Town took forty-five minutes, and as we neared the Grand Parade we could see an enormous crowd. The driver was meant to turn right and skirt its edges, but instead he inexplicably plunged straight into the sea of people. Immediately the crowd surged forward and enveloped the car. We inched forward for a minute or two but were then forced to stop by the sheer press of bodies. People began knocking on the windows, and then on the boot and the bonnet. Inside, it sounded like a massive hailstorm. Then people began to jump on the car in their excitement. Others began to shake it and at that moment I began to worry. I felt as though the crowd might very well kill us with their love.

The driver was even more anxious than Winnie and I, and he was clamouring to jump out of the car. I told him to stay calm and remain inside, that others from the cars behind us would come to our rescue. Allan Boesak and others began to attempt to clear a way for our vehicle and push the people off the car; but with little success. We sat inside—it would have been futile even to attempt to open the door, so many people were pressing on it—for more than an hour, imprisoned by thousands of our own supporters. The time for the scheduled beginning of the speech had long passed.

Several dozen marshals eventually came to the rescue and managed slowly to clear an exit path. When we finally broke free, the driver set off at great speed in the opposite direction from the City Hall. 'Man, where are you going?' I asked him in some agitation. 'I don't know!' he said, his voice tense with anxiety. 'I've never experienced anything like this before,' he said, and then continued driving without any destination in mind.

When he began to calm down I gave him

directions to the house of my friend and attorney Dullah Omar, who lived in the Indian area of the city. We could go there, I said, and relax for a few minutes. This appealed to him. Fortunately, Dullah and his family were home, but they were more than a bit surprised to see us. I was a free man for the first time in twenty-seven years, but instead of greeting me, they said with some concern, 'Aren't you meant to be at the Grand Parade?'

We were able to have some cold drinks at Dullah's, but we had only been there a few minutes when Archbishop Tutu telephoned. How he knew we were there I do not know. He was quite distressed, and said, 'Nelson, you must come back to the Grand Parade immediately. The people are growing restless. If you do not return straightaway, I cannot vouch for what will happen. I think there might be an uprising!' I said I would return at once.

Our problem was the driver: he was deeply reluctant to return to the Grand Parade. But I remonstrated with him and soon we were on our way back to City Hall. The building was surrounded by people on all sides, but it was not as dense at the back, and the driver managed to make his way through to the rear entrance. It was almost dusk when I was led up to the top floor of this stately building whose halls had always been filled with shuffling white functionaries. I walked out on to the balcony and saw a boundless sea of people cheering, holding flags and banners, clapping and laughing.

I raised my fist to the crowd, and the crowd responded with an enormous cheer. Those cheers fired me anew with the spirit of the struggle. *'Amandla!'* I called out. *'Ngawethu!'* they responded. *'iAfrika!'* I yelled; *'Mayibuye!'* they answered. Finally, when the crowd had started to settle down, I took out my speech and then reached into my breast pocket for my glasses. They were not there; I had left them at Victor Verster. I knew Winnie's glasses had a similar prescription, and I borrowed hers.

> Friends, comrades and fellow South Africans. I greet you all in the name of peace, democracy and freedom for all! I stand here before you not as a prophet but as a humble servant of you, the people. Your tireless and heroic sacrifices have made it possible for me to be here today. I therefore place the remaining years of my life in your hands.

I spoke from the heart. I wanted first of all to tell the people that I was not a messiah, but an ordinary man who had become a leader because of extraordinary circumstances. I wanted immediately to thank the people all over the world who had campaigned for my release. I thanked the people of Cape Town, and I saluted Oliver Tambo and the African National Congress, Umkhonto we Sizwe, the South African Communist Party, the UDF, the South African Youth Congress, COSATU, the Mass Democratic Movement, the National Union of South African Students, and the Black Sash, a group formed by women that had long been a voice of conscience. I also publicly expressed my gratitude to my wife and family, saying, 'I am convinced that [their] pain and suffering was far greater than my own.'

I told the crowd in no uncertain terms that

364

apartheid had no future in South Africa, and that the people must not scale down their campaign of mass action. 'The sight of freedom looming on the horizon should encourage us to redouble our efforts.' I felt it was important publicly to explain my talks with the government. 'Today,' I said, 'I wish to report to you that my talks with the government have been aimed at normalizing the political situation in the country. I wish to stress that I myself have at no time entered into negotiations about the future of our country except to insist on a meeting between the ANC and the government.'

I said I hoped that a climate conducive to a negotiated settlement could soon be achieved, ending the need for the armed struggle. The steps to achieving such a climate, I said, had been outlined in the ANC's 1989 Harare Declaration. As a condition to real negotiations, I said, the government must immediately end the State of Emergency and free all political prisoners.

I told the people that de Klerk had gone further than any other Nationalist leader to normalize the situation and then, in words that came back to haunt me, I called Mr de Klerk 'a man of integrity'. These words were flung back at me many times when Mr de Klerk seemed not to live up to them.

It was vital for me to show my people and the government that I was unbroken and unbowed, and that the struggle was not over for me but beginning anew in a different form. I affirmed that I was 'a loyal and disciplined member of the African National Congress'. I encouraged the people to return to the barricades, to intensify the struggle, and we would walk the last mile together.

*　　*　　*

It was evening by the time my speech was finished, and we were hustled back into our cars for the trip to Bishopscourt. As we entered its pristine environs, I saw hundreds of black faces waiting to greet me. When they saw us, the people burst into song. When I greeted Archbishop Tutu, I enveloped him in a great hug; here was a man who had inspired an entire nation with his words and his courage, who had revived the people's hope during the darkest of times. We were led inside the house, where more family and friends met us but, for me, the most wonderful moment was when I was told that I had a telephone call from Stockholm. I knew immediately who it was. Oliver Tambo's voice was weak but unmistakable, and to hear him after all those years filled me with great joy. Oliver was in Sweden recuperating from a debilitating stroke he had suffered in August 1989. We agreed to meet as soon as possible.

My dream upon leaving prison was to take a leisurely drive down to the Transkei and visit my birthplace, the hills and streams where I had played as a boy, and the burial ground of my mother, which I had never seen. But my dream had to be deferred, for I learned very quickly of the extensive plans that the ANC had for me, and none of them involved a relaxing journey to the Transkei.

101

I was scheduled to hold a press conference the afternoon after my release, and in the morning I met a number of my colleagues to talk about scheduling and strategy. A small mountain of telegrams and messages of congratulations had arrived, and I tried to review as many of these as possible. They came from all over the world, from presidents and prime ministers, but I remember one in particular from a white Cape Town housewife that amused me greatly. It read: 'I am very glad that you are free, and that you are back among your friends and family, but your speech yesterday was very boring.'

Before I went to prison I had never held such a press conference as I did that day. In the old days there were no television cameras, and most ANC press conferences were conducted clandestinely. That afternoon, there were so many journalists, from so many different countries, I did not know whom to speak to. I was pleased to see a high percentage of black journalists among the throng. At the press conference I was once again keen to reassert a number of themes: first, that I was a loyal and disciplined member of the ANC. I was mindful of the fact that the most senior ANC people would be watching my release from abroad, and attempting to gauge my fidelity from a distance. I was aware that they had heard rumours that I had strayed from the organization, that I was compromised, so at every turn I sought to reassure them. When asked what role I would play in the

367

organization, I told the press that I would play whatever role the ANC ordered.

I told the reporters that there was no contradiction between my continuing support for the armed struggle and my advocating negotiations. It was the reality and the threat of the armed struggle that had brought the government to the verge of negotiations. I added that when the state stopped inflicting violence on the ANC, the ANC would reciprocate with peace. Asked about sanctions, I said the ANC could not yet call for the relaxation of sanctions, because the situation that caused sanctions in the first place—the absence of political rights for blacks—was still the status quo. I might be out of jail, I said, but I was not yet free.

I was asked as well about the fears of whites. I knew that people expected me to harbour anger towards whites. But I had none. In prison, my anger towards whites decreased, but my hatred for the system grew. I wanted South Africa to see that I loved even my enemies while I hated the system that turned us against one another.

I wanted to impress upon the reporters the critical role of whites in any new dispensation. I have tried never to lose sight of this. We did not want to destroy the country before we freed it, and to drive the whites away would devastate the nation. I said that there was a middle ground between white fears and black hopes, and we in the ANC would find it. 'Whites are fellow South Africans,' I said, 'and we want them to feel safe and to know that we appreciate the contribution that they have made towards the development of this country.' Any man or woman who abandons apartheid will be embraced in our struggle for a democratic, non-racial South Africa; we must do everything we could to persuade our white compatriots that a new, non-racial South Africa would be a better place for all.

From my very first press conference I noticed that journalists were as eager to learn about my personal feelings and relationships as my political thoughts. This was new to me; when I went to prison, a journalist would never have thought of asking questions about one's wife and family, one's emotions, one's most intimate moments. While it was understandable that the press might be interested in these things, I nevertheless found their curiosity difficult to satisfy. I am not and never have been a man who finds it easy to talk about his feelings in public. I was often asked by reporters how it felt to be free, and I did my best to describe the indescribable, and usually failed.

After the press conference, Archbishop Tutu's wife telephoned us from Johannesburg to say that we must fly there straightaway. Winnie and I had hoped to spend a few days in Cape Town relaxing, but the message we were receiving was that the people of Johannesburg were getting restless and there might be chaos if I did not return at once. We flew to Johannesburg that evening, but I was informed that there were thousands of people surrounding our old home, No. 8115 Orlando West, which had been reconstructed, and that it would be unwise to go there. I reluctantly acceded; I yearned to spend my second night of freedom under my own roof. Instead, Winnie and I stayed in the northern suburbs at the home of an ANC supporter.

The following morning we flew by helicopter to

the First National Bank stadium in Soweto. We were able to make an aerial tour of Soweto, the teeming metropolis of matchbox houses, tin shanties and dirt roads, the mother city of black urban South Africa, the only home I ever knew as a man before I went to prison. While Soweto had grown, and in some places prospered, the overwhelming majority of the people remained dreadfully poor, without electricity or running water, eking out an existence that was shameful in a nation as wealthy as South Africa. In many places, the poverty was far worse than when I went to prison..

*   *   *

We circled over the stadium, overflowing with 120,000 people, and landed in the centre. The stadium was so crowded, with people sitting or standing in every inch of space, that it looked as though it would burst. I expressed my delight to be back among them, but I then scolded the people for some of the crippling problems of urban black life. Students, I said, must return to school. Crime must be brought under control. I told them that I had heard of criminals masquerading as freedom fighters, harassing innocent people and setting alight vehicles; these rogues had no place in the struggle. Freedom without civility, freedom without the ability to live in peace, was not true freedom at all.

Today, my return to Soweto fills my heart with joy. At the same time I also return with a deep sense of sadness. Sadness to learn that you are

370

still suffering under an inhuman system. The housing shortage, the schools crisis, unemployment and the crime rate still remain . . . Proud as I am to be part of the Soweto community, I have been greatly disturbed by the statistics of crime that I read in the newspapers. Although I understand the deprivations our people suffer, I must make it clear that the level of crime in the township is unhealthy and must be eliminated as a matter of urgency.

I ended by opening my arms to all South Africans of goodwill and good intentions, saying that 'no man or woman who has abandoned apartheid will be excluded from our movement towards a non-racial, united and democratic South Africa based on one-person one-vote on a common voters' roll.' That was the ANC's mission, the goal that I had always kept before me during the many lonely years in prison, the goal that I would work towards during the remaining years of my life. It was the dream I cherished when I entered prison at the age of forty-four, but I was no longer a young man, I was seventy-one, and I could not afford to waste any time.

*   *   *

That night, I returned with Winnie to No. 8115 in Orlando West. It was only then that I knew in my heart that I had left prison. For me, No. 8115 was the centrepoint of my world, the place marked with an X in my mental geography. The four-roomed house had been soundly rebuilt after the fire. When

I saw it, I was surprised by how much smaller and humbler it was than I remembered it being. Compared with my cottage at Victor Verster, No. 8115 could have been the servants' quarters at the back. But any house in which a man is free is a castle when compared with even the plushest prison.

That night, happy as I was to be home, I had a sense that what I most wanted and longed for was going to be denied me. I yearned to resume a normal and ordinary life, to pick up some of the old threads from my life as a young man, to be able to go to my office in the morning and return to my family in the evening, to be able to pop out and buy some toothpaste at the pharmacy, to visit old friends in the evening. These ordinary things are what one misses most in prison, and dreams about doing when one is free. But I quickly realized that such things were not going to be possible. That night, and every night for the next weeks and months, the house was surrounded by hundreds of well-wishers. People sang and danced and called out, and their joy was infectious. These were my people, and I had no right and no desire to deny myself to them. But in giving myself to my people, I could see that I was once again taking myself away from my family.

We did not sleep much that night, as the singing continued until the early hours, when members of the ANC and UDF who were guarding the house begged the crowd to remain quiet and allow us to rest. There were many in the ANC who advised me to move to the home a few blocks away, in Diepkloof extension, that Winnie had built while I was in prison. It was a grand place by Soweto standards, but it was a house that held no meaning or memories for me. Moreover, it was a house that because of its size and expense seemed somehow inappropriate for a leader of the people. I rejected that advice as long as I could. I wanted to live not only among my people, but like them.

102

My first responsibility was to report to the leadership of the ANC, and on 27 February, when I had been out of prison a little over two weeks, I flew to Lusaka for a meeting of the National Executive Committee. It was a wonderful reunion to be with old comrades whom I had not seen in decades. A number of African heads of state were also in attendance, and I had brief talks with Robert Mugabe of Zimbabwe, Kenneth Kaunda of Zambia, Quett Masire of Botswana, Joaquim Chissano of Mozambique, José Eduardo Dos Santos of Angola, and Yoweri Museveni of Uganda.

While the members of the Executive were pleased that I had been freed, they were also eager to evaluate the man who had been released. I could see the questions in their eyes. Was Mandela the same man who went to prison twenty-seven years before, or was this a different Mandela, a reformed Mandela? Had he survived or had he been broken? They had heard reports of my conversations with the government and they were rightly concerned. I had not only been out of touch with the situation on the ground—since 1984 I had not been able to communicate even with my colleagues in prison.

I carefully and soberly explained the nature of my talks with the government. I described the demands I had made, and the progress that had been achieved. They had seen the memoranda I had written to Botha and de Klerk, and knew that these documents adhered to ANC policy. I knew that over the previous few years some of the men who had been released had gone to Lusaka and whispered, 'Madiba has become soft. He has been bought off by the authorities. He is wearing three-piece suits, drinking wine and eating fine food.' I knew of these whispers, and I intended to refute them. I knew that the best way to disprove them was simply to be direct and honest about everything that I had done.

At that session of the NEC I was elected deputy president of the organization while Alfred Nzo, the organization's secretary-general, was named acting president while Oliver was recuperating. At a press conference after our meeting, I was asked about a suggestion made by Dr Kaunda, the president of Zambia and a long-time supporter of the Congress, that the ANC should suspend armed operations inside South Africa now that I had been released. I replied that while we valued Dr Kaunda's wisdom and support, it was too soon to suspend the armed struggle, for we had not yet achieved the goal for which we had taken up arms; it was not the ANC's job, I said, to help Mr de Klerk to placate his right-wing supporters.

I began a tour of Africa, which included many countries. During the first six months after my release, I spent more time abroad than at home. Nearly everywhere I went there were great enthusiastic crowds so that even if I felt weary, the people buoyed me. In Dar es Salaam I was met by a crowd estimated at half a million.

I enjoyed my travels immensely. I wanted to see new—and old—sights, taste different foods, speak with all manner of people. I very quickly had to acclimatize myself to a world radically different from the one I had left. With changes in travel, communication and mass media, the world had accelerated; things now happened so fast that it was sometimes difficult to keep up with them. Winnie tried to get me to slow down, but there was simply too much to do; the organization wanted to make sure we took advantage of the euphoria generated by my release.

In Cairo, the day after a private meeting with the Egyptian president, Hosni Mubarak, I was scheduled to address a large meeting in a local hall. When I arrived, the crowd seemed to be spilling out of the building and there was precious little security. I mentioned to a policeman that I thought he needed reinforcements, but he merely shrugged. Winnie and I waited in a room behind the hall, and at the appointed hour a policeman motioned for me to go in. I told him to escort the rest of my delegation in first because I feared that when I went in there would be pandemonium and they would be cut off. But the policeman urged me to go first, and indeed as soon as I was in the hall, the crowd surged forward and overcame the cordon of policemen. In their enthusiasm, I was jostled and a bit shaken, and at one point I lost my shoe in the general confusion. When things began to calm down a few minutes later, I found that neither my shoe nor my wife could be located. Finally, after nearly half an hour, Winnie was brought on to the stage with me, quite cross that she had been lost. I was not even able to address the crowd, for they were shouting 'Mandela! Mandela!' so furiously that I could not be heard above the din, and finally I left, without my shoe and with an uncharacteristically silent wife.

While in Cairo I held a press conference in which I said the ANC was 'prepared to consider a cessation of hostilities'. This was a signal to the government. Both the ANC and the government were engaged in creating a climate whereby negotiations would succeed. While the ANC was demanding that the government normalize the situation in the country by ending the State of Emergency, releasing all political prisoners and repealing all apartheid laws, the government was intent on first persuading the ANC to suspend the armed struggle. While we were not yet ready to announce such a suspension, we wanted to provide Mr de Klerk with enough encouragement to pursue his reformist strategies. We knew that eventually we would suspend the armed struggle, in part to facilitate more serious negotiations and in part to allow Mr de Klerk to go to his own constituency, the white voters of South Africa, and say, 'Look, here are the fruits of my policy.'

After my last stop in Africa, I flew to Stockholm to visit Oliver. Seeing my old friend and law partner was the reunion I most looked forward to. Oliver was not well, but when we met we were like two young boys in the veld who took strength from our love for each other. We began by talking of old times, but when we were alone, the first subject he raised was the leadership of the organization.

'Nelson,' he said, 'you must now take over as president of the ANC. I have been merely keeping the job warm for you.' I refused, telling him that he had led the organization in exile far better than I ever could have. It was neither fair nor democratic for a transfer to occur in such a manner. 'You have been elected by the organization as the president,' I said. 'Let us wait for an election; then the organization can decide.' Oliver protested, but I would not budge. It was a sign of his humility and selflessness that he wanted to appoint me president, but it was not in keeping with the principles of the ANC.

In April 1990, I flew to London to attend a concert at Wembley, held in my honour. Many international artists, most of whom I didn't know, were performing and the event was to be televised worldwide. I took advantage of this to thank the world's anti-apartheid forces for the tremendous work they had done in pressurising for sanctions, for the release of myself and fellow political prisoners, and for the genuine support and solidarity they had shown the oppressed people of my country.

103

When I emerged from prison, Chief Mangosuthu Buthelezi, head of the Inkatha Freedom Party and the chief minister of KwaZulu, was one of the premier players on the South African political stage. But within ANC circles, he was a far from popular figure. Chief Buthelezi was descended from the great Zulu king Cetywayo, who had defeated the British at the Battle of Isandlwana in 1879. As a young man, he attended Fort Hare and then joined the ANC Youth League. I saw him as one of the movement's upcoming young leaders. He had become chief minister of the KwaZulu homeland with the tacit support of the ANC, and even his launching of Inkatha as a Zulu cultural organization was unopposed by the organization. But, over the years, Chief Buthelezi drifted away from the ANC. Though he resolutely opposed apartheid and refused to allow KwaZulu to become an 'independent' homeland as the government wished, he was a thorn in the side of the democratic movement. He opposed the armed struggle. He criticized the 1976 Soweto uprising. He campaigned against international sanctions. He challenged the idea of a unitary state of South Africa. Yet Chief Buthelezi had consistently called for my release and refused to negotiate with the government until I and other political prisoners were liberated.

Chief Buthelezi was one of the first people I telephoned after my release to thank him for his long-standing support. My inclination was to meet the chief as soon as possible to try to resolve our differences. During my initial visit to Lusaka I brought up the idea of such a meeting, and it was voted down. While I was at Victor Verster, Walter had been invited by the Zulu king, Goodwill Zwelithini, to visit him in Ulundi, KwaZulu's capital, and I urged him to accept. I thought it was an excellent opportunity to influence the head of one of the most respected and powerful royal families in the country. The visit was tentatively approved by the NEC, provided Walter went to the king's palace in Nongoma; it was thought that going to Ulundi would suggest recognition of the authority of the homeland.

When I returned from Lusaka I phoned both Chief Buthelezi and the king, and explained that Walter would be coming to see the king, not in Ulundi but in Nongoma. The king said he would not accept Walter coming to see him anywhere but in the capital. 'I am the king,' he said. 'I have invited him to see me in Ulundi, and he has no right to say I will see you elsewhere.' 'Your Majesty,' I said, 'we are facing a wall of opposition from our membership who did not want Mr Sisulu to go to KwaZulu at all. We managed to get this compromise approved; surely you can bend as well?' But he could not, and he refused to see Walter.

Relations deteriorated after this, and in May I persuaded the ANC of the need for me to make a visit to the king and Buthelezi. The king approved, but a week or so before the visit I received a letter from him to say I must come alone. This proved to be the last straw, and the NEC would not give in to such a demand. I told the king that I could not come unless I was accompanied by my colleagues; the king regarded this as another slight and cancelled the visit.

My goal was to forge an independent relationship with the king, separate from my relationship with Chief Buthelezi. The king was the true hereditary leader of the Zulus, who loved and respected him. Fidelity to the king was far more widespread in KwaZulu than allegiance to Inkatha.

In the meantime, Natal became a killing-ground.

379

Heavily armed Inkatha supporters had in effect declared war on ANC strongholds across the Natal Midlands region and around Pietermaritzburg. Entire villages were set alight, dozens of people were killed, hundreds were wounded and thousands became refugees. In March 1990 alone, 230 people lost their lives in this internecine violence. In Natal, Zulu was murdering Zulu, for Inkatha members and ANC partisans are Zulus. In February, only two weeks after my release, I went to Durban and spoke to a crowd of over 100,000 people at King's Park, almost all of whom were Zulus. I pleaded with them to lay down their arms, to take each other's hands in peace: 'Take your guns, your knives and your pangas, and throw them into the sea! Close down the death factories. End this war now!' But my call fell on deaf ears. The fighting and dying continued.

I was so concerned that I was willing to go to great lengths to meet Chief Buthelezi. In March, after one particularly horrifying spasm of violence, I announced on my own that I would meet him at a mountain hamlet outside Pietermaritzburg. On a personal level, my relations with the chief were close and respectful, and I hoped to capitalize on that. But I found that such a meeting was anathema to the ANC leaders in Natal. They considered it dangerous, and vetoed my meeting. I did go to Pietermaritzburg, where I saw the burned remains of ANC supporters and tried to comfort their grieving families, but I did not see Chief Buthelezi.

104

In March, after much negotiation within our respective parties, we scheduled our first face-to-face meeting with Mr de Klerk and the government. These were to be 'talks about talks', and the meetings were to begin in early April. But on 26 March, in Sebokeng township, about thirty miles south of Johannesburg, the police opened fire without warning on a crowd of ANC demonstrators, killing twelve and wounding hundreds more, most of them shot in the back as they were fleeing. Police had used live ammunition in dealing with the demonstrators, which was intolerable. The police claimed that their lives were endangered, but many demonstrators who were shot in the back had no weapons. You cannot be in danger from an unarmed man who is running away from you. The right to assemble and demonstrate in support of our just demands was not a favour to be granted by the government at its discretion. This sort of action angered me like no other, and I told the press that every white policeman in South Africa regarded every black person as a military target. After consultation with the NEC, I announced the suspension of our talks and warned Mr de Klerk that he could not 'talk about negotiations on the one hand and murder our people on the other'.

But despite the suspension of our official talks, with the approval of the leadership, I met privately with Mr de Klerk in Cape Town in order to keep up the momentum for negotiations. Our discussions centred primarily on a new date, and we agreed on early May. I brought up the appalling behaviour at Sebokeng and the police's unequal treatment of blacks and whites; police used live ammunition on black demonstrators, while they never unsheathed their guns at white right-wing protests.

The government was in no great rush to begin negotiations; they were counting on the euphoria that greeted my release to die down. They wanted to allow time for me to fall on my face and show that the former prisoner hailed as a saviour was a highly fallible man who had lost touch with the present situation.

Despite his seemingly progressive actions, Mr de Klerk was by no means the great emancipator. He was a gradualist, a careful pragmatist. He did not make any of his reforms with the intention of putting himself out of power. He made them for precisely the opposite reason: to ensure power for the Afrikaner in a new dispensation. He was not prepared to negotiate the end of white rule.

His goal was to create a system of power-sharing based on group rights, which would preserve a modified form of minority power in South Africa. He was decidedly opposed to majority rule, or 'simple majoritarianism', as he sometimes called it, because that would end white domination in a single stroke. We knew early on that the government was fiercely opposed to a winner-take-all Westminster parliamentary system, and advocated instead a system of proportional representation with built-in structural guarantees for the white minority. Although he was prepared to allow the black majority to vote and create legislation, he wanted to retain a minority veto. From the start I would have no truck with this plan. I described it to Mr de Klerk as apartheid in disguise, a 'loser-takes-all' system.

The Nationalists' long-term strategy to overcome our strength was to build an anti-ANC alliance with the Inkatha Freedom Party and to lure the Coloured Afrikaans-speaking voters of the Cape into a new National Party. From the moment of my release, they began wooing both Buthelezi and the Coloured voters of the Cape. The government attempted to scare the Coloured population into thinking the ANC was anti-Coloured. They supported Chief Buthelezi's desire to retain Zulu power and identity in a new South Africa by preaching to him the doctrine of group rights and federalism.

*   *   *

The first round of talks with the government was held over three days in early May. Our delegation consisted of Walter Sisulu, Joe Slovo, Alfred Nzo, Thabo Mbeki, Ahmed Kathrada, Joe Modise, Ruth Mompati, Archie Gumede, the Reverend Beyers Naude, Cheryl Carolus and me. The setting was Groote Schuur, the Cape-Dutch-style mansion that was the residence of South Africa's first colonial governors, among them Cecil Rhodes. Some of our delegation joked that we were being led into an ambush on the enemy's ground.

But the talks, contrary to expectation, were conducted with seriousness and good humour. Historic enemies who had been fighting each other for three centuries met and shook hands. Many

383

wondered out loud why such discussions had not taken place long before. The government had granted temporary indemnities to Joe Slovo, the general secretary of the Communist Party, and Joe Modise, the commander of MK, and to see these two men shaking hands with the National Party leaders who had demonized them for decades was extraordinary. As Thabo Mbeki later said to reporters, each side had discovered that the other did not have horns.

The very fact of the talks themselves was a significant milestone in the history of our country; as I pointed out, the meeting represented not only what the ANC had been seeking for so many years, but an end to the master/servant relationship that characterized black and white relations in South Africa. We had come to the meeting not as supplicants or petitioners, but as fellow South Africans who merited an equal place at the table.

The first day was more or less a history lesson. I explained to our counterparts that the ANC from its inception in 1912 had always sought negotiations with the government in power. Mr de Klerk, for his part, suggested that the system of separate development had been conceived as a benign idea, but had not worked in practice. For that, he said, he was sorry, and hoped the negotiations would make amends. It was not an apology for apartheid, but he went further than any other National Party leader ever had.

The primary issue discussed was the definition of political prisoners and political exiles. The government argued for a narrow definition, wanting to restrict the number of our people who would qualify for an indemnity. We argued for the

384

broadest possible definition and said that any person who was convicted of an offence that was politically motivated should qualify for an indemnity. We could not agree on a mutually satisfactory definition of 'politically motivated' crimes, and this would be an issue that would bedevil us for quite a while to come.

At the end of the three-day meeting, we agreed on what became known as the Groote Schuur Minute, pledging both sides to a peaceful process of negotiations and committing the government to lifting the State of Emergency, which they shortly did everywhere except for the violence-ridden province of Natal. We agreed to set up a joint working group to resolve the many obstacles that still stood in our way.

When it came to constitutional issues, we told the government we were demanding an elected constituent assembly to draw up a new constitution; we believed that the men and women creating the constitution should be the choice of the people themselves. But before the election of an assembly, it was necessary to have an interim government that could oversee the transition until a new government was elected. The government could not be both player and referee, as it was now. We advocated the creation of a multi-party negotiating conference to set up the interim government and set out the guiding principles for the functioning of a constituent assembly.

105

Although I had wanted to go to Qunu immediately after my release from prison, it was not until April that I was able to travel. I could not pick up and leave whenever I wanted; security had to be arranged, as well as speeches prepared for local organizations. By April, the ANC and General Bantu Holomisa, the military leader of the Transkei and an ANC loyalist, had arranged for a visit. But what was foremost in my mind and heart was paying my respects to my mother's grave.

I went first to Qunu and the site where my mother was buried. Her grave was simple and unadorned, covered only by a few stones and some upturned bricks, no different from the other graves at Qunu. I find it difficult to describe my feelings: I felt regret that I had been unable to be with her when she died, remorse that I had not been able to look after her properly during her life and a longing for what might have been had I chosen to live my life differently.

In seeing my village again after so many years, I was greatly struck by what had changed and what had not. When I had been young, the people of Qunu were not at all political; they were unaware of the struggle for African rights. People accepted life as it was and did not dream of changing it. But, when I returned, I heard the schoolchildren of Qunu singing songs about Oliver Tambo and Umkhonto we Sizwe, and I marvelled at how knowledge of the struggle had by then seeped into every corner of African society.

What had endured was the warmth and simplicity of the community, which took me back to my days as a boy. But what disturbed me was that the villagers seemed as poor if not poorer than they had been then. Most people still lived in simple huts with dirt floors, with no electricity and no running water. When I was young, the village was tidy, the water pure and the grass green and unsullied as far as the eye could see. Kraals were swept, the topsoil was conserved, fields were neatly divided. But now the village was unswept, the water polluted and the countryside littered with plastic bags and wrappers. We had not known of plastic when I was a boy, and though it surely improved life in some ways, its presence in Qunu appeared to me to be a kind of blight. Pride in the community seemed to have vanished.

*   *   *

That month I had another homecoming: I returned to Robben Island in order to persuade twenty-five MK political prisoners to accept the government's offer of an amnesty and leave the island. Though I had left the island eight years before, my memories of prison were still fresh and untinged by nostalgia. After all the years of being visited by others, it was a curious sensation to be a visitor on Robben Island.

But that day I did not have much opportunity to sightsee, for I immediately met the men protesting at the government's offer of an amnesty. They maintained that they would leave only after a victory on the battlefield, not the negotiating table. They were fiercely opposed to this particular

387

settlement, in which they had to enumerate their crimes before receiving indemnity. They accused the ANC of retreating from the Harare Declaration demand for an unconditional, blanket amnesty covering political prisoners and exiles. One man said, 'Madiba, I have been fighting the government all my life, and now I have to ask for a pardon from them.'

I could sympathize with their arguments, but they were being unrealistic. Every soldier would like to defeat his enemy on the field but, in this case, such a victory was out of reach. The struggle was now at the negotiating table. I argued that they were not advancing the cause by remaining in jail. They could be of greater service outside than inside. In the end, they agreed to accept the government's offer.

*   *   *

In early June I was scheduled to leave on a six-week tour of Europe and North America. Before going, I privately met Mr de Klerk, who wanted to discuss the issue of sanctions. Based on the changes he had made in South Africa, he asked me to modify the call for the continuation of international sanctions. While we were mindful of what Mr de Klerk had done, in our view sanctions remained the best lever to force him to do more. I was aware that the European Community and the USA were inclined to relax sanctions based on Mr de Klerk's reforms. I explained to Mr de Klerk that we could not tell our supporters to do so until he had completely dismantled apartheid and a transitional government was in place. While he was

388

disappointed at my response, he was not surprised.

The first leg of the trip took Winnie and me to Paris, where we were treated in very grand style by François Mitterrand and his charming wife Danielle, a long-time ANC supporter. This was not my first trip to the continental mainland, but I was still entranced by the beauties of the Old World. Although I do not want to decry the loveliness of the City of Light, the most important event that occurred while I was in France was that the government announced the suspension of the State of Emergency. I was pleased, but well aware that they had taken this action while I was in Europe in order to undermine my call for sanctions.

After stops in Switzerland, Italy and the Netherlands, I went to England, where I spent two days on a visit to Oliver and Adelaide. My next stop was the United States, but I would be returning to England on my way back to South Africa, which is when I was scheduled to meet Mrs Thatcher. As a courtesy, however, I phoned her before I left, and she proceeded to give me a stern but well-meaning lecture: she said she had been following my travels and noting how many events I attended each day. 'Mr Mandela, before we discuss any issues,' she said, 'I must warn you that your schedule is too heavy. You must cut it in half. Even a man half your age would have trouble meeting the demands that are being made on you. If you keep this up, you will not come out of America alive. That is my advice to you.'

*   *   *

I had read about New York City since I was a

389

young man, and finally to see it from the bottom of its great glass-and-concrete canyons while millions upon millions of pieces of ticker tape came floating down was a breathtaking experience. It was reported that as many as a million people personally witnessed our procession through the city, and to see the support and enthusiasm they gave to the anti-apartheid struggle was truly humbling. I had always read that New York was a hard-hearted place, but I felt the very opposite of that on my first full day in the city.

The following day I went up to Harlem, an area that had assumed legendary proportions in my mind since the 1950s when I watched young men in Soweto emulate the sharp fashions of Harlem dandies. Harlem, as my wife said, was the Soweto of America. I spoke to a great crowd at Yankee Stadium, telling them that an unbreakable umbilical cord connected black South Africans and black Americans, for we were together children of Africa. There was a kinship between the two, I said, that had been inspired by such great Americans as W.E.B. Du Bois, Marcus Garvey and Martin Luther King Jr. As a young man, I idolized the Brown Bomber, Joe Louis, who took on not only his opponents in the ring but racists outside it. In prison, I followed the struggle of black Americans against racism, discrimination and economic inequality. To us, Harlem symbolized the strength of resistance and the beauty of black pride. This was brought home to me by a young man I had seen the previous day who wore a T-shirt that read, 'BLACK BY NATURE, PROUD BY CHOICE'. We were linked by nature, I said, but we were proud of each other by choice.

After journeying to Memphis and Boston, I went to Washington to address a joint session of Congress and attend a private meeting with President Bush. I thanked the US Congress for its anti-apartheid legislation and said the new South Africa hoped to live up to the values that had created the two chambers before which I spoke. I said that as freedom fighters we could not have known of such men as George Washington, Abraham Lincoln and Thomas Jefferson 'and not been moved to act as they were moved to act'. I also delivered a strong message on sanctions, for I knew that the Bush administration felt it was time to loosen them. I urged Congress not to do so.

Even before meeting George Bush, I had formed a positive impression of him, for he was the first world leader to telephone me with congratulations after I left prison. From that point on, President Bush included me on his short list of world leaders whom he briefed on important issues. In person, he was just as warm and thoughtful, though we differed markedly on the issues of the armed struggle and sanctions. He was a man with whom one could disagree and then shake hands.

From the United States I proceeded to Canada, where I had a meeting with Prime Minister Mulroney and also addressed their Parliament. We were due to go to Ireland next, and before crossing the Atlantic, our plane, a small jet, stopped for refuelling in a remote place north of the Arctic Circle called Goose Bay. I felt like having a walk in the brisk air, and as I was strolling on the tarmac, I noticed some people standing by the airport fence. I asked a Canadian official who they were.

'Eskimos,' he said.

In my seventy-two years on earth I had never met an Innuit, and never imagined that I would. I headed over to that fence and found a dozen or so young people in their late teens who had come out to the airport because they had heard our plane was going to stop there. As a boy I had read about the Innuit (the name 'Eskimo' was given to them by the colonists), and the impression I received from the racist colonialist texts was that they were a very backward people.

But in talking with these bright young people, I learned that they had watched my release on television and were familiar with events in South Africa. 'Viva ANC!' one of them said. The Innuit are an aboriginal people historically mistreated by a white settler population; there were parallels between the plights of black South Africans and the Innuit people. What struck me so forcefully was how small the planet had become during my decades in prison; it was amazing to me that a teenage Innuit living at the roof of the world could watch the release of a political prisoner on the southern tip of Africa. Television had shrunk the world, and had in the process become a great weapon for eradicating ignorance and promoting democracy.

*　　　*　　　*

After Dublin I went to London, where I had a three-hour meeting with Mrs Thatcher. Standing out in the cold talking with the young Innuits had given me a chill. On the day I was to see Mrs Thatcher it was wintry and raining and, as we were leaving, Winnie told me I must take a raincoat. We were already in the lobby of the hotel, and if I went back for my coat we would be late. I am a stickler about punctuality, not only because I think it is a sign of respect to the person you are meeting but in order to combat the Western stereotype of Africans as being notoriously tardy. I told Winnie we did not have time, and instead I stood out in the rain signing autographs for some children. By the time I got to Mrs Thatcher I was feeling poorly, and was later diagnosed as having a mild case of pneumonia.

But it did not interfere with our meeting, except that she chided me like a schoolmarm for not taking her advice and cutting down on my schedule. Even though Mrs Thatcher was on the opposite side of the ANC on many issues such as sanctions, she was always a forthright and solicitous lady. In our meeting that day, though, I could not make the slightest bit of headway with her on the question of sanctions.

106

When I returned to South Africa in July, after brief trips to Uganda, Kenya and Mozambique, I requested a meeting with Mr de Klerk. Violence in the country was worsening; the death toll in 1990 was already over fifteen hundred, more than all the political deaths of the previous year. After conferring with my colleagues, I felt it necessary to speed up the process of normalization. Our country was bleeding to death, and we had to move ahead faster.

Mr de Klerk's lifting of the State of Emergency in June seemed to set the stage for a resumption of talks, but in July government security forces arrested about forty members of the ANC, including Mac Maharaj, Pravin Gordhan, Siphiwe Nyanda and Billy Nair, claiming that they were part of a Communist Party plot called Operation Vula to overthrow the government. De Klerk called for an urgent meeting with me and read to me from documents he claimed had been confiscated in the raid. I was taken aback because I knew nothing about it.

After the meeting I wanted an explanation, and called Joe Slovo. Joe explained that the passages read by Mr de Klerk had been taken out of context and that Vula was a moribund operation. But the government was intent on using this discovery to try to prise the ANC away from the SACP and keep Joe Slovo out of the negotiations. I went back to Mr de Klerk and told him that he had been misled by his own police and that we had no intention of parting ways with the SACP or dropping Joe Slovo from our negotiating team.

In the middle of July, shortly before a scheduled meeting of the National Executive Committee, Joe Slovo came to me privately with a proposition. He suggested we voluntarily suspend the armed struggle in order to create the right climate to move the negotiation process forward. Mr de Klerk, he said, needed to show his supporters that his policy had brought benefits to the country. My first reaction was negative; I did not think the time was ripe.

But the more I thought about it, the more I

realized that we had to take the initiative and this was the best way to do it. I also recognized that Joe, whose credentials as a radical were above dispute, was precisely the right person to make the proposal. He could not be accused of being a dupe of the government or of having gone soft. The following day I told Joe that if he brought up the idea in the NEC, I would support him.

When Joe raised the idea in the NEC the next day there were some who firmly objected, claiming that we were giving de Klerk's supporters a reward, but not our own people. But I defended the proposal, saying the purpose of the armed struggle was always to bring the government to the negotiating table, and now we had done so. I argued that the suspension could always be withdrawn, but it was necessary to show our good faith. After several hours, our view prevailed.

This was a controversial move within the ANC. Although MK was not active, the aura of the armed struggle had great meaning for many people. Even when cited merely as a rhetorical device, the armed struggle was a sign that we were actively fighting the enemy. As a result, it had a popularity out of proportion to what it had achieved on the ground.

On 6 August in Pretoria, the ANC and the government signed what became known as the Pretoria Minute in which we agreed to suspend the armed struggle. As I was to say over and over to our followers, although we had suspended armed action, we had not terminated the armed struggle. The agreement also set forth target dates for the release of political prisoners and the granting of certain types of indemnity. The process of indemnity was scheduled to be completed by May

1991, and the government also agreed to review the Internal Security Act.

*   *   *

Of all the issues that hindered the peace process, none was more devastating and frustrating than the escalation of violence in the country. We had all hoped that as negotiations got under way, violence would decrease. But in fact the opposite happened. The police and security forces were making very few arrests. People in the townships were accusing them of aiding and abetting the violence. It was becoming more and more clear to me that there was connivance on the part of the security forces. Many of the incidents indicated to me that the police, rather than quelling violence, were fomenting it.

Over the next few months, I visited townships all across the violence-racked Vaal Triangle south of Johannesburg, comforting wounded people and grieving families. Over and over again I heard the same story: the police and the defence force were destabilizing the area. I was told of the police confiscating weapons one day in one area, and then Inkatha forces attacking our people with those stolen weapons the next day. We heard stories of the police escorting Inkatha members to meetings and on their attacks.

In September I gave a speech in which I said there was a hidden hand behind the violence and suggested that there was a mysterious 'Third Force', which consisted of renegade men from the security forces who were attempting to disrupt the negotiations. I could not say who the members of the Third Force were, for I did not know myself, but I was certain that they existed and that they were murderously effective in their targeting of the ANC and the liberation struggle.

I came to this conclusion after becoming personally involved in two specific incidents. In July 1990 the ANC received information that hostel-dwellers belonging to the Inkatha Freedom Party were planning a major attack on ANC members in Sebokeng township in the Vaal Triangle on 22 July. Through our attorneys, we notified the minister of law and order, the commissioner of police and the regional commissioner, warning them of the impending attacks and urging them to take the proper action. We asked the police to prevent armed Inkatha members from entering the township to attend an Inkatha rally.

On 22 July busloads of armed Inkatha members, escorted by police vehicles, entered Sebokeng in broad daylight. A rally was held, after which the armed men went on a rampage, murdering approximately thirty people in a dreadful and grisly attack. I visited the area the next day and witnessed scenes I have never before seen and hope never to see again. At the morgue were bodies of people who had been hacked to death; a woman had both her breasts cut off with a machete. Whoever these killers were, they were animals.

I requested a meeting with Mr de Klerk the following day. When I saw him, I angrily demanded an explanation. 'You were warned in advance,' I told him, 'and yet did nothing. Why is that? Why is it that there have been no arrests? Why have the police sat on their hands?' I then told him that in any other nation where there was a tragedy of this magnitude, when more than thirty people had been slain, the head of state would make some statement of condolence, yet he had not uttered a word. He had no reply to what I said. I asked de Klerk to furnish me with an explanation, and he never did.

*　　*　　*

The second incident occurred in November, when a group of Inkatha members entered a squatters' camp known as Zonkizizwe (Zulu for 'the place where all nations are welcome') outside the city of Germiston, east of Johannesburg, and drove ANC people out, killing a number of them in the process. Inkatha members then proceeded to occupy the abandoned shacks and confiscate all the property. Residents of the area said that the Inkatha members were accompanied by the police. Once again, in the wake of this tragedy, the police and the government took no action. Black life in South Africa had never been so cheap.

Again, I met Mr de Klerk and his minister of law and order, Adriaan Vlok. Again, I asked Mr de Klerk why no action had been taken by the police in the aftermath of these crimes. I said the attackers could easily be found because they were now occupying the shacks of the people they had killed. Mr de Klerk asked Mr Vlok for an explanation and then Vlok, in a rather rude tone, asked me on whose property the shacks were located, the implication being that these people were squatters and therefore had no rights. In fact, I told him, the land had been made available to these people by the local authorities. His attitude was that of many Afrikaners who simply believed that black tribes had been killing each other since time immemorial. Mr de Klerk again told me he would investigate and respond, but never did.

*   *   *

During this time, the government took another action that added fuel to the flames. It introduced a regulation permitting Zulus to carry so-called 'traditional weapons' to political rallies and meetings in Natal and elsewhere. These weapons, assegais, which are spears, and knobkerries, wooden sticks with a heavy wooden head, are actual weapons with which Inkatha members killed ANC members. This gave me grave doubts about Mr de Klerk's peaceful intentions.

Those opposed to negotiations benefited from the violence, which always seemed to flare up when the government and the ANC were moving towards an agreement. These forces sought to ignite a war between the ANC and Inkatha, and I believe many members of Inkatha connived at this as well. Many in the government, including Mr de Klerk, chose to look the other way or ignore what they knew was going on under their noses. We had no doubts that men at the highest levels of the police and the security forces were aiding the Third Force. These suspicions were later confirmed by newspaper reports disclosing that the South African police had secretly funded Inkatha.

As the violence continued to spiral, I began to have second thoughts about the suspension of the armed struggle. Many of the people in the ANC were restive, and in September, at a press conference, I said that the continuing violence might necessitate taking up arms once more. The situation looked very grim, and any understanding that had been achieved with the government seemed lost.

107

In December 1990 Oliver returned to South Africa, having been in exile from his native land for three decades. It was wonderful to have him near. He returned for an ANC consultative conference in Johannesburg, which was attended by over fifteen hundred delegates from forty-five different regions, from home and abroad.

At the meeting I spoke in tribute to Oliver as the man who had led the ANC during its darkest hours and never let the flame go out. Now, he had ushered us to the brink of a future that looked bright and hopeful. During the twenty-seven years that I was in prison, it was Oliver who saved the ANC and then built it into an international organization with power and influence. He took up the reins when most of its leaders were either in prison or in exile. He was a soldier, a diplomat, a statesman.

Although I criticized the government for its orchestrated campaign of counter-revolutionary activities, it was Oliver's address that created a storm. He opened the meeting with a controversial speech in which he called for our sanctions policy to be re-evaluated. The ANC, he maintained, faced 'international marginalization' unless it took the initiative to de-escalate sanctions. The European Community had already begun to scale down sanctions. The countries in the West, particularly the United Kingdom and the United States, wanted to reward Mr de Klerk for his reforms, believing that this would encourage him to go further. We felt this was the wrong strategy, but we had to recognize international realities.

Although Oliver's speech had been discussed and approved by the NEC, his proposal was met with indignation by ANC militants, who insisted that sanctions must be maintained unchanged. The conference decided to retain the sanctions policy as it was.

I myself was the target of complaints by those who charged that the negotiators were out of touch with the grass roots and that we spent more time with National Party leaders than with our own people. I was also criticized at the conference for engaging in 'personal diplomacy' and not keeping the rank-and-file of the organization informed. As a leader of a mass organization, one must listen to the people, and I agreed that we had been remiss in not keeping the entire organization informed about the course of the negotiations. But I also knew the delicacy of our talks with the government; any agreements that we arrived at depended in part on their confidentiality. Although I accepted the criticism, I believed we had no alternative but to advance on the same course. I knew that I had to be more inclusive, brief more people as to our progress, and I proceeded with that in mind.

*   *   *

Each day, each weekend, the newspapers were filled with fresh reports of new and bloody violence in our communities and townships. It was clear that violence was the number one issue in the country. In many communities in Natal and on the Reef around Johannesburg, a poisonous mixture of crime, political rivalries, police brutality and shadowy death squads made life brutish and untenable. As long as the violence was not dealt with, the progress to a new dispensation would remain uneven and uncertain.

To try to arrest the spiral of violence, I contacted Chief Buthelezi to arrange a meeting. We met at Durban's Royal Hotel in January. Chief Buthelezi spoke first to assembled delegates and the media, and in the process opened old wounds rather than healing them. He catalogued the verbal attacks the ANC had made on him and criticized the ANC's negotiating demands. When it was my turn to speak, I chose not to respond to his remarks but to thank him for his efforts over many years to secure my release from prison. I cited our long relationship and underlined the many matters that united our two organizations rather than divided us.

Progress was made during our private talks, and Chief Buthelezi and I signed an agreement that contained a code of conduct covering the behaviour of our two organizations. It was a fair accord, and I suspect that if it had been implemented it would indeed have helped to staunch the bloodletting. But, as far as I could tell, Inkatha never made any effort to implement the accord, and there were also violations on our own side.

The violence continued between our two organizations. Each month people were dying by the hundreds. In March, Inkatha members launched an attack in Alexandra township north of Johannesburg in which forty-five people were killed over three days of fighting. Again, no one was arrested.

I could not sit idly by as the violence continued, and I sought another meeting with Chief Buthelezi. In April I went down to Durban, and we again made strong statements and signed another agreement. But, again, the ink was no sooner dry than it was drenched in blood. I was more convinced than ever that the government was behind much of the violence and that the violence was impeding the negotiations. Mr de Klerk's failure to respond put our own relationship in jeopardy.

In April, at a two-day meeting of the National Executive Committee, I discussed my doubts about Mr de Klerk. The NEC believed that the government was behind the violence and that the violence was upsetting the climate for negotiations. In an open letter to the government, we called for the dismissal of Magnus Malan, the minister of defence, and Adriaan Vlok, the minister of law and order; the banning of the carrying of traditional weapons in public; the phasing out of the migrant-worker hostels, where so many Inkatha members lived in the townships around Johannesburg; the dismantling of secret government counter-insurgency units; and the appointment of an independent commission to probe complaints of misconduct on the part of the security forces.

We gave the government until May to meet our

demands. Mr de Klerk responded by calling for a multiparty conference on violence to be held in May but I replied that this was pointless, since the government knew precisely what it had to do to end the violence. In May we announced the suspension of talks with the government.

*   *   *

In July 1991 the ANC held its first annual conference inside South Africa in thirty years. The conference was attended by 2,244 voting delegates who were democratically elected at ANC branches at home and abroad. At the conference I was elected president of the ANC without opposition. Cyril Ramaphosa was elected secretary-general, evidence that the torch was being passed from an older generation of leadership to a younger one. Cyril, whom I met only upon my release from prison, was a worthy successor to a long line of notable ANC leaders. He was probably the most accomplished negotiator in the ranks of the ANC, a skill he honed as general secretary of the National Mine Workers' Union.

In my speech I expressed my appreciation for the great honour that had been bestowed on me, and spoke of how difficult it would be to follow in the great footsteps of my predecessor, Oliver Tambo. Though we were then at loggerheads with the government, negotiations in and of themselves, I said, constituted a victory. The mere fact that the government was engaged in negotiations at all was a sign that they did not have the strength to sustain apartheid. I reiterated that the process would not be smooth, as we were dealing with politicians who do not want to negotiate themselves out of power. 'The point which must be clearly understood is that the struggle is not over, and negotiations themselves are a theatre of struggle, subject to advances and reverses as any other form of struggle.'

But negotiations could not wait. It was never in our interest to prolong the agony of apartheid for any reason. It was necessary, I said, to create a transitional government as soon as possible.

*   *   *

The conference underlined one of the most important and demanding tasks before the ANC: to transform an illegal underground liberation movement into a legal mass political party. For thirty years the ANC had functioned clandestinely in South Africa; those habits and techniques were deeply ingrained. We had to reconstruct an entire organization, from the smallest local branch to the National Executive. And we had to do so in a matter of months during a period of extraordinary change.

A large part of the ANC and Communist Party leadership had been in exile. Most of them had returned for the conference in July. They were unfamiliar with present-day South Africa; it was a new-found land for them as well as me. There was, however, an extraordinary crop of young leaders of the United Democratic Front and COSATU who had remained in the country, who knew the political situation in a way that we did not. These organizations had in some measure been surrogates for the ANC inside South Africa during the 1980s. The ANC had to integrate these men and women into the organization as well.

We faced not only logistical problems but philosophical ones. It is a relatively simple proposition to keep a movement together when you are fighting a common enemy. But creating a policy when that enemy is across the negotiating table is another matter altogether. In the new ANC, we had to integrate not only many different groups, but many different points of view. We needed to unite the organization around the idea of negotiations.

In the first seventeen months of legal activity, the ANC had recruited 700,000 members. This was impressive, but there was no room for complacency. A proportionately low number of these members were from the rural areas, the regions where the ANC had historically been weakest. At the same time, the National Party was throwing open its doors to non-whites and was busily recruiting disaffected Coloureds and Indians.

*   *   *

Ever since my release from prison, the state had continued its campaign to discredit my wife. After the alleged kidnapping of four youths who were staying in the Diepkloof house and the death of one of them, Winnie had first been vilified by a whispering campaign and was then charged with four counts of kidnapping and one of assault. The continuing aspersions cast on her character were such that both Winnie and I were eager for her to have her day in court and prove her innocence of

406

the charges.

My wife's formal trial began in February in the Rand Supreme Court in Johannesburg. I attended on the first day, as did many senior figures in the ANC, and I continued to attend as often as I could. I did this both to support my wife and to show my belief in her innocence. She was ably defended by George Bizos, who attempted to demonstrate that Winnie had had no involvement with either the kidnappings or beatings.

After three and a half months, the court found her guilty of kidnapping charges and being an accessory to assault. The judge, however, acknowledged that she had not taken part in any assault herself. She was sentenced to six years in prison, but was released on bail pending her appeal. As far as I was concerned, verdict or no verdict, her innocence was not in doubt.

108

On 20 December 1991, after more than a year and a half of talks about talks, the real talks began: CODESA—the Convention for a Democratic South Africa—represented the first formal negotiations forum between the government, the ANC and other South African parties. All our previous bilateral discussions had been laying the groundwork for these talks, which took place at the World Trade Centre, a modern exhibition centre near Jan Smuts airport in Johannesburg. CODESA comprised eighteen delegations covering the gamut of South African politics, plus observers from the

United Nations, the Commonwealth, the European Community and the Organization of African Unity. It was the widest cross-section of political groups ever gathered in one place in South Africa.

The opening of such talks was a historic occasion, certainly the most important constitutional convention since that of 1909 when the British colonies of the Cape and Natal and the former Boer republics of the Transvaal and the Orange Free State agreed to form a single union. Of course, that convention was not a tribute to democracy but a betrayal of it, for none of the representatives there that day was black. In 1991, the majority of them were.

Our planning delegation, led by Cyril Ramaphosa and including Joe Slovo and Valli Moosa, had been engaged in weekly discussions with the government on the issues of elections, the constitution, a constituent assembly and a transitional government. Delegates from twenty different parties including the homeland governments had already agreed on the ground rules for the convention.

The optimism at the opening of the talks could not be dampened even by a few spoilers. The PAC decided to boycott the talks, accusing the ANC and the National Party of conspiring together to set up a multi-racial government. This occurred despite the formation, a month before, of the Patriotic Front, an alliance of the ANC, the PAC and the Azanian People's Organization around a declaration of common goals. The PAC feared democratic elections because they knew that such a vote would expose their meagre popular support. Chief Buthelezi also boycotted the talks on the ground that he was not permitted three delegations: for Inkatha, the KwaZulu government and King Zwelithini. We argued that the king should be above politics, and that if he were included then every tribe in South Africa should be able to send their paramount chief.

There was not only a sense of history at the World Trade Centre, but of self-reliance. Unlike the negotiations preceding new dispensations in African states like Zimbabwe and Angola, which required outside mediators, we in South Africa were settling our differences among ourselves. Mr de Klerk talked about the need for a transitional, 'power-sharing' government on a democratic basis. The National Party's chief delegate to the talks, Dawie de Villiers, even offered an apology for apartheid.

In my own opening remarks I said that, with the dawn of CODESA, progress in South Africa had at last become irreversible. Governments, I said, derive their authority and legitimacy from the consent of the governed, and we had assembled to create such a legitimate authority. I said that CODESA marked the beginning of the road to an elected assembly that would write a new constitution, and I did not see any reason why an election for such a constituent assembly could not occur in 1992. I called on the government to usher in an interim government of national unity to supervise such an election, control the state media and the military and generally oversee the transition to a new, non-racial, democratic South Africa.

On the convention's first day, the lion's share of the participating parties, including the National

Party and the ANC, endorsed a Declaration of Intent, which committed all parties to support an undivided South Africa whose supreme law would be a constitution safeguarded by an independent judiciary. The country's legal system would guarantee equality before the law, and a bill of rights would be drawn up to protect civil liberties. In short there would be a multi-party democracy based on universal adult suffrage on a common voters' roll. As far as we were concerned, this was the minimum acceptable constitutional threshold for a new South Africa. Inkatha refused to sign on the ground that the phrase an 'undivided' South Africa implied that a federal system was off limits.

The convention created five working groups that would meet in early 1992 to prepare the way for the second round of CODESA scheduled for May 1992. The groups would explore the question of creating a free political climate, the future of the homelands, the restructuring of the South African Broadcasting Corporation, the examination of various constitutional principles such as federalism, and the creation and installation of an interim government. The parties agreed that decisions would be taken by 'sufficient consensus', which was never defined, but in practice meant an agreement between the government and the ANC and a majority of the other parties.

The first day of CODESA 1 was uneventful, until it came to a close. The night before the convention I had been negotiating with Mr de Klerk on the telephone until after 8 in the evening. Mr de Klerk asked me whether or not I would agree to permit him to be the final speaker the next day. Though I was scheduled to give the concluding remarks, I told him that I would take up the matter with our National Executive. I did so that evening and, despite their misgivings, I persuaded them to permit Mr de Klerk to have the last word. I did not see the issue as a vital one, and I was prepared to do Mr de Klerk the favour.

At the end of the session, all seemed well; I spoke about the importance of the talks and I was followed by Mr de Klerk. He proceeded to underline the historic significance of the occasion and discussed the need for overcoming mutual distrust. But then he did a curious thing. He began to attack the ANC for not adhering to the agreements that we had made with the government. He began to speak to us like a schoolmaster admonishing a naughty child. He berated the ANC for failing to disclose the location of arms caches and then rebuked us for maintaining a 'private army', Umkhonto we Sizwe, in violation of the National Peace Accord of September 1991. In intemperate language, he questioned whether the ANC was honourable enough to abide by any agreements it signed.

This was more than I could tolerate and I would now be damned if I would permit Mr de Klerk to have the last word. When he finished, the meeting was meant to be over. But the room had grown very quiet; instead of allowing the session to end, I walked to the podium. I could not let his remarks go unchallenged. My voice betrayed my anger.

I am gravely concerned about the behaviour of Mr de Klerk today. He has launched an attack on the ANC and in doing so he has been less than frank. Even the head of an

411

illegitimate, discredited minority regime, as his is, has certain moral standards to uphold. He has no excuse just because he is the head of such a discredited regime not to uphold moral standards . . . If a man can come to a conference of this nature and play the type of politics he has played—very few people would like to deal with such a man.

The members of the government persuaded us to allow them to speak last. They were very keen to say the last word here. It is now clear why they did so. He has abused his position, because he hoped that I would not respond. He was completely mistaken. I respond now.

I said it was unacceptable for Mr de Klerk to speak to us in such language. I reiterated that it was the ANC, not the government, that started the initiative of peace discussions, and it was the government, not the ANC, who time and again failed to live up to its agreements. I had told Mr de Klerk before that it served no useful purpose to attack the ANC publicly, yet he continued to do so. I noted that we had suspended our armed struggle to show our commitment to peace, yet the government was still colluding with those waging war. We told him that we would turn in our weapons only when we were a part of the government collecting those weapons, and not until then.

I added that it was apparent the government had a double agenda. They were using the negotiations not to achieve peace, but to score their own petty political gains. Even while negotiating, they were secretly funding covert organizations that committed violence against us. I mentioned the recent revelations about million-rand pay-offs to Inkatha that Mr de Klerk claimed not to have known about. I stated that if a man in his position 'doesn't know about such things, then he is not fit to be the head of government'.

I knew I had been harsh, but I did not want to capsize the whole ship of negotiations, and I ended on a more conciliatory note.

I ask him to place his cards on the table face upwards. Let us work together openly. Let there be no secret agendas. Let him not persuade us that he would be the last speaker because he wants to abuse that privilege and attack us in the hope that we won't respond. I am prepared to work with him in spite of all his mistakes.

CODESA convened the following day for its final session, and both Mr de Klerk and I took pains to show that no irreparable harm had been done. At the beginning of the session, he and I publicly shook hands and said we would work together. But much trust had been lost, and the negotiations were now in a state of disarray.

*   *   *

Six weeks after the opening of CODESA 1, the National Party contested an important by-election in Potchefstroom, a conservative university town in the Transvaal, traditionally the party's stronghold. In a stunning upset, the Nationalists were defeated by the candidate of the right-wing Conservative

Party. The Conservatives resolutely opposed the government's policy of negotiations with the ANC, and were composed mainly of Afrikaners who felt that Mr de Klerk was giving away the store. The election result seemed to cast doubt on Mr de Klerk's policy of reform and negotiations. The National Party was alarmed; these were their own voters in their own heartland rejecting their policies.

Mr de Klerk decided to gamble. He announced that as a result of the by-election in Potchefstroom he would call a nationwide all-white referendum for 17 March so that the people of South Africa could vote on his reform policy and on negotiations with the ANC. He stated that if the referendum was defeated, he would resign from office. The referendum asked a plain and direct question of all white voters over the age of eighteen: 'Do you support the continuation of the reform process which the state president began on 2 February 1990 which is aimed at a new constitution through negotiation?'

The ANC opposed the referendum on the principle that it was a vote that excluded all non-whites. At the same time, we were realistic: we certainly did not want white voters to rebuff Mr de Klerk's efforts to pursue negotiations. Though we disdained the election on principle, we urged whites to vote 'yes'. We saw such a vote as a signal of support for negotiations, not necessarily for de Klerk.

We watched Mr de Klerk's campaign with interest and some consternation. He and the National Party conducted a sophisticated, expensive, American-style political campaign accompanied by extensive newspaper and television advertisements, bumper stickers and colourful rallies. We saw this as a dress rehearsal for the campaign Mr de Klerk would wage against us.

In the end, 69 per cent of the white voters supported negotiations, giving de Klerk a great victory. He felt vindicated; I think the margin even swelled his head a bit. His hand was strengthened, and as a result, the Nationalists toughened their negotiating positions. This was a dangerous strategy.

109

On 13 April 1992 at a press conference in Johannesburg, flanked by my two oldest friends and comrades, Walter and Oliver, I announced my separation from my wife. The situation had grown so difficult that I felt that it was in the best interests of all concerned—the ANC, the family and Winnie—that we part. Although I discussed the matter with the ANC, the separation itself was made for personal reasons.

I read the following statement:

The relationship between myself and my wife, Comrade Nomzamo Winnie Mandela, has become the subject of much media speculation. I am issuing this statement to clarify the position and in the hope that it will bring an end to further conjecture.

Comrade Nomzamo and myself contracted

our marriage at a critical time in the struggle for liberation in our country. Owing to the pressures of our shared commitment to the ANC and the struggle to end apartheid, we were unable to enjoy a normal family life. Despite these pressures our love for each other and our devotion to our marriage grew and intensified . . .

During the two decades I spent on Robben Island she was an indispensable pillar of support and comfort to myself personally . . . Comrade Nomzamo accepted the onerous burden of raising our children on her own . . . She endured the persecutions heaped upon her by the Government with exemplary fortitude and never wavered from her commitment to the freedom struggle. Her tenacity reinforced my personal respect, love and growing affection. It also attracted the admiration of the world at large. My love for her remains undiminished.

However, in view of the tensions that have arisen owing to differences between ourselves on a number of issues in recent months, we have mutually agreed that a separation would be best for each of us. My action was not prompted by the current allegations being made against her in the media . . . Comrade Nomzamo has and can continue to rely on my unstinting support during these trying moments in her life.

I shall personally never regret the life Comrade Nomzamo and I tried to share together. Circumstances beyond our control however dictated it should be otherwise. I part from my wife with no recriminations. I embrace her with all the love and affection I have nursed for her inside and outside prison from the moment I first met her. Ladies and gentlemen, I hope you will appreciate the pain I have gone through.

Perhaps I was blinded to certain things because of the pain I felt for not being able to fulfil my role as a husband to my wife and a father to my children. But just as I am convinced that my wife's life while I was in prison was more difficult than mine, my own return was also more difficult for her than it was for me. She married a man who soon left her; that man became a myth; and then that myth returned home and proved to be just a man after all.

As I later said at my daughter Zindzi's wedding, it seems to be the destiny of freedom fighters to have unstable personal lives. When your life is the struggle, as mine was, there is little room left for family. That has always been my greatest regret, and the most painful aspect of the choice I made.

'We watched our children growing without our guidance,' I said at the wedding, 'and when we did come out [of prison], my children said, "We thought we had a father and one day he'd come back. But to our dismay, our father came back and he left us alone because he has now become the father of the nation."' To be the father of a nation is a great honour, but to be the father of a family is a greater joy. But it was a joy I had far too little of.

110

In May 1992, after a four-month interruption, the multi-party conference held its second plenary session at the World Trade Centre. Known as CODESA 2, the talks had been prepared by secret meetings between negotiators from both the ANC and the government as well as discussions between the ANC and other parties. These meetings culminated in a final session between Mr de Klerk and me the day before the opening of CODESA 2, the first time the two of us had met since before CODESA 1.

Only days before CODESA 2 was to begin, the government was hit by two scandals. The first involved the revelation of massive corruption and bribery at the Department of Development Aid, which was responsible for improving black life in the homelands, and the second was the implication of high government security officials in the 1985 murder of four of the UDF, the best known of whom was Matthew Goniwe. These revelations were added to the recent evidence implicating the police in murders in Natal and suspicions that the Department of Military Intelligence was conducting covert operations against the ANC. These two scandals coming together undermined the credibility of the government and strengthened our hand.

Over the previous months, the government had made numerous proposals that fell by the wayside. Most of them, like the idea of a rotating presidency, sought to preserve their power. But through negotiations over the past months, the ANC and government teams had put together a tentative agreement involving a two-stage transitional period to a fully democratic South Africa. In the first stage, a multi-party 'transitional executive council' would be appointed from the CODESA delegations to function as a temporary government in order to 'level the playing-field' for all parties and create an interim constitution. In the second stage, general elections would be held for a constituent assembly and legislature in which all political parties winning 5 per cent or more of the vote would participate in the cabinet. Half the members of the assembly would be elected on a national basis and half on a regional one, and the assembly would be empowered both to write a new constitution and to pass legislation. An independent commission would preside over the election and make sure it was free and fair.

Yet there were many matters on which the ANC and the government could not reach agreement, such as the percentage of voting necessary in the assembly to decide constitutional issues and to agree on a bill of rights. Only days before CODESA 2, the government proposed a second body, a senate, composed of regional representatives, as a way of ensuring a minority veto. They also proposed that, before all this, CODESA 2 first agree on an interim constitution, which would take months to draw up.

All of this bargaining was going on behind the scenes, and by the time CODESA 2 opened on 15 May 1992, the prospects for agreement looked bleak. What we disagreed about was threatening all that we had agreed upon. Mr de Klerk and I had

419

not managed to find a consensus on most of the outstanding issues. The government seemed prepared to wait indefinitely; their thinking was that the longer we waited, the more support we would lose.

The convention was deadlocked at the end of the first day. At that time, the two judges presiding over the talks told Mr de Klerk and me to meet that evening to attempt to find a compromise. We did meet that night over coffee, and though we did not find a way out of the impasse, we agreed that the negotiations must not founder. 'The whole of South Africa and the world is looking at you and me,' I told Mr de Klerk. 'Let us save the peace process. Let us reach some kind of agreement. Let us at least fix a date for the next round of talks.' We decided that we would each speak the following day in a spirit of constructive compromise.

The next afternoon we spoke in the reverse order that we had agreed to at CODESA 1: Mr de Klerk first, and I last. In his remarks, Mr de Klerk insisted that the National Party did not seek a 'minority veto', but that he did want a system of 'checks and balances' so that the majority would not be able 'to misuse its power'. Although this certainly sounded to me like outright opposition to the idea of majority rule, when I spoke after Mr de Klerk I merely said we needed to work in a constructive manner and dispel the tensions around the negotiations.

Despite our attempts to put a positive face on the matter, the convention ended the second day in a stalemate. The impasse, as I saw it, was caused by the National Party's continuing reluctance to submit their fate to the will of the majority. They simply could not cross that hurdle.

Ultimately, CODESA 2 broke down on four fundamental issues: the government's insistence on an unacceptably high percentage of votes in the assembly to approve the constitution (essentially a back-door veto); entrenched regional powers that would be binding on a future constitution; an undemocratic and unelected senate that had veto power over legislation from the main chamber; and a determination to make an interim constitution negotiated by the convention into a permanent constitution.

These were all difficult issues, but not insoluble ones, and I was determined not to let the deadlock at CODESA 2 subvert the negotiation process. The government and the ANC agreed to continue bilateral talks to work towards a solution. But, then, other matters intruded to render this impossible.

*   *   *

With negotiations stalled, the ANC and its allies agreed on a policy of 'rolling mass action', which would display to the government the extent of our support around the country and show that the people of South Africa were not prepared to wait forever for their freedom. The mass action consisted of strikes, demonstrations and boycotts. The date chosen for the start of mass action was 16 June 1992, the anniversary of the 1976 Soweto revolt, and the campaign was meant to culminate in a two-day national strike set for 3 and 4 August.

But before that happened, another event occurred that drove the ANC and the government even further apart. On the night of 17 June 1992, a heavily armed force of Inkatha members secretly raided the Vaal township of Boipatong and killed forty-six people. Most of the dead were women and children. It was the fourth mass killing of ANC people that week. People across the country were horrified by the violence and charged the government with complicity. The police did nothing to stop the criminals and nothing to find them; no arrests were made, no investigation began. Mr de Klerk said nothing. I found this to be the last straw, and my patience snapped. The government was blocking the negotiations and at the same time waging a covert war against our people. Why then were we continuing to talk with them?

Four days after the murders, I addressed a crowd of twenty thousand angry ANC supporters and told them I had instructed the ANC secretary-general Cyril Ramaphosa to suspend direct dealings with the government. I also announced an urgent meeting of the National Executive Committee to examine our options. It was as if we had returned to the dark days of Sharpeville. I likened the behaviour of the National Party to the Nazis in Germany, and publicly warned de Klerk that if he sought to impose new measures to restrict demonstrations or free expression, the ANC would launch a nationwide defiance campaign with myself as the first volunteer.

At the rally, I saw signs that read, 'MANDELA, GIVE US GUNS' and 'VICTORY THROUGH BATTLE NOT TALK'. I understood such sentiments; the people were frustrated. They saw no positive results of the negotiations. They were beginning to think that the only way to overthrow apartheid was through the barrel of a gun. After Boipatong, there were those in the NEC who said, 'Why did we abandon the armed struggle? We should abandon negotiations instead; they will never advance us to our goal.' I was initially sympathetic to this group of hardliners, but gradually realized that there was no alternative to the process. It was what I had been urging for so many years, and I would not turn my back on negotiations. But it was time to cool things down. Mass action in this case was a middle course between armed struggle and negotiations. The people must have an outlet for their anger and frustration, and a mass action campaign was the best way to channel those emotions.

When we informed the government that we were suspending talks, we sent Mr de Klerk a memo outlining the reasons for our withdrawal. In addition to resolving the constitutional deadlocks at CODESA 2, we demanded that the people responsible for the violence be tracked down and brought to justice and that some mechanism be found for fencing in and policing the hostels, the seedbeds of so much violence. Mr de Klerk sent us back a memo asking for a face-to-face meeting with me, which we rebuffed. I felt such a meeting would suggest that we had something to talk about, and at the time we did not.

*   *   *

The mass action campaign culminated in a general strike on 3 and 4 August in support of the ANC's negotiation demands and in protest against state-supported violence. More than four million workers stayed at home in what was the largest political strike in South African history. The centrepiece of the strike was a march of one hundred thousand people to the Union Buildings in Pretoria, the imposing seat of the South African government, where we held an enormous outdoor rally on the great lawn in front of the buildings. I told the crowd that one day we would occupy these buildings, as the first democratically elected government of South Africa.

In the face of this mass action, Mr de Klerk said that if the ANC made the country ungovernable, the government might be forced to consider some unpleasant options. I warned Mr de Klerk that any anti-democratic actions would have serious repercussions. It was because of such threats, I said, that it was absolutely critical to set up a transitional government.

Inspired by the success of the mass action campaign, a group within the ANC decided to march on Bisho, the capital of the Ciskei homeland in the eastern Cape, a Bantustan led by Brigadier Oupa Gqozo. The Ciskei had a history of repression against the ANC and in 1991 Brigadier Gqozo had declared a State of Emergency in the homeland to curtail what he called ANC-sponsored terrorism. On the morning of 7 September 1992, seventy thousand protesters set out on a march to Bisho's main stadium. When a group of marchers attempted to run through an opening in a fence and take a different path to town, the poorly trained homeland troops opened fire on the marchers and killed twenty-nine people, wounding over two hundred. Now Bisho joined Boipatong as a byword for brutality.

*　　*　　*

Like the old proverb that says the darkest hour is before the dawn, the tragedy of Bisho led to a new opening in the negotiations. I met de Klerk in order to find common ground and avoid a repetition of another tragedy like Bisho. Our respective negotiators began meeting regularly. Both sides were making an effort in good faith to get the negotiations back on track, and on 26 September de Klerk and I met for an official summit.

On that day he and I signed the Record of Understanding, an agreement which set the mould for all the negotiations that followed. The agreement established an independent body to review police actions, created a mechanism to fence in the hostels and banned the display of 'traditional weapons' at rallies. But the real importance of the Record of Understanding was that it broke the constitutional deadlock of CODESA 2. The government finally agreed to accept a single, elected constitutional assembly, which would adopt a new constitution and serve as a transitional legislature for the new government. All that was left to negotiate was a date for the election of the assembly and the percentage of majorities necessary for it to reach its decisions. We were now aligned on the basic framework that would take the country into a democratic future.

The Record of Understanding prompted Inkatha to announce its withdrawal from all negotiations involving the government and the

ANC. The agreement infuriated Chief Buthelezi, who severed relations with the NP and formed an alliance with a group of discredited homeland leaders and white right-wing parties solely concerned with obtaining an Afrikaner homeland. Chief Buthelezi called for the abolition of the Record of Understanding, the ending of CODESA and the disbanding of Umkhonto we Sizwe.

Just as Joe Slovo had taken the initiative concerning the suspension of the armed struggle, he again took the lead in making another controversial proposal: a government of national unity. In October, Joe published a paper in which he wrote that negotiations with the government were not armistice talks in which we could dictate terms to a defeated enemy. It would probably take years for the ANC to control the levers of government, even after an election. An ANC government would still require much of the present civil service to run the country. Joe proposed a 'sunset clause' providing for a government of national unity that would include power-sharing with the National Party for a fixed period of time, an amnesty for security officers and the honouring of contracts of civil servants. 'Power-sharing' was a debased term within the ANC, considered a code-phrase for the government's quest for a minority veto. But in this context it merely meant that the National Party would be part of any popularly elected government, provided it polled enough votes.

After much discussion, I supported Joe's proposal and it was endorsed by the National Executive on 18 November. The NEC agreed to support power-sharing, provided the minority parties did not have a veto. In December we began a new round of secret bilateral talks with the government. These were held over a five-day period at a game lodge in the bush. The talks proved to be critical, for they built on the foundation established in the Record of Understanding. At this bush meeting we agreed in principle on a five-year government of national unity in which all parties polling over 5 per cent in a general election would be proportionally represented in the cabinet. After five years, the government of national unity would become a simple majority-rule government. In February the ANC and the government announced an agreement in principle on the five-year government of national unity, a multi-party cabinet and the creation of a transitional executive council. Elections would be held as early as the end of 1993.

111

I have always believed that a man should have a home within sight of the house where he was born. After being released from prison, I set about plans to build a country house for myself in Qunu. By autumn 1993, the house was complete. It was based on the floor plan of the house I had lived in at Victor Verster. People often commented on this, but the answer was simple: the Victor Verster house was the first spacious and comfortable home I ever stayed in, and I liked it very much. I was familiar with its dimensions, so at Qunu I would not have to wander at night looking for the kitchen.

In April, I was at my house in the Transkei on a brief holiday. On the morning of 10 April I had just gone outside to greet some members of the Transkei police rugby team when my housekeeper ran out and informed me of an urgent telephone call. She was weeping. I excused myself from the young men and learned from a colleague that Chris Hani, the secretary-general of the SACP, the former chief of staff of MK and one of the most popular figures in the ANC, had been shot at point-blank range in front of his home in Boksburg, Johannesburg, a mostly white working-class suburb that Chris was seeking to integrate.

Chris's death was a blow to me personally and to the movement. He was a soldier and patriot, for whom no task was too small. He was a great hero among the youth of South Africa, a man who spoke their language and to whom they listened. If anyone could mobilize the unruly youth behind a negotiated solution, it was Chris. South Africa was now deprived of one of its greatest sons, a man who would have been invaluable in transforming the country into a new nation.

The country was fragile. There were concerns that Hani's death might trigger a racial war, with the youth deciding that their hero should become a martyr for whom they would lay down their own lives. I first flew via helicopter to pay my respects to Chris's eighty-two-year-old father in Sabalele, a tiny, dusty town in the Cofimvaba district in the Transkei, a place well known to me because it was the home region of the Matanzima family. As I arrived in this village with no running water or electricity, I marvelled at how this poor and tiny place could produce a man like Chris Hani, a man who stirred the entire nation with his passion and ability. His concern for the rural poor came from his childhood in Sabalele, for his roots were deep and true, and he never lost them. Chris's father spoke eloquently of the pain of losing a son, but with satisfaction that he had died in the struggle.

Upon my return to Johannesburg I learned that the police had arrested a member of the militant right-wing Afrikaner Weerstandsbeweging (AWB), a Polish immigrant to South Africa who had been captured after a courageous Afrikaner woman had phoned the police with the killer's licence-plate number. The murder was an act of mad desperation, an attempt to derail the negotiation process. I was asked to speak on the SABC that night to address the nation. In this instance, it was the ANC, not the government, that sought to calm the people.

I said that the process of peace and negotiations could not be halted. With all the authority at my command, I said, 'I appeal to all our people to remain calm and to honour the memory of Chris Hani by remaining a disciplined force for peace.'

Tonight I am reaching out to every single South African, black and white, from the very depths of my being. A white man, full of prejudice and hate, came to our country and committed a deed so foul that our whole nation now teeters on the brink of disaster. A white woman, of Afrikaner origin, risked her life so that we may know, and bring to justice, this assassin . . . Now is the time for all South Africans to stand together against those who, from any quarter, wish to destroy what Chris

Hani gave his life for—the freedom of all of us.

The assassination of Chris was an attempt by white supremacists to arrest the inevitable. They preferred that the country descend into civil war rather than have majority rule by peaceful means.

We adopted a strategy to deal with our own constituency in the ANC. In order to forestall outbreaks of retaliatory violence, we arranged a week-long series of mass rallies and demonstrations throughout the country. This would give people a means of expressing their frustration without resorting to violence. Mr de Klerk and I spoke privately and agreed that we would not let Hani's murder derail the negotiations.

We learned within days that a member of the Conservative Party, Clive Derby-Lewis, had been arrested in connection with the murder. More confirmation of a Third Force. It was Chris himself who had criticized a recent theft of weapons from an air force base; preliminary police reports suggested that the gun that killed him had come from that stockpile.

*　　　*　　　*

Exactly two weeks later, there was another significant passing. This one did not shake the nation as Chris's had, but it shook me. Oliver Tambo had not been well for a long time, but the stroke that killed him occurred suddenly and without warning. His wife Adelaide phoned me early in the morning and I rushed to Oliver's bedside. I did not have a chance to say a proper

430

good-bye, for he was already gone.

In Plato's allegory of the metals, the philosopher classifies men into groups of gold, silver and lead. Oliver was pure gold; there was gold in his intellectual brilliance, gold in his warmth and humanity, gold in his tolerance and generosity, gold in his unfailing loyalty and self-sacrifice. As much as I respected him as a leader, that is how much I loved him as a man.

Though we had been apart for all the years that I was in prison, Oliver was never far from my thoughts. In many ways, even though we were separated, I kept up a life-long conversation with him in my head. Perhaps that is why I felt so bereft when he died. I felt, as I told one colleague, like the loneliest man in the world. It was as though he had been snatched away from me just as we had finally been reunited. When I looked at him in his coffin, it was as if a part of myself had died.

Though we were not yet in power, I wanted Oliver to have a state funeral, and that is what the ANC gave him. At a mass rally at a stadium in Soweto, hundreds of dignitaries from foreign governments gathered to pay their respects to the man who kept the ANC alive during its years of exile. MK troops marched in his honour and a twenty-one-gun salute was given at his graveside. Oliver had lived to see the prisoners released and the exiles return, but he had not lived to cast his vote in a free and democratic South Africa. That was what remained to be accomplished.

112

Although few people will remember 3 June 1993, it was a landmark in South African history. On that day, after months of negotiations at the World Trade Centre, the multi-party forum voted to set a date for the country's first national, non-racial, one-person-one-vote election: 27 April 1994. For the first time in South African history, the black majority would go to the polls to elect their own leaders. The agreement was that voters would elect four hundred representatives to a constituent assembly, which would both write a new constitution and serve as a parliament. After convening, the first order of business for the assembly would be to elect a president.

The talks had reconvened in April. This time, the twenty-six parties included Inkatha, the Pan-Africanist Congress and the Conservative Party. We had been pressing the government to establish a date for months, and they had been stalling. But now the date was written in stone.

A month later, in July, the multi-party forum agreed on a first draft of an interim constitution. It provided for a bicameral parliament with a four-hundred-member national assembly elected by proportional representation from national and regional party lists, and a senate elected indirectly by regional legislatures.

Elections to regional legislatures would take place at the same time as national elections, and the regional bodies could draw up their own constitutions consistent with the national constitution.

Chief Buthelezi wanted a constitution drawn up before the election and walked out in protest against the setting of an election date before a constitution was finalized. A second draft interim constitution in August gave greater powers to the regions, but this did not placate either Chief Buthelezi or the Conservative Party. The Conservative Party described the resolutions as hostile to Afrikaner interests. A group called the Afrikaner Volksfront, led by General Constand Viljoen, a former chief of the South African Defence Force, was formed to unite conservative white organizations around the idea of a *volkstaat*, a white homeland.

Just after midnight on 18 November an interim constitution was approved by a plenary session of the multiparty conference. The government and the ANC had cleared the remaining hurdles. The new cabinet would be composed of those winning more than 5 per cent of the vote and would make decisions by consensus, rather than the two-thirds majority proposed by the government; national elections would not take place until 1999, so that the government of national unity would serve for five years; finally, the government gave way on our insistence on a single ballot paper for the election, rather than separate ballots for national and provincial legislatures. Two ballot papers would only confuse a majority of voters, most of whom would be voting for the first time in their lives. In the period leading up to the election, a Transitional Executive Council with members from each party would ensure the right climate for the elections. In effect, the TEC would be the government between

22 December and the election on 27 April. An Independent Electoral Commission with extensive powers would be responsible for the administration of the election. We were truly on the threshold of a new era.

* * *

I have never cared very much for personal prizes. A man does not become a freedom fighter in the hope of winning awards, but when I was notified that I had won the 1993 Nobel Peace Prize jointly with Mr de Klerk, I was deeply moved. The Nobel Peace Prize had a special meaning to me because of its involvement with South African history.

I was the third South African since the end of the Second World War to be so honoured by the Nobel Committee. Chief Albert Luthuli was awarded the prize in 1960. The second was Archbishop Desmond Tutu, who selflessly fought the evils of racism during the most terrible days of apartheid, and won the prize in 1984.

The award was a tribute to all South Africans and especially to those who had fought in the struggle; I would accept it on their behalf. But the Nobel award was one I had never thought about. Even during the bleakest years on Robben Island, Amnesty International would not campaign for us on the ground that we had pursued an armed struggle, and their organization would not represent anyone who had embraced violence. It was for that reason that I assumed the Nobel Committee would never consider for the peace prize the man who had started Umkhonto we Sizwe.

I had tremendous respect for the nations of Norway and Sweden. In the 1950s and 1960s, when we went to Western governments seeking contributions to the ANC, we were turned down flat. But in Norway and Sweden we were greeted with open arms and given assistance and scholarships and money for legal defence and humanitarian aid for political prisoners.

I used my speech in Norway not only to thank the Nobel Committee and sketch out a vision of a future South Africa that was just and equitable, but to pay tribute to my fellow laureate, Mr F.W. de Klerk.

> He had the courage to admit that a terrible wrong had been done to our country and people through the imposition of the system of apartheid. He had the foresight to understand and accept that all the people of South Africa must, through negotiations and as equal participants in the process, together determine what they want to make of their future.

I was often asked how I could accept the award jointly with Mr de Klerk after I had criticized him so severely. Although I would not take back my criticisms, I could say that he had made a genuine and indispensable contribution to the peace process. I never sought to undermine Mr de Klerk, for the practical reason that the weaker he was, the weaker the negotiations process. To make peace with an enemy, one must work with that enemy, and that enemy becomes your partner.

Although the official campaign for the national assembly was not scheduled to begin until February 1994, we started to campaign in earnest after the new constitution was ratified. That did not give us a head start; the National Party began its campaign the day they released me from prison.

Although the polls showed the ANC with a healthy margin, we never took victory for granted. I counselled everyone against over-optimism. We had all read dozens of accounts of parties favoured to win who subsequently came in second. We faced an experienced, well-organized and well-financed rival.

Our campaign was under the capable leadership of Popo Molefe, Terror Lekota and Ketso Gordhan, all veteran UDF activists adept at mass mobilization. The task was a formidable one. We estimated that there would be over twenty million people going to the polls, most of them voting for the first time. Many of our voters were illiterate, and were likely to be intimidated by the mere idea of voting. According to the Independent Electoral Commission, there would be ten thousand polling stations around the country. We sought to train over a hundred thousand people to assist with voter education.

The first stage of our election effort was what were known as People's Forums. ANC candidates would travel all over the country and hold meetings in towns and villages in order to listen to the hopes and fears, the ideas and complaints, of our people. The People's Forums were similar to the town meetings that candidate Bill Clinton held in

America on his way to the presidency. The forums were parliaments of the people, not unlike the meetings of chiefs at the Great Place that I witnessed as a boy.

I revelled in the People's Forums. I began in Natal in November, and then went to the PWV area, the northern Transvaal and the Orange Free State. I attended as many as three or four forums in a day. The people themselves enjoyed them immensely. No one had ever come to solicit their opinion on what should be done in their own country.

After incorporating the suggestions from the forums, we travelled the country delivering our message to the people. Some in the ANC wanted to make the campaign simply a liberation election, and tell the people: Vote for us because we set you free. We decided instead to offer them a vision of the South Africa we hoped to create. We wanted people to vote for the ANC not simply because we had fought apartheid for eighty years, but because we were best qualified to bring about the kind of South Africa they hoped to live in. I felt that our campaign should be about the future, not the past.

The ANC drafted a 150-page document known as the Reconstruction and Development Programme, which outlined our plan to create jobs through public works; to build a million new houses with electricity and flush toilets; to extend primary health care and provide ten years of free education to all South Africans; to redistribute land through a land claims court; and to end the value-added tax on basic foodstuffs. We were also committed to extensive affirmative action measures in both the private and public sectors. This document was translated into a simpler manifesto called 'A Better Life for All', which in turn became the ANC's campaign slogan.

Just as we told the people what we would do, I felt we must also tell them what we could not do. Many people felt life would change overnight after a free and democratic election, but that would be far from the case. Often, I said to the crowds, 'Do not expect to be driving a Mercedes the day after the election or swimming in your own backyard pool.' I told our supporters, 'Life will not change dramatically, except that you will have increased your self-esteem and become a citizen in your own land. You must have patience. You might have to wait five years for results to show.' I challenged them; I did not patronize them: 'If you want to continue living in poverty without clothes and food,' I told them, 'then go and drink in the shebeens. But if you want better things, you must work hard. We cannot do it all for you; you must do it yourselves.'

I told white audiences that we needed them and did not want them to leave the country. They were South Africans just like ourselves and this was their land, too. I would not mince words about the horrors of apartheid, but I said, over and over, that we should forget the past and concentrate on building a better future for all.

Each rally was also designed to teach people how to vote. The ballot itself was a long, narrow piece of paper with the parties listed in descending order to the left, and then the symbol of the party and a picture of its leader to the right. Voters were to place an X in the box next to the party of their choice. I would tell audiences, 'On election day, look down your ballot and when you see the face of a young and handsome man, mark an X.'

113

The road to freedom was far from smooth. Although the Transitional Executive Council began functioning in the new year, some parties opted out. Inkatha rejected participation in the election and gave itself over to the politics of resistance. King Zwelithini, supported by Chief Buthelezi, called for an autonomous and sovereign KwaZulu, and discouraged everyone in his province from voting. The white right called the elections a betrayal and clamoured for a *volkstaat*, yet they still had not proposed where it would be located or how it would work. There was no magisterial district in the whole of South Africa where whites constituted a majority of residents.

12 February 1994 was the deadline for registration of all parties, and on that day Inkatha, the Conservative Party and the Afrikaner Volksfront failed to sign. The government of the Bophuthatswana homeland also refused to participate and resisted reincorporation into a united South Africa. I was disturbed that these important groups were choosing not to participate. To bring them on board, we proposed certain significant compromises: we agreed to the use of double ballots for provincial and national legislatures; guarantees of greater provincial powers; the renaming of Natal province as

KwaZulu/Natal; and the affirmation that a principle of 'internal' self-determination would be included in the constitution for groups sharing a common cultural and language heritage.

I arranged to meet Chief Buthelezi in Durban on 1 March. 'I will go down on my knees to beg those who want to drag our country into bloodshed,' I told a rally before this meeting. Chief Buthelezi agreed to register provisionally for the elections in exchange for a promise to subject our differences over constitutional issues to international mediation. To this I gladly assented. Before the final registration deadline, General Viljoen also registered under a new party known as the Freedom Front.

Though Lucas Mangope, the president of Bophuthatswana, had chosen to keep his homeland out of the election, the tide of events soon altered the situation. I spoke to him on a number of occasions urging him to let his people decide, but he would not listen. Those who wanted to participate launched mass demonstrations and strikes, which soon spread to the Bophuthatswana civil service. The radio and television networks went off the air. On the streets of Mafikeng, battles broke out between the homeland police and striking workers and students. Mangope called in military help from his white right-wing allies. Soon his own forces deserted him and he was ousted in a coup in early March. A few weeks later, Brigadier Gqozo in the Ciskei capitulated and asked South Africa to take over the homeland.

Violence in Natal worsened. Inkatha supporters were blocking our efforts to campaign in Natal. Fifteen ANC election workers were shot and hacked to death after putting up ANC posters. In March, Judge Johann Kriegler reported to me and Mr de Klerk that because of the lack of cooperation from the KwaZulu government, free elections could not be held there without direct political intervention. To demonstrate our strength in Natal, the ANC held a mass march through the centre of Durban. Then Inkatha attempted to do the same in Johannesburg, with dire results.

On 28 March thousands of Inkatha members brandishing spears and knobkerries marched through Johannesburg to a rally in the centre of town. At the same time an armed Inkatha group attempted to enter Shell House, the ANC headquarters, but was repulsed by armed guards. Shots by unidentified gunmen were also fired in the city centre, and altogether fifty-three people died. It was a grisly spectacle that made South Africa appear as if it was on the brink of internal war. Inkatha was attempting to postpone the election, but neither Mr de Klerk nor I would budge. That day was sacrosanct.

I had agreed to international mediation, and on 13 April a delegation arrived led by Lord Carrington, the former British foreign secretary, and Henry Kissinger, the former American secretary of state. But when Inkatha was informed that the election date was not subject to mediation, they refused to see the mediators, who left without talking to anyone. Now Chief Buthelezi knew the election would take place no matter what. On 19 April Chief Buthelezi accepted the offer of a constitutional role for the Zulu monarchy and agreed to participate.

Ten days before the vote, Mr de Klerk and I held our single television debate. I had been a fair debater at Fort Hare, and in my early years in the organization I had engaged in many impassioned debates on the platform. On Robben Island we had honed our debating skills while we chipped away at limestone. I was confident, but the day before, we held a mock debate in which the journalist Allister Sparks ably performed as Mr de Klerk. Too ably, according to my campaign advisers, for they chided me for speaking too slowly and not aggressively enough.

When the time came for the actual debate, however, I attacked the National Party quite firmly. I accused the National Party of fanning race hatred between Coloureds and Africans in the Cape by distributing an inflammatory comic book that said the ANC's slogan was 'Kill a Coloured, kill a farmer'. 'There is no organization in this country as divisive as the new National Party,' I declared. When Mr de Klerk criticized the ANC's plan to spend billions of dollars on housing and social programmes, I scolded him, saying he was alarmed that we would have to devote so many of our resources to blacks.

But as the debate was nearing an end, I felt I had been too harsh with the man who would be my partner in a government of national unity. In summation, I said, 'The exchanges between Mr de Klerk and me should not obscure one important fact. I think we are a shining example to the entire world of people drawn from different racial groups who have a common loyalty, a common love, to their common country . . . In spite of criticism of Mr de Klerk,' I said, and then looked over at him, 'sir, you are one of those I rely upon. We are going to face the problem of this country together.' At which point I reached over to take his hand and said, 'I am proud to hold your hand for us to go forward.' Mr de Klerk seemed surprised, but pleased.

114

I voted on 27 April, the second of the four days of voting (certain categories including the elderly, the disabled and South Africans voting abroad were allowed to vote on 26 April). I chose to vote in Natal to show the people in that divided province that there was no danger in going to the polling stations. I voted at Ohlange High School in Inanda, a green and hilly township just north of Durban, for it was there that John Dube, the first president of the ANC, was buried. This African patriot had helped found the organization in 1912, and casting my vote near his graveside brought history full circle, for the mission he began eighty-two years before was about to be achieved.

As I stood over his grave, on a rise above the small school below, I thought not of the present but of the past. When I walked to the voting station, my mind dwelt on the heroes who had fallen so that I might be where I was that day, the men and women who had made the ultimate sacrifice for a cause that was now finally succeeding. I thought of Oliver Tambo, Chris Hani, Chief Luthuli and Bram

Fischer. I thought of our great African heroes, who had made great sacrifices so that millions of South Africans could be voting on that very day; I thought of Josiah Gumede, G. M. Naicker, Dr Abdullah Abdurahman, Lilian Ngoyi, Helen Joseph, Yusuf Dadoo, Moses Kotane. I did not go into that voting station alone on 27 April; I was casting my vote with all of them.

Before I entered the polling station, an irreverent member of the press called out, 'Mr Mandela, who are you voting for?' I laughed. 'You know,' I said, 'I have been agonizing over that choice all morning.' I marked an X in the box next to the letters ANC and then slipped my folded ballot paper into a simple wooden box; I had cast the first vote of my life.

*   *   *

The images of South Africans going to the polls that day are burned in my memory. Great lines of patient people snaking through the dirt roads and streets of towns and cities; old women who had waited half a century to cast their first vote saying that they felt like human beings for the first time in their lives; white men and women saying they were proud to live in a free country at last. The mood of the nation during those days of voting was buoyant. The violence and bombings ceased, and it was as though we were a nation reborn. Even the logistical difficulties of the voting, misplaced ballots, pirate voting stations and rumours of fraud in certain places could not dim the overwhelming victory for democracy and justice.

It took several days for the results to be counted.

We polled 62.6 per cent of the national vote, slightly short of the two-thirds needed had we wished to push through a final constitution without support from other parties. That percentage qualified us for 252 of 400 seats in the national assembly. The ANC thoroughly dominated the northern and eastern Transvaal, the northwest, the eastern Cape and the Free State. We won 33 per cent of the vote in the western Cape, which was won by the National Party, which did extremely well among Coloured voters. We captured 32 per cent in KwaZulu/Natal, which was won by Inkatha. In Natal, fear of violence and intimidation kept many of our voters at home. There were charges, as well, of vote fraud and vote rigging. But, in the end, that did not matter. We had underestimated Inkatha's strength in KwaZulu, and they had demonstrated it on election day.

Some in the ANC were disappointed that we did not cross the two-thirds threshold, but I was not one of them. In fact I was relieved; had we won two-thirds of the vote and been able to write a constitution unfettered by input from others, people would argue that we had created an ANC constitution, not a South African constitution. I wanted a true government of national unity.

*   *   *

On the evening of 2 May Mr de Klerk made a gracious concession speech. After more than three centuries of rule, the white minority was conceding defeat and turning over power to the black majority. That evening the ANC was planning a victory celebration at the ball-room of the Carlton

445

Hotel in downtown Johannesburg. I was suffering from a bad case of flu and my doctors ordered me to remain at home. But there was nothing that could keep me away from that party. I went on stage at about nine o'clock and faced a crowd of happy, smiling, cheering faces.

I explained to the crowd that my voice was hoarse from a cold and that my physician had advised me not to attend. 'I hope that you will not disclose to him that I have violated his instructions,' I told them. I congratulated Mr de Klerk for his strong showing. I thanked all those in the ANC and the democratic movement who had worked so hard for so long. Mrs Coretta Scott King, the wife of the great freedom fighter Martin Luther King Jr, was on the podium that night, and I looked over to her as I made reference to her husband's immortal words.

This is one of the most important moments in the life of our country. I stand here before you filled with deep pride and joy—pride in the ordinary, humble people of this country. You have shown such a calm, patient determination to reclaim this country as your own, and now the joy that we can loudly proclaim from the rooftops—Free at last! Free at last! I stand before you humbled by your courage, with a heart full of love for all of you. I regard it as the highest honour to lead the ANC at this moment in our history. I am your servant . . . It is not the individuals that matter, but the collective . . . This is a time to heal the old wounds and build a new South Africa.

From the moment the results were in and it was apparent that the ANC was to form the government, I saw my mission as one of preaching reconciliation, of binding the wounds of the country, of engendering trust and confidence. I knew that many people, particularly the minorities, whites, Coloureds and Indians, would be feeling anxious about the future, and I wanted them to feel secure. I reminded people again and again that the liberation struggle was not a battle against any one group or colour, but a fight against a system of repression. At every opportunity, I said all South Africans must now unite and join hands and say we are one country, one nation, one people, marching together into the future.

115

10 May dawned bright and clear. For the past few days I had been pleasantly besieged by dignitaries and world leaders who were coming to pay their respects before the inauguration. The inauguration would be the largest gathering ever of international leaders on South African soil.

The ceremonies took place in the lovely sandstone amphitheatre formed by the Union Buildings in Pretoria. For decades this had been the seat of white supremacy, and now it was the site of a rainbow gathering of different colours and nations for the installation of South Africa's first democratic, non-racial government.

On that lovely autumn day I was accompanied by

447

my daughter Zenani. On the podium, Mr de Klerk was first sworn in as second deputy president. Then Thabo Mbeki was sworn in as first deputy president. When it was my turn, I pledged to obey and uphold the constitution and to devote myself to the well-being of the republic and its people. To the assembled guests and the watching world, I said:

Today, all of us do, by our presence here . . . confer glory and hope to newborn liberty. Out of the experience of an extraordinary human disaster that lasted too long, must be born a society of which all humanity will be proud.

. . . We, who were outlaws not so long ago, have today been given the rare privilege to be host to the nations of the world on our own soil. We thank all of our distinguished international guests for having come to take possession with the people of our country of what is, after all, a common victory for justice, for peace, for human dignity.

We have, at last, achieved our political emancipation. We pledge ourselves to liberate all our people from the continuing bondage of poverty, deprivation, suffering, gender and other discrimination.

Never, never, and never again shall it be that this beautiful land will again experience the oppression of one by another . . . The sun shall never set on so glorious a human achievement.

Let freedom reign. God bless Africa!

A few moments later we all lifted our eyes in awe

as a spectacular array of South African jets, helicopters and troop carriers roared in perfect formation over the Union Buildings. It was not only a display of pinpoint precision and military force, but a demonstration of the military's loyalty to democracy, to a new government that had been freely and fairly elected. Only moments before, the highest generals of the South African Defence Force and police, their chests bedecked with ribbons and medals from days gone by, saluted me and pledged their loyalty. I was not unmindful of the fact that not so many years before they would not have saluted but arrested me. Finally a chevron of Impala jets left a smoke trail of the black, red, green, blue and gold of the new South African flag.

The day was symbolized for me by the playing of our two national anthems, and the vision of whites singing 'Nkosi Sikelel' iAfrika' and blacks singing 'Die Stem', the old anthem of the republic. Although that day neither group knew the lyrics of the anthem they once despised, they would soon know the words by heart.

*   *   *

On the day of the inauguration, I was overwhelmed with a sense of history. In the first decade of the twentieth century, a few years after the bitter Anglo-Boer war and before my own birth, the white-skinned peoples of South Africa patched up their differences and erected a system of racial domination against the dark-skinned peoples of their own land. The structure they created formed the basis of one of the harshest, most inhumane, societies the world has ever known. Now, in the last decade of the twentieth century, and my own eighth decade as a man, that system had been overturned forever and replaced by one that recognized the rights and freedoms of all peoples regardless of the colour of their skin.

That day had come about through the unimaginable sacrifices of thousands of my people, people whose suffering and courage can never be counted or repaid. I felt that day, as I have on so many other days, that I was simply the sum of all those African patriots who had gone before me. That long and noble line ended and now began again with me. I was pained that I was not able to thank them and that they were not able to see what their sacrifices had wrought.

The policy of apartheid created a deep and lasting wound in my country and my people. All of us will spend many years, if not generations, recovering from that profound hurt. But the decades of oppression and brutality had another, unintended, effect, and that was that it produced the Oliver Tambos, the Walter Sisulus, the Chief Luthulis, the Yusuf Dadoos, the Bram Fischers, the Robert Sobukwes of our time—men of such extraordinary courage, wisdom and generosity that their like may never be known again. Perhaps it requires such depths of oppression to create such heights of character. My country is rich in the minerals and gems that lie beneath its soil, but I have always known that its greatest wealth is its people, finer and truer than the purest diamonds.

It is from these comrades in the struggle that I learned the meaning of courage. Time and again, I have seen men and women risk and give their lives for an idea. I have seen men stand up to attacks and torture without breaking, showing a strength and resilience that defies the imagination. I learned that courage was not the absence of fear, but the triumph over it. I felt fear myself more times than I can remember, but I hid it behind a mask of boldness. The brave man is not he who does not feel afraid, but he who conquers that fear.

I never lost hope that this great transformation would occur. Not only because of the great heroes I have already cited, but because of the courage of the ordinary men and women of my country. I always knew that deep down in every human heart, there was mercy and generosity. No one is born hating another person because of the colour of his skin, or his background, or his religion. People must learn to hate, and if they can learn to hate, they can be taught to love, for love comes more naturally to the human heart than its opposite. Even in the grimmest times in prison, when my comrades and I were pushed to our limits, I would see a glimmer of humanity in one of the guards, perhaps just for a second, but it was enough to reassure me and keep me going. Man's goodness is a flame that can be hidden but never extinguished.

We took up the struggle with our eyes wide open, under no illusion that the path would be an easy one. As a young man, when I joined the African National Congress, I saw the price my comrades paid for their beliefs, and it was high. For myself, I have never regretted my commitment to the struggle, and I was always prepared to face the hardships that affected me personally. But my family paid a terrible price, perhaps too dear a price, for my commitment.

451

In life, every man has twin obligations—obligations to his family, to his parents, to his wife and children; and he has an obligation to his people, his community, his country. In a civil and humane society, each man is able to fulfil those obligations according to his own inclinations and abilities. But in a country like South Africa, it was almost impossible for a man of my birth and colour to fulfil both of those obligations. In South Africa, a man of colour who attempted to live as a human being was punished and isolated. In South Africa, a man who tried to fulfil his duty to his people was inevitably ripped from his family and his home and was forced to live a life apart, a twilight existence of secrecy and rebellion. I did not in the beginning choose to place my people above my family, but in attempting to serve my people, I found that I was prevented from fulfilling my obligations as a son, a brother, a father and a husband.

In that way, my commitment to my people, to the millions of South Africans I would never know or meet, was at the expense of the people I knew best and loved most. It was as simple and yet as incomprehensible as the moment a small child asks her father, 'Why can you not be with us?' And the father must utter the terrible words: 'There are other children like you, a great many of them . . .' and then one's voice trails off.

*   *   *

I was not born with a hunger to be free. I was born free—free in every way that I could know. Free to run in the fields near my mother's hut, free to swim in the clear stream that ran through my village, free to roast mealies under the stars and ride the broad backs of slow-moving bulls. As long as I obeyed my father and abided by the customs of my tribe, I was not troubled by the laws of man or God.

It was only when I began to learn that my boyhood freedom was an illusion, when I discovered as a young man that my freedom had already been taken from me, that I began to hunger for it. At first, as a student, I wanted freedom only for myself, the transitory freedoms of being able to stay out at night, read what I pleased and go where I chose. Later, as a young man in Johannesburg, I yearned for the basic and honourable freedoms of achieving my potential, of earning my keep, of marrying and having a family—the freedom not to be obstructed in a lawful life.

But then I slowly saw that not only was I not free, but my brothers and sisters were not free. I saw that it was not just my freedom that was curtailed, but the freedom of everyone who looked like I did. That is when I joined the African National Congress, and that is when the hunger for my own freedom became the greater hunger for the freedom of my people. It was this desire for the freedom of my people to live their lives with dignity and self-respect that animated my life, that transformed a frightened young man into a bold one, that drove a law-abiding attorney to become a criminal, that turned a family-loving husband into a man without a home, that forced a life-loving man to live like a monk. I am no more virtuous or self-sacrificing than the next man, but I found that I could not even enjoy the poor and limited freedoms I was allowed when I knew my people were not free. Freedom is indivisible; the chains on any one of my people were the chains on all of them, the chains on all of my people were the chains on me.

It was during those long and lonely years that my hunger for the freedom of my own people became a hunger for the freedom of all people, white and black. I knew as well as I knew anything that the oppressor must be liberated just as surely as the oppressed. A man who takes away another man's freedom is a prisoner of hatred, he is locked behind the bars of prejudice and narrow-mindedness. I am not truly free if I am taking away someone else's freedom, just as surely as I am not free when my freedom is taken from me. The oppressed and the oppressor alike are robbed of their humanity.

When I walked out of prison, that was my mission, to liberate the oppressed and the oppressor both. Some say that has now been achieved. But I know that that is not the case. The truth is that we are not yet free; we have merely achieved the freedom to be free, the right not to be oppressed. We have not taken the final step of our journey, but the first step on a longer and even more difficult road. For to be free is not merely to cast off one's chains, but to live in a way that respects and enhances the freedom of others. The true test of our devotion to freedom is just beginning.

I have walked that long road to freedom. I have tried not to falter; I have made missteps along the way. But I have discovered the secret that after climbing a great hill, one only finds that there are many more hills to climb. I have taken a moment here to rest, to steal a view of the glorious vista that surrounds me, to look back on the distance I have come. But I can rest only for a moment, for with freedom come responsibilities, and I dare not linger, for my long walk is not yet ended.